Church and Society in England, 1000–1500

Social History in Perspective
General Editor: Jeremy Black

Social History in Perspective is a series of in-depth studies of the
many topics in social, cultural and religious history.

PUBLISHED

John Belchem *Popular Radicalism in Nineteenth-Century Britain*
Andrew Brown *Church and Society in England, 1000–1500*
Sue Bruley *Women in Britain Since 1900*
Anthony Brundage *The English Poor Laws, 1700–1930*
Simon Dentith *Society and Cultural Forms in Nineteenth-Century England*
Joyce M. Ellis *The Georgian Town, 1680–1840*
Peter Fleming *Family and Household in Medieval England*
Ian Gazeley *Poverty in Britain, 1900–1965*
Kathryn Gleadle *British Women in the Nineteenth Century*
Harry Goulbourne *Race Relations in Britain since 1945*
Anne Hardy *Health and Medicine in Britain since 1860*
Tim Hitchcock *English Sexualities, 1700–1800*
Sybil M. Jack *Towns in Tudor and Stuart Britain*
Helen M. Jewell *Education in Early Modern England*
Alan Kidd *State, Society and the Poor in Nineteenth-Century England*
Peter Kirby *Child Labour in Britain, 1750–1870*
Arthur J. McIvor *A History of Work in Britain, 1880–1950*
Hugh McLeod *Religion and Society in England, 1850–1914*
Donald M. MacRaild *Irish Migrants in Modern Britain, 1750–1922*
Donald M. MacRaild and David E. Martin *Labour in Britain, 1830–1914*
Christopher Marsh *Popular Religion in the Sixteenth Century*
Michael A. Mullett *Catholics in Britain and Ireland, 1558–1829*
Richard Rex *The Lollards*
George Robb *British Culture and the First World War*
R. Malcolm Smuts *Culture and Power in England, 1585–1685*
John Spurr *English Puritanism, 1603–1689*
W.B. Stephens *Education in Britain, 1750–1914*
Heather Swanson *Medieval British Towns*
David Taylor *Crime, Policing and Punishment in England, 1750–1914*
N.L. Tranter *British Population in the Twentieth Century*
Ian D. Whyte *Migration and Society in Britain, 1550–1830*
Ian D. Whyte *Scotland's Society and Economy in Transition, c.1500–c.1760*
Andy Wood *Riot, Rebellion and Popular Politics in Early Modern England*

Please note that a sister series, *British History in Perspective*, is available,
covering key topics in British political history.

Social History in Perspective
Series Standing Order
ISBN 0–333–71694–9 hardcover
ISBN 0–333–69336–1 paperback
(outside North America only)

You can receive future titles in this series as they are published by placing a standing order.
Please contact your bookseller or, in case of difficulty, write to us at the address below with
your name and address, the title of the series and the ISBN quoted above.

Customer Services Department, Macmillan Distribution Ltd
Houndmills, Basingstoke, Hampshire RG21 6XS, England

Church and Society in England, 1000–1500

ANDREW BROWN

First published 2003 by
PALGRAVE MACMILLAN

Palgrave Macmillan in the UK is an imprint of Macmillan Publishers Limited, registered in England, company number 785998, of Houndmills, Basingstoke, Hampshire RG21 6XS.

Palgrave Macmillan in the US is a division of St Martin's Press LLC, 175 Fifth Avenue, New York, NY 10010.

Palgrave Macmillan is the global academic imprint of the above companies and has companies and representatives throughout the world.

Palgrave® and Macmillan® are registered trademarks in the United States, the United Kingdom, Europe and other countries.

ISBN-13: 978-0-3336-9144-1   hardback
ISBN-10: 0-3336-9144-X   hardback
ISBN-13: 978-0-3336-9145-8   paperback
ISBN-10: 0-3336-9145-8   paperback

This book is printed on paper suitable for recycling and made from fully managed and sustained forest sources. Logging, pulping and manufacturing processes are expected to conform to the environmental regulations of the country of origin.

A catalogue record for this book is available from the British Library.

A catalog record for this book is available from the Library of Congress.

Printed and bound in Great Britain by
Cpod, Trowbridge, Wiltshire

For Rebecca, George and Imogen with love

Contents

Acknowledgements

Were it not for the kindness and expertise of others, this book would have been much the poorer. To Ms Terka Acton and Ms Sonya Barker at Palgrave, I owe thanks for such efficient handling of my questions and for their impressive reserves of patience in waiting for the final text to arrive. To my father, Dr Barry Brown, I owe a good deal of thanks for taking parental duty to heroic lengths by reading a first draft in its entirety, and removing a large number of mistakes (and a superfluity of commas). I am also very grateful for the generosity of several of my colleagues at Edinburgh. Dr Tom Brown gave highly useful advice on Anglo-Saxon England. Dr Cordelia Beattie's perceptive comments on several chapters, particularly on late medieval England and on matters concerning gender, were invaluable. Professor Tony Goodman's critical suggestions on the whole text were as useful as his words of encouragement were inspiring. To Dr Gary Dickson – for his advice and questioning comments on almost every page of the entire text – I owe a particular debt for taking so much trouble. Had I been able to answer all his questions, this book would have been considerably improved.

I owe a special debt of gratitude to my wife, Dr Rebecca Reader. Without her the book would never have been finished. I have relied heavily on her historical and literary skills: her keen eye for a nonsensical or ugly sentence often revealed a humbling blindness in mine for either. I have also relied on her for support and encouragement, and for the task – far harder than writing any book – of bringing up two demanding but amazing children, George and Imogen, both born while this book was being written.

Andrew Brown

Introduction

So short a book is bound to raise a suspicion: that its themes will not be
as all-encompassing as the expansive title suggests. The suspicious will
not be disappointed. Discussion of the 'Church' as an institution is well
served elsewhere[1] (although this is the sense in which the term is generally used here). I have chosen instead to concentrate on the 'community
of the faithful' (which was in any case one contemporary definition of the
'Church'), and on how the religious practices and attitudes, principally
of lay people, changed over the period. The 'community of the faithful'
in medieval terms was of course 'society' itself (or at least 'Christian
society'); so to the crime of raising false expectations, the book's title
risks adding the sin of tautology. But more modern definitions tend to
allow the distinction, and what is attempted here is an overview of the
relationship (to some extent two-way) between religious practices and
their social setting: how they were affected by status and gender (and by
perceptions of them), and by the vast socio-economic changes which
took place over the whole period.

These themes are broad enough in themselves: the book could have
been longer. I have also relied heavily on the expertise of others, perch-
ing on 'shoulders of giants' (to borrow a medieval 'apology for short-
comings') without the pretence (often conceitedly implied by medieval
authors) that I have seen any further than they. But the point of taking
so long a period is that some of the continuities, as well as changes, might
also be discerned. 'Church and society' in the Anglo-Saxon period, or
even the twelfth and thirteenth centuries, is often cut off, historiograph-
ically speaking, from the fourteenth and fifteenth; while the latter two
centuries used to be treated as a depressing finale to the 'medieval
period' or as a curtain-raiser to the upheavals of the Reformation in the

1

sixteenth century. There were indeed continuities over the whole period, and ones which did not lead, as though towards some inexorable conclusion, to the kind of Reformation which happened in England. In the past, Catholicism was viewed from the perspective of a Reformation which was itself judged to have broken a monopoly of religious power wielded by the Church over the laity. A wealth of recent research into the later Middle Ages, especially on the vitality and depth of lay involvement in Catholic practices, has rendered this traditional perspective difficult to sustain (so difficult that it might seem a puzzle now why the Reformation happened at all).[2] It is worth looking at this lay involvement from an even longer-term perspective: it forms one of the continuities over the whole period, albeit in changing forms. Another continuity too is that however much the Church changed as an institution – and undoubtedly it became a more powerful and centralized one – its monopoly over 'religion' was always limited, partly because 'society' changed around it too, and partly because the 'religion' it advocated was not a monolithic ideology, and could lead in directions which undermined the very basis of clerical power. Before these themes can be developed, further comment is needed on the variety of approaches to 'Church', 'religion' and 'society'.

(i) Church and Religion

Analysis of 'religion' tends to proceed along two interrelated lines: what it is and what it does. From a modern rather than a medieval perspective,[3] 'religion' is defined as an abstraction, a system of prescribed rites, symbols and beliefs, which attempts to structure and explain the nature of the human condition. This may seem uncontroversial (if too reductionist and secularized) a statement, but even this definition brings its own baggage of problematic assumptions. An older tradition of anthropology readily distinguished 'religion' from 'magic' (and both from 'rational science');[4] and although modern commentary has tended to dismiss the validity of this approach – not least because all three categories might be described as 'modes of rationality' – these distinctions are worth recalling because they have left lingering traces in the historiography of medieval Catholicism.

A Protestant tradition was inclined to dismiss late medieval Catholicism in particular as 'magical' and 'superstitious' to explain why a Reformation was so badly needed by the sixteenth century. Prayers, blessings, holy objects and even the Host were being used by the 'ignorant' peasant to secure the health of his crops: such 'coercion' (rather than petitioning) of divine power was a gross abuse which the Catholic Church was encouraging and for its own fraudulent purposes.[5] But more sensitive readings of Catholic practices have shown how misleading this characterization is. On the one hand, medieval churchmen criticized 'abuses', and also used different criteria in assessing their validity. Some practices later dismissed as 'magical' were not, even to churchmen, 'magical' at all. Prayers which encouraged a good harvest were acceptable if tapping into the God-given potential of nature, but unacceptable if seeking to tap the power of the devil. So if 'magic' is supposed to be 'coercive' of divine power, it was an integral part of medieval 'religion'. Historians do best to avoid any implied distinction between 'religion' and 'magic' in describing religious practices.[6] On the other hand, medieval 'peasants' were a good deal less 'ignorant' than some descriptions of their practices would imply. It is no longer convincing to dismiss the medieval Church, in 'Protestant' terms, as a source or purveyor of 'magic', but hints that Catholicism, on the eve of the Reformation, was 'vulnerable' to a 'rationalistic critique' can still inform present debate.[7]

There is another reason for recalling the traditional distinction between 'religion' and 'magic' or 'superstition'. Medieval churchmen too could distinguish between the Christian faith, as expounded in councils and sermons, and the 'superstitions' of certain lay people. Some of this 'superstition' was denounced as little more than 'paganism'. Once again, it is quite plausible to dismiss these labels used by medieval churchmen as so much polemic, as part of a Catholic rhetoric of reform.[8] But the implied distinction between churchmen and laity has also informed another kind of historiographical debate. For some historians, it suggests a difference between clergy and laity, between an 'elite' religion developing more systematically especially from the twelfth century onwards, and a 'popular' one which, even if increasingly influenced by 'elite' ideologies, was still rooted in a pagan (or 'primitive') past.[9] For others, differences between the two lie more in a distinction between a ritualistic or 'cultic' religion of the people and a more internalized creed of an educated elite.[10] However, the validity of any such distinction has also been questioned, if not flatly denied.[11] The 'repertoire of inherited beliefs and symbols' to be found in the liturgy, writes Eamon Duffy, was a 'reservoir', certainly by the later Middle Ages, 'shared' by priest and 'peasant' alike. There was 'no substantial gulf between the religion of the clergy and the educated elite on the one hand and that of the people at large on the other'. Although religious symbols were 'capable of enormous flexibility and variety', it is the homogeneity of late medieval religion, across the social spectrum, which stands out.[12]

Such an approach has undoubtedly developed a more empathetic understanding of the richness and depth of late medieval religious culture. It has tempted some historians to speak of a 'Christian' Middle Ages,[13] and to speak of religious practices which struck Protestants as particularly dubious (such as 'peasant abuse' of the Host) not as vestigial paganism or superstitious folklore but as 'lay Christianity'. There are those who are healthily sceptical about the depth of spirituality amongst the majority – preferring to identify a certain 'comfortable' air, or 'complacency' and 'lukewarmness' about the religion of fifteenth-century English people (men in particular).[14] Assessing depth of belief, however, is not straightforward. Still at issue too is the extent of the homogeneity of late medieval religion. 'No substantial gulf', to use Duffy's phrase once more, suggests a 'gulf' none the less; the 'flexibility and variety' may in the end seem more significant than the apparent uniformity of the whole.

Diversity rather than uniformity is one of the themes emphasized in this book. From the eleventh century a drive to a more 'universal' Church, uniform in doctrine, law and cult, was indeed apparent in the papal curia and beyond. Homogeneity was increasingly encouraged and developed around the liturgy and mass. The Church, it was asserted with greater vigour, was one body, the body of the faithful, in which Christ was 'priest' and his body 'sacrifice' at the mass. Yet despite vigorous efforts, a 'universal' Church was never fully established in practice; and however much the 'body of Christ' was developed as a symbol to assert both the unity and hegemony of the Church, it also generated associations and meanings which defied the assertion of either. The articles of faith and the practices required of every Christian were formalized as never before, but 'religion' did not become a monolithic system of belief. Differences over interpretation of doctrine developed, even around one so central as the Eucharist.[15]

One line of 'postmodernist' thought takes this line of argument much further. The culturally relative nature of any form of 'language' prevents fixed meaning: religious beliefs and actions are thus inherently open to reinterpretation. So, for instance, it is possible for different audiences to take different meanings from their readings of saints' lives; or for different pilgrims to find alternative meanings at the shrine to which they journeyed.[16] Such an approach is helpful, although its logical extreme – that any belief or action can have any meaning imposed on them – seems too nihilistic: within a particular social context the range of plausible meanings might be limited, or a consensus of views might seem to prevail. But at the very least, a certain sensitivity is required to the variety of ways in which religious doctrines or attitudes could be reinterpreted.

The 'religion' of the Church, moreover, was not just about the prescription of formal doctrine and beliefs. It was also about the expression of spiritual ideals and standards of holy living which were often more difficult to define and institutionalize. Some of these ideals even worked against the Church as an institutional structure. The 'imitation of Christ' (especially His 'poverty') was an inspiration for reform and renewal within the Church throughout the period, but an inspiration too for enthusiasms it could not always contain, and for denunciations of the whole apparatus of ecclesiastical organization (see Chapter 6: iv).

It is difficult to see religion, even in the late medieval period, as homogeneous; but the extent to which greater homogeneity had been achieved by then raises other questions. If it existed, how was it engineered, and if so, how and by whom? Did communal ideals serve the good of 'society' as a whole or the interests of particular groups within in it?[17] And what did expressions of communal ideals – whether at mass or other liturgical occasions – mean within a contemporary context? These questions lead to a wider debate about the social dimension of religion, in which discussion tends to shift away from what religion 'is' to what it 'does'.

(ii) Religion and Society

There is a long tradition of anthropological and social theory which categorizes religion, in some form or other, as a mirror of social aspirations. Durkheim classically defined religion as the projection of the social order onto the divine, a system of ideas with which individuals represent to themselves, often in 'ritual' activity, the society of which they are members. Religion thus functions as a force for social cohesion and control: participation in sacred acts and rituals was a means by which members would experience the meaning and moral power of their society.[18] Although this has seemed too crude a formulation of both 'religion' and 'society' (and Durkheim's ideas are often more subtle than this), it is undeniable that social relations affected perceptions of the supernatural order and the structures of religious practices.[19] Thus historians (whether Durkheimian or not) have characterized, for instance, the relationship between saint and client as an extension of existing 'social relations beyond human society'; or have illuminatingly described certain liturgical processions as the sacramental embodiment of social reality.[20] Take the Corpus Christi processions in late medieval towns, during which the mayor was stationed closest to the paraded Host, and craft guilds were strung out in front: the carefully calibrated hierarchy allowed different groups to display their standing within the urban 'community'. Even historians with an empathetic eye for 'pious' motives and spiritual ideals recognize the force of social pressures on religious belief and practice. As Duffy writes, the liturgy and the service of mass with its emphasis on the need for 'charity' among those attending, might well allow its participants a means through which to 'articulate their experience of community'.[21]

But what was this 'experience of community' and why did it need articulating? Durkheim tended (although not always) to regard 'society' as an organic totality; but historians who regard 'society' as an arena of conflicting interest groups (especially those drawing upon Marx or Weber), reach different conclusions about the function of 'religion' within it. Rather than the projection of 'society' as a whole, 'religion' is the instrument by which one group asserts control over another, as justification of social hierarchy and hegemony.[22] There are indeed occasions when certain religious practices appear to function in just this way. The adaption of the feast of Corpus Christi within the late medieval towns enshrined a corporate but also hierarchical vision of urban society. Perhaps, then, a 'sense of community' was articulated in the interests of hierarchy.

But before characterizing medieval society any further, it needs emphasizing that if 'religion' articulated anything, it did not do so in straightforward ways. Weber himself had a good deal more to say about the relationship between religion and particular social groups; and on how the 'charisma' of individuals might transcend the established order and generate religious change. In any case, rituals, symbols and beliefs could not be appropriated at will by those in power. There is little agreement on how rituals actually work and what they do (or even what they are), beyond a sense that they can be complicated processes which are often ambiguous in meaning and indeterminate in result.[23] They may even be self-defeating of the authority who promote them: the effect of projecting social structures on to the unseen world or on to visible rituals may have the more subtle effect, deliberate or otherwise, of questioning the nature and validity of those structures. Moreover, the interplay in ritualized activity between agents and participants is often more dynamic than any simple imposition of 'social control' by the one over the other. So the late medieval Corpus Christi procession might be viewed not as an assertion of social dominance but as a vision of the social order itself under dispute, or a site of negotiation between the civic elite and lower ranks resistant to domination.[24] And again, the occasions when rituals fail to work, or become appropriated to subvert rather than support social hierarchy, tend to demonstrate the potential instability of the ritual process.

Just as 'religion' was not a monolithic system of belief, so religious rituals were not simple mechanisms of 'social control'. But there were certainly religious ideas which were used to support hierarchy and which constructed categories of social groups in certain ways; and there were also social reasons why those in authority might have cause to assert them. How did contemporaries perceive 'society' and how do these perceptions square with modern historical analysis?

(iii) Medieval Perceptions of Society

For medieval churchmen, 'society' meant the community of Christians, but there were several ways in which people were categorized within it. One model conceptualized society as a 'body', the different members of society, like limbs and organs, making up the functioning whole. But a more dominant model, already emerging in England by the ninth century, was to place people in one of three estates or orders – those who prayed, fought or worked. Although a bipartite theory of division was also used (between clergy and laity), the tripartite division began to dominate from the twelfth century, and was emphasized even more strongly in the later Middle Ages.[25]

Schematic views like these did not mean that other more practical kinds of criteria were ignored. For legal or fiscal purposes, people were arranged according to hierarchies of social or economic status: within records of landlords' properties by tenure, or in taxation surveys by wealth.[26] As society became more complex (see Introduction: iv) these categories received more attention, but without bringing about a significant reassessment of 'estates' theory. Diversification of occupations and professions did not lead to a multiplication of 'estates': new groups were usually placed (although sometimes awkwardly) within the tripartite framework. So too, generally, were women. Occasionally they appear as a separate group, almost a 'fourth estate', with their own subdivisions, but usually they were integrated (if discussed at all) within the categories of 'those who prayed', 'those who worked', and in association with 'those who fought'.

Such theorizing undoubtedly tended to reinforce hierarchy and inequality within society: as part of a 'body' or within an 'estate' everyone had a natural and fixed place. It could also reinforce patriarchy. The occlusion of women in much theorizing about estates is telling in itself, but so too is the tendency, when women are explicitly placed within the three orders, to categorize them differently from men. In the late twelfth-century estates handbook of Cicely, countess of Hereford, men are listed by occupation, women by moral criteria – in which the faithful wife is held up as the morally desirable model for lay women.[27]

The subordination in 'estates' theory of women to men, or of 'labourer' to lord, makes it difficult to avoid the conclusion that the 'three orders' were the 'projections of dominant groups' used to enforce their dominance. Yet there were ambiguities even within so hierarchic a scheme. Authority also meant responsibility, and if peasants were morally reprehensible for rebelling, their masters also deserved to be called to account. Clerical writers were almost unanimous in condemning as unnatural the most serious rebellion against lordship in late medieval England, the Peasants' Revolt in 1381; yet according to John Gower part of the blame was to be laid at the feet of lords whose moral turpitude had allowed the brutish anarchy of the rebellion to erupt.[28] Such commentary did not justify revolt, but it points to alternative perceptions of society which were much more equivocal about hierarchies within it.

A strong line of Christian thought regarded mankind as inherently sinful and the world inherently corrupt. Although such a perspective was concentrated within the monastic tradition, it was also one that influenced the Church as a whole during this period. Pastoral effort had the salvation of mankind as its ultimate mission; the offices of the Church were to assist in the process of combatting sin, and during an intense period of pastoral reform in the twelfth and thirteenth centuries, discussion and definition of sin and the need for penance received unprecedented attention (see Chapter 2: iii). In the growing quantity of penitential literature which assisted priests in the administering of confession, great emphasis was placed on the need to look behind the outer facade to locate the nature of sin within. Moreover, incorporated within penitential literature was also another kind of 'estates' theory, different from three orders, and with its own alternative hierarchy. The three 'estates' of the flesh ('virginity', 'chastity' and 'marriage') categorized individuals not by social function but according to a sliding scale based on levels of holy living and sin.[29] These alternative perceptions could still bear the impression of hierarchical divisions of society. Manuals of confession increasingly targeted the vices of particular social groups, subliminally underpinning social and patriarchal hierarchies: peasants, for instance, might be questioned on whether they had paid their dues to their manorial lord; women on their obedience to husbands.[30] Yet an emphasis on sin and the sinfulness of society also had the powerful effect of cutting across social hierarchies; and the discourse of penitential reform provided a commentary on society which was inherently critical of worldly values. Part of this discourse too, was that these values could infect the Church itself. Confessors were to consider the particular sins of the clergy as well as the laity. In this respect, 'religion' was anything but supportive of the social order and of the Church's place within it.

Contemporary views of society, then, were both hierarchical and equivocal of social hierarchy. But what of the views of modern historians, and how do these views change an understanding of the function of religion within medieval society? It is important to set Church and religion firmly within the context of English society as it changed during the period.

(iv) Medieval Society from a Modern Perspective

Up to a point, the categories of the 'three orders' did correspond, roughly speaking, to social 'realities'.[31] It makes a good deal of sense to distinguish 'those who fought' from 'those who worked', and to place the landed aristocracy in the first category and the landless serf in the second. Throughout the period, landowning remained the key determinant in the exercise of power, even if trade and money increasingly offered alternative avenues of social advancement. Yet medieval estates theory, from a modern standpoint, distorts social 'reality' in two fundamental ways. On the one hand, it is a model of implied stasis which obscures the enormous social changes that took place over the period; on the other, it is also a model which, in its supposition of harmony and mutual interdependence amongst its members, hides antagonisms between and within the estates.

So much has been written on the changes in medieval society, so much too on regional differences and anomalies, that a brief summary of them all will be inadequate.[32] But a few features of these changes are worth stressing because they can cast significant light on the nature of religious practices within England. Society was becoming more complex and diversified. At the beginning of our period a fundamental divide existed between the great landlord and the slave who worked his land; but even in the eleventh century, an expanding number of 'thegns' between the great landowner and the family farmer was complicating distinctions between 'those who worked' and 'those who fought'. More urbanized settlements or proto-towns made for different social set-ups from the countryside. The rapid increase in population from this period, the increasing cultivation and production of land, the expansion of trade, and the growing commercialization of the economy accelerated social change still further. All had an effect on the character of Church and religion in late Anglo-Saxon society (see Chapter 1).

The demand for goods and services stimulated markets and occupational specialization. By the end of the thirteenth century, town life was less localized and exceptional, although English towns (outside London) never became as heavily capitalized as those in the Low Countries or Northern Italy. This may have a bearing on the character of religious life in England compared with these other regions (see Chapters 3: ii–v; 6: iv). Even so, the political and economic privileges that English towns accumulated and the plethora of crafts they came to contain, made them distinctive and socially diverse environments. In more rural regions, great landlords were able to profit from expanding markets and control their labour force on their manors: although 'slaves' disappear, a distinction between 'free' and 'unfree' still remained at the end of the thirteenth century. But between these two extremes, an expanding diversity of other groups is evident: 'knights' appear below the rank of aristocrats, but below them there are free tenant-farmers, with 'franklins' at their head, and below them poorer groups of 'peasants' amongst whom a thriving land market is already apparent. It is not insignificant that this growing diversity took place at a time when the Church too was in the process of expansion, in its system of government, and in developing doctrines and forms of religious life which were applicable to social changes (see Chapter 2). Whether the Church was able to harness these changes and control all forms of religious practice is a recurring theme of this book.

Changes in economy and society did not reduce social inequality. Lordship may have become less arbitrary, but coercion could be replaced by more legalistic devices of control. Connected with a rapidly expanding economy was a developing need to use written records to formalize and document economic transactions and social arrangements.[33] At the highest level, royal authority was extended through bureaucratic, legalistic and administrative means. Indeed, one of the striking features of English society, already evident in the Anglo-Saxon period, is the relative strength of royal control even over religious life. Such control may well have made aspects of religious practice in England different from many other parts of Europe – although the limitations of this control and the extent of regional diversity must also be emphasized (see Chapters 1: ii; 3: ii; 4: ii; 5: ii; 6: iv–ix).

Other kinds of lordship exerted powerful influences. Manorial lords could exploit markets by commuting labour rents for cash or enforcing control over tenants in manorial courts. But the pressure of lordship had other effects on society. Also apparent by the thirteenth century is the growing capacity among other social groups for collective action. The acquisition of 'borough' privileges by towns was often the result of lordly initiative, but townsmen with their own economic interests, could assert themselves against seigneurial control. Within a rural setting, manorial records demonstrate 'communal' responses of tenants to landlord demands. In any case, increasing pressure on land with the continuing rise in population made collective arrangements over 'common' fields essential. Regional diversity however makes these generalizations unsound. We find lordship rather lighter in East Anglia than in 'champion' regions of England where nucleated villages were often more tightly bound to lordly manors. But such variation does not alter the general picture of a society increasingly diverse in its hierarchical structure.

How social hierarchy and diversity impacted upon religious practice (and a sense of 'community') is another question to be pursued (see especially Chapters 4: ix; 5: v, viii; 6: ii, viii). But a preliminary exploration of the nature of divisions within society is required. Whether social groups were fundamentally antagonistic towards each other is a matter of vigorous debate.[34] A stratified society need not have meant a fractured one: a sense of mutual interdependence or deference may well have promoted consensus across unequal social groups. Perhaps the stratas in society should be seen as gradations on a sliding scale of hierarchy, based on status, rather than as separate 'classes' polarized against each other (as a Marxist would have it) because of economic division. Conflict between them, when it did occur, was thus sporadic rather than fundamental. And yet extremes of wealth and power were so great that it is difficult to escape the conclusion (whether we adopt a Marxist perspective or not), that if conflicts were few, it was because resistance was suppressed by the strong hand of lordship. A Marxist model would also categorize the contrast between great landowners and 'peasants' as the fundamental divide in this society, and attribute each group with their own 'class' consciousness; and although it is easier to detect such a consciousness within the former, bound by a 'chivalric' culture and buoyed up by its economic power, the cooperative efforts of the latter make it possible to discern common interests among the 'peasantry' too. Not all historians would agree. The 'dominant elite' was divided within itself: there were great contrasts in wealth and outlook among the clergy, for instance between bishop and parish priest; there were potentially great conflicts of interest between churchman (however lordly and powerful) and secular aristocrat. In any case, the penumbra of social groups which seem to straddle 'classes' of 'lord' and 'peasant' blurs distinctions between them. Amongst the 'peasantry', differences between a village elite and poorer groups, or within towns between 'guilds merchant', craft guilds and journeymen, may seem more important than any collective antipathy amongst them against seigneurial lordship. Nevertheless, on balance it is more convincing to argue that antagonism towards lordship among these lesser groups was stronger than tensions within them; but it is worth bearing in mind (when discussing corporate religious practices) that significant antagonisms could develop within groups which intrinsically had more to unite them than divide.

The nature of divisions within society is made more complicated by issues of gender. Perhaps women should be seen as a separate social group; perhaps they had concerns which linked them across any social divide. A powerful tradition of misogyny, reaching back to a classical past, may have encouraged a sense of female gender identity. Certainly this tradition usually prevented women from wielding significant political or economic power. Socio-economic changes may also have affected women in particular ways or at particular moments of the life-cycle more than was the case for men. On the other hand, there may be a stronger case for arguing that women in this period were more divided by their social status than united by their gender.[35] Discussion about the existence of any shared sense of womanhood among women also raises related but different questions about the nature of 'gender' and 'gender identity', male and female. Much recent debate has tended to highlight the complexity of these issues especially if the gender of an individual is seen as a matter of 'performance' rather than biological essence.[36] Commentary on norms or attitudes about 'gender' has also emphasized complexity within apparently straightforward stereotyping: ideologies which at first

glance appear irredeemably misogynistic were open to alternative interpretation, while assertions of gender difference could hide other kinds of
agenda. These issues will need further discussion because 'gender' could
have a significant impact both on choices and on perceptions of religious
behaviour, ideal as well as practical (see Chapters 4: ix; 6: ii, viii, ix).
Suffice it to note here that gender (whether we mean the biological differences
between men and women or the gendered identities and norms that men
or women could adopt) could cut across social status, as well as vice versa:
divisions within society cannot be seen simply as socio-economic ones.

In the later Middle Ages, the potential for social mobility and tension
was increased[37] – with some significant implications, as we shall see, for
religious practices. Some of the conditions which had previously promoted social change were reversed. Population levels were already
declining in the early fourteenth century, and were severely reduced after
the Black Death in 1348–49 which killed off at least a third of the population. It may still be debated whether plague was the root cause of subsequent changes, and whether it was continuing visitations of plague
which prevented demographic recovery until late into the fifteenth
century.[38] But the changes which did occur made for significant
alterations in social structures and attitudes. Late medieval society was
certainly more fluid. Depressed population levels meant an overall
decline in production; yet some regions (particularly in the south and
around London), and some industries (such as the cloth trade) were able
to thrive; commercial opportunities allowed some individuals to increase
per capita wealth; labour shortages meant a potential rise in income for
the agricultural labourer or urban artisan who could command higher
wages, and may even have allowed women a greater economic freedom;[39]
and such was the need for landlords to adjust to new 'market-forces' that
serfdom had virtually disappeared by the end of the fifteenth century. It
is not surprising to find greater social diversity: new gradations of 'gentlemen' and 'esquires' below aristocrats; and below them, 'yeomen' and
'husbandmen' whose exploitation of the land market lifted them above
other 'peasants' in rural society; or to find, within towns, merchants
whose wealth placed them on a par with gentry. It was also a period in
which levels of literacy and opportunities for education, especially in
the larger towns, were increasing, with potentially far-reaching social
implications: for one thing, the traditional distinction made between
orders of clergy and laity – the one 'literate', the other 'illiterate' – was a
distinction increasingly difficult to make, and one (in the minds of some
churchmen) which had alarming implications (see Chapter 6: iii, iv).

Fluidity created opportunity, but tension too. Some changes did not come without delay or without reaction. Landlords in the 1350s and 1360s sought to prevent serfs or labourers profiting from changing conditions with statutory legislation. A fundamental rift between great landlord and 'peasant' is still observable in the Peasants' Revolt of 1381: even if short-term events (not least the imposition of the Poll Tax) helped trigger the uprising, it is inexplicable without reference to the effects of lordly repression on both the 'free' and 'unfree' within rural society.[40] The revolt was put down with further repression, and although it may have finally forced landlords to relax manorial restrictions, the frightening spectacle of revolt continued to haunt the imagination of the seigneurial elite.

Conversely the Revolt perhaps contributed to a tradition of dissent among 'peasants'.[41] But although there are moments, especially in 1381, when a 'class consciousness' is apparent among social groups united by a common sense of oppression, solidarity within rural 'communities' is hard to find. Village elites may have joined in with the rebellion in 1381, but their attitudes to repression were ambivalent, not least because as employers themselves they might welcome and enforce the Statute of Labourers. There were other ways, after the mid-fourteenth century, that social cohesion within villages tended to become eroded, especially in areas (notably around London) where new markets offered opportunity for individual enterprise. Manorial court records seem to show greater evidence of insistence on individual rights at the expense of communal ones.[42]

Urban society from the late fourteenth century was also affected by social divisions. Post-plague conditions caused some towns to 'decline' and enabled others to prosper, while the retreat of seigneurial authority allowed more towns to acquire borough privileges. But within most, antagonisms seem to have increased. Town governments had good reason to fret about the problems of labour shortage and artisanal behaviour, especially after the Peasants' Revolt which had involved urban as well as rural unrest. Opportunities for a mercantile elite to accumulate capital also contributed to an increase in oligarchic control within many towns. Oligarchies were themselves subject to faction: the uprising at York during the Peasants' Revolt was as much a result of dissension among the mercantile elite as it was an artisanal rebellion against the city rulers.[43] But the sense of collective urgency among the urban elite is evident in attempts to enforce labour legislation to control the distribution of wealth within towns and to weaken the potential for corporate identity among artisans as a whole. In York, the town council institutionalized craft guilds in 1363–64 and restricted individual membership to one trade. A parliamentary statute of 1436 required registration of all guilds with town councils (or local JPs), making them subject to closer authoritarian scrutiny.[44] At a national and local level, regulation attempting to control social mobility of all kinds was increasing. It appears in sumptuary legislation which denounced the idle luxury of parvenus who had the audacity to ape the sartorial and dietary habits of their social superiors. It appears in legislation and literature denouncing the 'idle' poor and 'vagrants' who disguised their indigency as holy poverty. It appears too in attitudes to women: from the sharper segregation of prostitutes in towns, to the 'protective' moralizing on respectable female behaviour evident in certain 'courtesy' texts. Social unrest and social mobility from the late fourteenth century provoked a reaction, amongst those in authority, of a repressive and moralizing kind. Demographic recovery (and in some places economic contraction) by the later fifteenth century did not soften such attitudes; indeed by then concern in some towns with moral and sexual misbehaviour was sharper than before.[45] All these developments made an impact on late medieval religious practices both of a corporate and more personal nature, and have a significant bearing on how we might characterize those practices (see Chapters 5: vii, viii; 6: viii, ix).

(v) The Social Dimension of Religion

The changes within English society obviously cast a different light on medieval perceptions of society. The fractured nature of relations between different social groups makes the harmonious model of the three orders an even more specious one: emphasis on the model in the twelfth century already seems a response to social mobility, and renewed emphasis on its divine purpose from the mid-fourteenth seems even more a rearguard reaction to rapid change.[46]

For the purposes of this book, however, there are more significant reasons why the nature of society needs emphasis. After all, religious practices were rooted in a social context. Since 'society' itself was cast as 'Christian', social regulation inevitably had a moralizing edge, and religious behaviour a social dimension. Going to church was not simply a matter of personal piety. It might have a gendered aspect: church-going is made a particular female virtue in 'courtesy' texts. It also had other social implications. The parish church was not just an arena of communal worship but a space in which lordship or other local hierarchies could assert themselves.[47] In the climate of fear at popular unrest in the late fourteenth century, attendance at church might be perceived as part of social discipline. One petition to Parliament in 1390 connected a fear of social mobility with concern about communal worship: it claimed that 'low persons' on holy days went hunting – an aristocratic pursuit – when 'good Christians' were at church.[48]

So how 'homogeneous', in the end, was medieval religion in this kind of society? In the late medieval period, when evidence for religious practices at a local level is much more abundant, an emphasis on 'community' is indeed striking. The elaboration of the liturgy and setting for mass, the most important of all services, seems testimony to the depth of Christian culture within late medieval society and to strong collective desire for religious and social harmony. Such a view seems predicated on an assumption that common bonds outweighed any antagonisms between different groups.[49] It also suggests that religion functioned as some kind of benign social cement between these groups. But to regard late medieval society as essentially fractured offers alternative perspectives on contemporary religion: it alerts us to the ways in which the desire for harmony might be the product of social anxiety, the expression of 'community' the assertion of hierarchy, and communal practices the sites of contention.[50]

None of this need imply that religious beliefs and practices should be fitted neatly into social categories, as though predetermined by social context, or imply that every mass attended was an occasion for fraught dispute. We should stop short too of regarding 'religion' as a whole as the instrument of dominant social groups.[51] These groups had their own conflicts of interest which divided them internally. Certain religious ideas and practices were undoubtedly exploited in the interests of hierarchy and authority, but if 'dominant' social groups used religion in this fashion it was because they did not always feel dominant. And for all its core doctrines, beliefs and rituals, medieval Catholicism was too diverse in the way these were interpreted and practised to be viewed as a simple adjunct of power and social relations.

We should also stop short of regarding individuals as social automata, as though their piety was merely the unconscious product of their place in society. To penetrate the inner beliefs of most people in this period may be impossible, but it is a mistake to assume that beliefs did not matter, and that these beliefs might not lead an individual to question the nature of his or her values and place in society. What is possible for the historian to observe, without ignoring the importance of beliefs, is the social implications of religious ideas and actions and how these in their turn might condition social behaviour; and the ways in which choices of religious behaviour were shaped (rather than determined) by a great variety of influences. Doctrines preached from the pulpit or enjoined at confession; moral prescriptions of religious and secular authorities; patterns of piety practised locally; perceptions and habits conditioned by status, gender and social change: all played a part in the 'religion of the laity'.

The social dimension of religion in England and the social forces that shaped it are, then, the particular concerns of this book. Chapter 1 looks at 'Church and society' as a whole, taking as a starting point the late Anglo-Saxon period; from then on the chapters deal with issues more thematically from the eleventh to the fifteenth centuries. Chapter 2 concentrates on the development of a universal Church and the pastoral efforts to instruct the laity. In subsequent chapters, the responses of lay people to prescription, their religious activities, beliefs and attitudes, are the focus of attention. Chapter 3 looks at manifestations of the 'holy' – the appearance of saints and cults, lay and clerical perceptions of them, and at potential tensions between the universal Church and local churches. Chapter 4 concentrates on the more corporate forms of lay religious activity, especially within the parish; Chapter 5 on how these were affected by attitudes to death. The final chapter examines more 'personal' forms of devotion, and the effects of literacy, nonconformity and heresy on the ideals and practice of living a 'holy' life within the world.

Chapter 1: Anglo-Saxon Church and Society c.1000

About the year 1001, a peasant ploughing a field at Slepe, in a manor belonging to the abbey of Ramsey, stumbled upon the bones of four bodies hidden in the soil. One set of bones was extravagantly identified in a dream as those of St Ivo, a Persian bishop, no less, who had spent his last days in England as a hermit. A great crowd witnessed the translation of these relics from Slepe to the abbey. So that the relics would be accessible for public veneration, the sarcophagus containing them was allowed to protrude through the abbey walls into the world outside. A spring gushed from the sepulchre and became the source of many cures. Some people were sceptical: a foreign monk suspected the cult to be nothing more than the product of silly, superstitious rustics, who were habitually deceived out of heathen error into making cults of springs and bones. But his objections were stilled by the spring's miraculous powers.[1]

Envisage multitudes of pious peasants flocking to monasteries and their relics: does this epitomize the place of the Church in late Anglo-Saxon society? Alas, the attempt to peer through the miracle story into a field of common folk meets a reflection of the abbey's own traditions, fears and ambitions. St Ivo's story was written down by Goscelin in the late 1080s at the request of the community at Ramsey, at a difficult time in the monastery's history.[2] The Norman conquest did seem to pose a threat to cherished Anglo-Saxon cults; Ramsey's hold over the manor of Slepe had been disputed. The miracles 'authenticated' the cult for a new Norman abbot and a wider foreign elite; it established the monastery's claim to the manor. The miracles followed a long tradition of hagiography in which crowds of pious peasants, as well as objections to cults, were *de rigueur*. The picture of superstitious 'rustics' and of a sepulchre, both inside and outside the cloister walls, is not a description of 'fact', but a textual construction of corporate identity in which the contours of monastic life are set in high relief against the world outside. The story of St Ivo at Ramsey reflects a genre rather than describes a 'reality'.

There are other problems. Even at face value, the story offers an ambiguous picture of lay religion: pious crowds awaiting miracles, and yet, according to the sceptical monk, an underworld of semi-heathen rustics. Was late Anglo-Saxon England 'Christian' at all? Church organization in Roman Britain had been all but destroyed in the wake of pagan Germanic invaders and settlers after the fifth century; in the more recent past, Viking settlement in the Danelaw region of the north in the ninth century had disrupted ecclesiastical life. We might expect to encounter pagan survivals or Scandinavian religion. But the nature and depth of belief among lay people is hard to assess, as we shall see. To begin with, it is easier to gauge the place of the Church in Anglo-Saxon society, by looking at the more tangible evidence for its influence: evidence such as the buildings, personnel and organization showing the reach of its ministry, and evidence such as its pronouncements and instructive literature expressing its ideals.

(i) The Church and Pastoral Reform

The potential influence of Christianity was certainly far greater in the eleventh century than it had been in the seventh or eighth. By then church buildings were much thicker on the ground. In the sixth century, Pope Gregory had envisaged the establishment of a network of bishoprics, centred on Canterbury, to accomplish the process of conversion, but although bishops did become heavily involved in pastoral efforts and created a diocesan structure, Christianity had spread to the countryside largely through the establishment of monastic houses or 'minsters' (and under the inspiration too of 'Celtic' missionaries detached from the Roman tradition).[3] There is still some dispute over the nature and function of these churches.[4] A 'monasterium' or 'minster' could refer interchangeably to a church staffed by regular monks or by secular clergy. Either way 'monks' might perform similar tasks to the 'secular clergy': the Benedictine ideal itself had never precluded pastoral activity from a life of ascetic withdrawal. The early minsters seem to have established large 'parochiae', along existing regional boundaries, royal vills or large agrarian estates; many may well have acted as a base for an itinerant team ministry to carry out pastoral work in remoter areas. Perhaps such work was not the function of all minsters, but the siting of many of them does suggest a deliberate pastoral scheme: most of the inhabitants of Surrey by the tenth century, for instance, would have been within a short morning's walk of such a church.[5]

Pastoral effort, however, should not be seen as the product of a single clerical will. The Anglo-Saxon 'Church' was not the 'Universal Church' of later centuries (see Chapter 2), and its diversity within regions is often more striking than unity across them. The pattern of minster creation was variable. It is more evident in Hampshire than in Yorkshire; and while in Kent and Surrey there appears to be a close relation between minster and 'hundred' boundaries, the correlation is not so evident in Devon. In fact the minster 'system' was established late in Devon and later still in Cornwall, where Celtic influences and missionary activity had been particularly strong. Devon was not absorbed into the Anglo-Saxon kingdom of Wessex until the seventh century, Cornwall not till the tenth, and the early chapel baptisteries or preaching stations set up by hermits and British monks in this region, established a pattern of churches (and an attachment to 'Celtic' saints) which was to linger late into the Middle Ages and beyond.[6] Viking invasions from the end of the eighth century also affected the pattern, especially in the northern and eastern regions of England (later the Danelaw) where ecclesiastical organization was severely disrupted. After the Viking threat had diminished, and the Danelaw began to be reabsorbed, a larger number of minsters is evident in all areas from the mid-ninth century onwards, although the extent of continuity between old and new minsters is not entirely clear.

By the eleventh century law codes which deal with the status of minsters also show a great variety in types of church.[7] Yet variety also meant abundance: regular contact between churchmen and people by then did not rely on larger minsters and teams of itinerant preachers. A process had begun by the tenth century in which the 'parochiae' of such minsters were fragmenting into a system of smaller proto-parishes, with their own churches or chapels: the proliferation of parish churches in the eleventh century was, it seems, a distinctively English phenomenon; and it should partly be set within the context of pastoral reform, for some of this fragmentation may have been planned. The difficulty of providing for the cure of souls in large or heavily populated areas could be solved with the foundation of churches in outlying villages or populous towns.

Pastoral reform was also bound up with other kinds of Church reform. In the mid-tenth century, especially under King Edgar (959–75), there had been a period of monastic expansion such that reformed Benedictine communities became numerous all over Wessex and the Midlands (though not in Northumbria), and in which a sharper distinction between secular and monastic clergy was enshrined. But a renewed emphasis on the ascetic ideal did not weaken the pastoral impulse. Indeed, monastic renewal was once again part of a wider movement of reform which was underway by the end of the tenth century. The reformed monasteries did not retreat from the world. Abbot Aelfric (d.1010) who founded the reformed monastery of Cerne Abbas, wrote letters in Old English to the bishops of Sherborne and Worcester with advice for the training of secular clergy and unprecedented detail on how they should fulfil their vocation: they were warned, for instance, not to let mouse droppings lie on the altar.[8]

More attention than ever before was also directed to the laity. Councils and synods legislated on the proper conduct of lay people, both in the payment of dues to support minster churches, and in duties such as abstaining from work on feast days. The homilies of Aelfric and Wulfstan made concerted use of the vernacular – more perhaps than any contemporary bishop on the continent – to communicate basic religious truths to the laity and stimulate the moral reform of the individual. Specific texts (books of the Old Testament) were written for ealdormen: the ideal life recommended to them was one in which monastic observances were followed as closely as a life lived in the world allowed. Such an ideal was apparently followed by the nobleman Leofric who heard two masses a day, fasted and prayed in secret while others slept.[9]

But such a life might be open only to the few, and the homiletic message was intended to reach a much broader, and largely illiterate, cross-section of society. Observances did not have to be as harsh. The laity were to learn the Pater Noster, the Creed, Ten Commandments; they were to attend communion, observe Sundays and festivals, confess sins to a local priest, and perform penances such as fasting or almsgiving for the good of their souls. Even if not enforced regularly the confessional was an opportunity to test a penitent's knowledge and to mould his moral behaviour. The laity were to be reminded about the fate of their souls if they remained unrepentant. There was not yet a fully developed ideal of purgatory, between heaven and hell, integrated into a system of penance (see Chapter 2: ii) – although visions of the afterlife could include a place of punishment that was 'not hell'.[10] In general homilies tended to adopt a more apocalyptic tone in describing punishment for the sinner: Abbot Aelfric's Catholic Homilies promised the 'surging fires of hell torment' for all those who did not repent before the Day of Judgment and the coming of the Antichrist. The vast accumulation of penitential literature from this period is testimony to the pastoral endeavour.[11]

Its impact among the laity is more easily gauged among the landowning elite. Some ealdormen or thegns had clearly requested specific instructional texts. Their wills evince an apprehension of the Day of Judgment and a concern to give land and money to monasteries or minsters, and their saints, 'for the fate of their souls'.[12] But a wider impact was envisaged through preaching. Bishop Oswald apparently preached in the cemetery of Worcester cathedral to large audiences; and his Life describes how in 991 he preached to a 'multitude' from five counties at the rededication of the church of St Mary, Ramsey, and how, at a rogation procession, the boat filled with his personal retinue almost capsized because it was so overloaded.[13]

Once again we are back in the midst of pious 'crowds'. Tenth-century monastic reform was accompanied by a growing interest in cults of saints, whose lives and miracles involved the laity in ever greater numbers. The public display of relics in translation processions seems to have become much more common by the end of the tenth century. The relics of Sts Swithun, Aethelwold and Oswald were all moved, sometimes more than once, between 971 and 1002, in public ceremonies attended by 'multitudes'. According to Aelfric, St Swithun's second translation in 975 to a new altar in Winchester was followed by an extension of his cult: the walls of his church became littered with crutches and stools hung there by cripples cured of their disabilities.[14]

Once again too, however, hagiographic convention and monastic concerns lay behind the 'popularity' of these cults. Most of the saints created were monks, and hagiography was still produced largely for a monastic audience. Crowds were 'manufactured'. They played their part in demonstrating divine approval of a community's possession of particular relics. The reformed monastic houses founded in the mid-tenth century gathered in relics from all parts of the country in a conscious bid to assert the legitimacy of the new order. Rightful possession of relics also guaranteed the patronage of the saint for the monastery to which they belonged: as an undying landlord a saint could be counted upon to protect his or her patrimony. St Ivo bestowed his blessing on Ramsey's possession of the manor of Slepe. Local groups of laity often feature in these accounts. Goscelin tells how the abbot of St Augustine, Canterbury, in the late eleventh century, personally interrogated a parishioner at Lyminge in an endeavour to disprove the claim made by St Gregory's priory that it had acquired St Mildrith's relics from that parish. Minster-in-Thanet had been the relics' resting place; and when these were translated to Canterbury, the monks of St Augustine were careful to leave some dust of St Mildrith's flesh to console the islanders in their grief at the removal of their saint's remains.[15]

The assertion that these cults enjoyed local support, outside monastic walls, may also reflect additional threats rather than a groundswell of popular devotion. The renewed assault of Viking raids from 980 which culminated in 1016 with the accession of a Danish king, Canute, appears in stories dated to that period. The body of St Edmund – and his miraculously talking head – had been translated to Bury St Edmund's c.915 following his martyrdom (869) at the hands of marauding Vikings; later, Danish raids forced further movement of his remains to London in 1010. There his cult also made its mark: Herman's Life (late eleventh century) recounts how Londoners refused to allow the same martyr's relics to be taken back to Bury St Edmund's in 1013. Ultimately though, the Danes did not represent the same kind of threat posed to the Church by early Viking raids in the eighth century. Church lands may well have been seized, but Canute rapidly reconciled himself to Christianity and its cults in England. In 1023 he had the relics of St Aelfheah (murdered by drunken Danes in 1011) transported from London to Canterbury in a dragon-prowed ship, filled with chanting monks and house carls.[16]

Yet there may be something more to 'crowds' of pious layfolk than monastic convention and wishful thinking. Perhaps worried monks consciously promoted – and perhaps could expect – the support of a broader spectrum of society. In the context of pastoral reform from the late tenth century, in which preaching, public processions, and duties to local churches were so strongly stressed, the more regular appearance in miracles of lay people, sensitized to cults of saints, is less implausible. But if this was so, it was not solely, or even largely, the result of an ecclesiastical propagation of the 'Christian' message. As we shall see, the Anglo-Saxon Church had relied on lay power, and with this reliance had come compromise with the world. The interests of lay groups in society, and their attitudes to the clergy, religious houses and the cults of saints did not necessarily accord with clerical reform.

(ii) Royal Power and the Church

Although on the continent – not least under Carolingian kings – the relationship between the Church and rulers had been close, in England it was closer still. The hierarchical structure of a metropolitan Church, centred on Canterbury, was a legacy of Pope Gregory's mission; and in his *Ecclesiastical History of the English People*, Bede had enshrined a vision of an intimate relationship between this ecclesiastical structure and the progression of royal authority. A shared sense of 'Englishness' first among the various Anglo-Saxon kingdoms and then, by the tenth century, in the region of England dominated by the house of Wessex, was a constructive legacy of this heritage. Ecclesiastical and royal power advanced one with the other: after Northumbria had fallen under West Saxon rule in 937, the Archbishop of York acted as the royal representative in the region.[17]

The main partnership between Church and kings had developed not through the diocesan structure, but through the minster 'system'. In exchange for royal patronage, the monastic house provided kings with an association with the saints and a burial place for the perpetuation of their fame. Many of the larger minsters by the early eighth century had been set up in royal administrative centres. As royal authority became more effective, and shire administration more centralized, so West Saxon kings established their hold over churches in southern England. The military organization – especially the burghal system – which eventually defeated the Vikings in the ninth century allowed West Saxon kings to develop a kingdom with a degree of centralization almost without parallel on the Continent.

Monastic reform in the tenth century had clerical and pastoral goals; but it was also the product of royal power. It was in the interest of kings to establish their patronage over a movement which sought to weaken (as we shall see) the control exercised by ealdormen over 'family' monasteries. In return, reformed monasteries offered special prayers for the king and queen every day; reforming clerics recognized the sacred authority of kings and queens in the development of the coronation ritual. Royal anointing may have implied that the spiritual blessing of kings was conferred by the Church alone, but kingship was quasi-sacerdotal: in 973 King Edgar was crowned at Bath in an 'imperial' style of coronation in which the king's functions were identified with those of Christ. The identification of royal power with reform of the Church is cemented in the *Regularis Concordia* of 973: in exchange for his patronage, essential for the well-being of the Church, Edgar was assured, as a faithful Christian king, of a glorious hegemony over the English and other peoples in the island of Britain.[18]

So closely were spiritual and temporal authority intertwined that King Ethelred at the Council of Bath, faced with the growing threat of the Vikings from the late tenth century, could order penitential processions throughout his kingdom. The martyred King Edmund, Christ-like in his suffering according to Abbo of Fleury's late tenth-century account, combined royal authority with the qualities of a saint.[19] Wulfstan's statement of ecclesiastical law in 1014 equated the laws of the king with the laws of Christ. Moreover, however fearful Wulfstan was of the Danish threat, the theocratic principle survived Danish accession and was enshrined in the secular and ecclesiastical laws of Canute. It appears too in the homiletic material of pastoral reformers: the 'Law of the Northumbrian Priests' (c.1020) ends with the assertion that there was ever to be one Christianity and one royal authority in the nation.[20]

Royal control over cults of saints and relics is evident. Perhaps the ideal of a united kingdom was encouraged by placing the newly reformed religious houses, themselves linked by royal patronage, under the protection of a primary cult, that of the Virgin Mary.[21] More strikingly, the cult of the royal martyr and saint seems to have been stronger in England than elsewhere, perhaps as a result of a tradition of strong kingship.[22] Possession of relics was as much a measure of power as of piety, and kings acquired new relics to enlarge their political authority. As West Saxon kings extended their control over the east and then the north of England, so they despoiled the local religious houses of their relics. King Eadred's Northumbria campaign of 948 was completed by the transference of the remains of St Wilfrid to Canterbury. The reformed monasteries of the south were often the recipients of this royal booty, their chroniclers offering justifications for these relic raids and locating the legitimacy of their reformed life in the acquisition of new relics: a version of the Life of St Wilfrid, commissioned shortly after the arrival of the saint's remains at Canterbury, justified the translation by denouncing the neglect of shrines in religious houses like Ripon. Divine approval for possession of relics could be extended to the kingdom at large: to Abbot Aelfric 'the English race is not deprived of the Lord's saints, since in this English land lie such saints as this holy king [St Edmund] and the blessed Cuthbert and Saint Aethelfryth in Ely ... for the strengthening of belief'.[23] Collectively they bestowed a divine destiny on England and the English under royal rule.

Changes of regime in the eleventh century did not alter the pattern of close royal control over cults. Canute's conversion to Christianity was also a conversion to Anglo-Saxon cults.[24] He decreed that the feast days of Edward the Martyr and St Dunstan be celebrated throughout England. He also became a benefactor of St Aelfheah, whom his own countrymen had murdered: his involvement in the translation of St Aelfheah's relics to Canterbury in 1023 was public demonstration of contrition and of the legitimacy of rule.

The precocious extent of royal authority over the Church and saints' cults was a feature of religion which is more striking in England than in any other region on the continent. From the very beginning of conversion, the pastoral efforts of churchmen were strongly aided, and constrained, by their royal masters. But the level of royal control over the sacred had its limits. The Church's assertion of special status or immunity was a theoretical counterweight to regal authority, and it would be stressed increasingly from the eleventh century. In any case, the image of kings as Christ-like figures was potentially two-edged: it raised a standard by which kings might all the more easily be judged unfavourably. Some royal saints might potentially have become focuses of anti-royal resistance: the cult of Edward the Martyr (the half-brother of Ethelred, murdered in 979) seems to have required careful handling. Monastic reform in the mid-tenth century had advanced hand in glove with royal power, but not without raising the hostilities of those vested interests which it had sought to overcome. The 'anti-monastic' reaction of some ealdormen, who resented the reduction of their rights over monasteries, affected royal as well as monastic power.[25] In any case, in a 'Church' which was still highly localized, with religious houses developing their own identities, even the relics of the most royal of saints could be absorbed into the traditions of houses that possessed them.[26] But it is also evident that both clerical institutions and royal power were constrained by wider social forces. As we shall see later, the character of religion in late Anglo-Saxon society was shaped by much more than an alliance of kings and churchmen.

(iii) Church and Social Order

The close identification of ecclesiastical with royal power was part of a wider integration of Church and clergy within society. At an ideological level, the division of society into three orders, those who 'laboured', 'prayed' or 'fought', seems to have occurred in England earlier than elsewhere. Again, the strength of kingship might provide an explanation, since this tripartite schema potentially underpinned royal power which could act as arbiter between all three 'estates'. But it also acted to support other kinds of hierarchy. According to Aelfric, the three estates were mutually interdependent. If one fell, they all fell. Or as the tract *Episcopus* emphasized, bishops were to labour for a just and ordered society in which slaves worked willingly for their lords.[27]

Other kinds of hierarchy were reinforced by religious reform and homiletic literature.[28] For Aelfric, 'those who prayed' were exclusively male monks. The monastic reform movement of the tenth century had not led to a burgeoning of female houses; and for Aelfric the ideal of virginity, even when exemplified in the lives of female martyrs, was identified as an attribute of male monasticism. Female sexuality was evidently more dangerous. The *Regularis Concordia* seems to exalt the special role of queens in the protection of nuns, yet it also identifies female houses as needful of more careful regulation. Patriarchal control asserted itself beyond the cloister – in homiletic advocation of obedience of wives to husbands, or in royal law codes which dealt specially with widows. Growing 'state' control in England seems to extend itself beyond religious and fiscal affairs and into the sexual identity of its members. Recent historiography can be gloomy about the 'freedoms' enjoyed by women in pre-Conquest society; and within this society, churchmen lent spiritual legitimacy to patriarchy.

Nevertheless, some constraints on women are more apparent than real. The relative absence of female religious houses, permanently endowed with land, may be offset by the presence of forms of religious life which, however ephemeral or fleetingly visible in surviving records, allowed certain women full expression for their spiritual aspirations.[29] The widowed vowess, provided for on her own lands, still a layperson but exalted in religious status, perhaps with a tiny household of other women, connected informally with a local monastic house, may have formed the focal point for what, in a later period, some historians would call a 'female subculture' (see Chapter 6: ii, viii). But evidence is fragmentary; and what such women read or which books they possessed is obscure indeed. Aelfric's sermons or lives of virgin martyrs would not have provided ready models validating female independence. On the other hand, women may have found in them meanings quite different from those intended by a patriarchal author. Again, evidence for a later period suggests that ideals could undergo considerable reinterpretation in different contexts: why not too in Anglo-Saxon England? The 'Life of Edward the Confessor' commissioned by his queen Edith (1065–66) suggests ways in which a powerful woman might construct herself as 'chaste virgin' to extend rather than limit her power.[30]

There were ways, too, in which religious attitudes were more ambivalent towards other kinds of hierarchy. Homiletic literature, in its emphasis on sin, was socially levelling. Wulfstan's 'Sermon of the Wolf to the English' (1014) decries the desertion of masters by slaves, but makes no social distinctions in reminding its audience of the fate of the Britons whose sinfulness had brought about their own destruction.[31] As a commentary on values and change in lay society, the religious ideals of reformers might be corrosive of the social order. Although Wulfstan does integrate the perceived neglect of rank and status into a picture of wider sinfulness, his 'Sermon' is by no means a confident assertion of hierarchy. An apocalyptic tone is adopted: social and moral harmony has indeed collapsed and English defeats at the hands of Vikings are a punishment for sins. Assertions of hierarchy and social order were perhaps the product of a fear that both were under threat: expressed ideals of hierarchy did not necessarily reflect social 'fact'.

(iv) Church and Lay Society

Churchmen had other anxieties about the distinctiveness of their place within society. There was a considerable distance between the reality and the assertion that 'those who prayed' constituted a separate 'order'. The clergy were not, as they were to become (in theory), a caste apart. The 'vertical' ties between local churches and the papacy in Rome, even if increasingly encouraged, were tenuous relative to the situation in later centuries.[32] Much stronger were the 'horizontal' ties between clergy and laity. Bishops, as royal appointees, played their part in the running of a secular government, attending royal councils and shire courts. The humbler clergy in the 'Law of the Northumbrian Priests', although given a sense of corporate solidarity, were subject to their kin-law. Even monks retained strong links with their aristocratic kin outside the cloister.

Such ties were an inevitable consequence of the early process of conversion: the establishment of religious houses had been dependent not only on kings but also on a warrior aristocracy who expected, besides the promise of spiritual reward, that monastic endowment would allow retention of wealth and estates for the future benefit of their kin. But though inevitable, these ties were not always welcomed. The intrusion of secular influence and values into religious life worried reformers. Eighth-century synods had already insisted on a greater separation of clergy from laity. Bede had attacked those 'monasteries' which were monastic only in name, and those clergy who retained close connections with founding families. Some thegns may well have converted their households into 'monasteries' to acquire the same landholding rights that might accrue to a religious foundation.[33] Monastic reform in the tenth century had attempted to sharpen the distinction between monks who held property in common and those not living under a monastic rule over whose personnel and lands secular families exercised a stronger hold. But eleventh-century reformers were to insist that this process had not gone far enough. Anglo-Saxon minsters (with clusters of clergy not bound by a Rule) were to be condemned as 'decadent'.

The necessary though, to some churchmen, disturbing interdependence of Church and laity is evident at every social level. The great expansion in the number of smaller churches, even by the eleventh century, may have been part of a pastoral programme, but the efforts in law codes to protect the financial rights of larger minsters in their 'parochiae' reflect an attempt to impose system on relative disorder, and a recognition of the growing independence of local churches. Just as the beginnings of the 'minster system' had followed in the footsteps of secular power and landholding, so its 'fragmentation' (especially in the Danelaw) was shaped by changes in landholding patterns.[34] A new 'class' of thegns, between the great landowner and family farmer, serving the law courts and shire administration of an expanding royal government, was already emerging in the tenth century. The break-up of large unitary estates into smaller manors in many areas, and the activity of thegns on the land market, was accompanied by the foundation of churches by the thegnly holders of these manors.[35] Motives are hard to read. Doubtless, a concern for the welfare of their souls prompted landowners to establish their own centres of spiritual insurance; and it is possible that these also served the pastoral needs of a wider local community. But local churches, with pretensions to independence from mother churches, also served as symbols of thegnly status. Spiritual and temporal motives coalesce in the proud inscription on the tower of the church of St Mary Wigford: 'Eirtig had me built and endowed to the glory of Christ and St Mary'.[36] Church land, building and priest who served it, were his property.

But the beginnings of the parish system was not just the product of thegnly power. The proliferation of churches in the countryside – and in urban settlements – was primarily the consequence of demographic and economic change. The rise in population from the ninth to at least the mid-twelfth century; the apparent improvement in climate and in productivity; the expansion of trade and urban markets: all had powerful effects on the character of the Church and religious practice. In the countryside (especially in eastern England), new communities emerged with the advance of land clearance, which old minster churches could find difficult to accommodate. Thegnly churches might serve the pastoral needs of a wider local manor or region. But groups of local inhabitants were also active. It was because their village was so far from the mother church of Sonning that those of Whistley (Berkshire) petitioned for burial rights c.1080 to be given to their own chapel.[37]

About 10 per cent of the population in England by the late eleventh century – particularly in the south and east of England – lived in towns or proto-urban areas.[38] Their density and social diversity usually translated into a heavier concentration of churches – the properties of local urban landowners, burgesses and even enclaves of foreign merchants (like the church of the Scandinavian saint Olaf outside the north gate of York). On occasion, local groups of neighbours must also have been responsible: some of the forty-nine churches and chapels counted in Winchester by 1088 were associated with local craftsmen. These churches were clearly regarded as the property of their founders, invested with a strong sense of local and corporate identity. When in the mid-eleventh century a priest Godric attempted to endow Peterborough abbey with a church at Lincoln in which he had served as priest, he met with the objections of citizens who claimed that no one could grant possession of property to bodies outside the city.[39] Official ecclesiastical direction might attempt to regularize the pressure to found churches, but it was a pressure that came from below.

The corporate expression of lay concerns is most vividly shown in the statutes of five guilds which survive before c.1100.[40] Membership of these guilds is not certain: at least three of them (at Abbotsbury, Cambridge and Exeter) included thegns (perhaps exclusively). The fourteen village guilds mentioned at Exeter appear less aristocratic. All of them were attached in some way to a minster church: at Abbotsbury for instance members made payments of candle wax and money to the mother church. Yet their activities show that dependence on the mother church for spiritual needs was not total. A guild at Exeter employed its own mass priest; and although none of the statutes refer to the building of independent chapels, such cooperative activity was clearly well within the scope of these guilds. Once more, we are observing, by the eleventh century, a transitional stage in a nascent parish system: from an affiliation to (sometimes distant) minster churches as primary units of pastoral care, towards an attachment to chapels and churches which local groups of lay people paid for themselves.

The guild statutes are revealing about other devotional concerns. The determination amongst the villagers of Whistley to ensure local provision for their corpses, is replicated in guild emphasis on burial and masses for the dead. The fourteen village guilds relied on the prayers of the minster clergy in return for their contributions. But other guilds took matters into their own hands. The Exeter guild expected two masses to be celebrated at each meeting, one for the living and one for the dead. Such was the concern of the Abbotsbury guild for fitting funerals, that they were prepared to fetch the bodies of members who had died up to thirty miles away from the minster church.

Whether the aims of these guilds were entirely at one with ecclesiastical concerns is not always clear. Preoccupation with the afterlife might have met with clerical approval; perhaps there is a link between the encouragement of penitential processions by reforming churchmen at the end of the tenth century, and a deeper appreciation of the penitential needs of the soul.[41] But guildsmen had other concerns too. A decent burial was a matter of worldly status as much as spiritual assurance: the thegn Ordnoth and his wife in their tenth-century will wished for transportation to the kind of resting place 'as is necessary for us in God's sight and fitting in the eyes of the world'.[42] The statutes of the thegnly guild at Cambridge have more to say about regulation of the blood feud than the fate of the soul, and although a goal of social harmony might be as much a clerical as a lay priority, some of the means to achieve it – the drinking and feasting emphasized in some of the guild statutes – did not always meet with clerical approval. There remained lingering concern that these groups of lay people might be agents of disruption rather than vehicles of the gospel message. In any case, commemoration of the dead might be all too redolent of a pagan past. How Christian indeed was Anglo-Saxon society?

(v) Beliefs: Pagan and Christian

In the eleventh century, churchmen still fretted about pagan practices. It was apparently necessary c.1020 for a law code to confirm that it was heathen practice to worship wells, stones or trees.[43] The manner of conversion had even encouraged the perpetuation of these beliefs. Rather than destroy pagan shrines, Pope Gregory himself had advised missionaries in England in 601 to convert them into Christian use.[44] Pagan practices like the sacrificing of animals might be tolerated if slaughtered for food and to the praise of God. 'Celtic' missionaries, outside the Roman tradition (and just as important in the conversion process), appear to have been more accommodating still of pagan practices. The process of conversion had been syncretic: the miracles produced by St Ivo's gushing spring may have 'Christianized' a pagan belief in water as an abode for deities.

But Christianized it was. It is the depth of this Christianization that is the issue. Most ecclesiastical prohibitions suggest not so much a 'rustic' adherence to an organized pagan religion as a lingering attachment to beliefs which may once have been part of regularly practised rites – beliefs that the landscape was filled with numinous sites, and that the forces of nature could be propitiated and harnessed for the improvement of conditions and the continuing passage of the seasons. If these beliefs remained influential (even if detached from a system of religion), they were also ones which churchmen themselves were prepared to encourage within a broadly Christian frame of reference. Field remedies to ensure healthy crops took on liturgical forms. At a time of drought in 1095, the bishop of Ely brought the body of St Edmund out from the church of Bury St Edmund's and preached a sermon before the people: holy martyrs, he said, had the power to call forth abundant rainfall. Other churchmen accepted that charms could ward off evil and effect cures – although Aelfric felt the need to clarify that the medicinal power of herbs came from God rather than heathen forces.[45]

The problem of 'pagan' survival is in part a semantic one. By a narrow definition of 'Christianity', the religion of 'rustics' (and perhaps even an Aelfric) might be deemed heathen. A less extreme view is that Christianity at this time was merely a crust on top of 'popular culture'. But the clerical 'crust' clearly appropriated this 'culture' and participated in it, despite the rhetoric which distinguished educated churchmen from superstitious 'rustics'. Some practices were clearly not tolerated, but sometimes it is churchmen themselves who appear to be under suspicion of deviant belief: Bishop Wulfstan reprimanded a priest Ailsi for an inordinate affection for a nut tree which grew in his cemetery.[46] Other recorded beliefs did go beyond the broadest definition of Christianity and proved persistent: William of Malmesbury in the twelfth century was to reckon it a peculiarly English belief that corpses could be reanimated by the power of the devil.[47] But it seems reasonable to call England by c.1000 a 'Christian' country, where surviving pagan beliefs were generally Christianized, if by 'Christian' we accept a broad and contemporary definition of the word.

Thus, the 'crowds' that gathered ever more frequently in hagiographical accounts may indeed reflect a deepening of the process of conversion. Perhaps these crowds were also capable of generating their own cults. There is less evidence for 'popular' cults in England than some parts of the continent, and once again the strength of royal and ecclesiastical control over cults provides a partial explanation. Yet even this control may have been asserted after a cult had sprung up more spontaneously: the early cult at Steyning of St Cuthman who was not of royal birth, may have been the eventual object, rather than the initial product, of official approval.[48] Conversely, officially promoted cults did not always develop 'popular' followings: although the cult of the Virgin Mary was central to reformed monastic houses, it does not appear to have become the focus of local cults – perhaps because these tended to coalesce more readily around saints whose corporeal relics had remained on earth.[49]

Other kinds of cult may also reflect local origins. Cult-sites embedded in the landscape emerged from a context which was less clerical in inspiration than those cults associated with the movable remains of a saint. Breton hagiography between the ninth and thirteenth centuries, for instance, seems to have preserved the influence of a more 'popular' and oral culture which did not need the bodies of saints themselves to effect miracles.[50] Places which are mentioned in the written sources as associated with local saints – including wells and springs – may preserve the memory of informal cult-sites which had not been clerically promoted, and predated the need for a written account. Areas of England with a strong Celtic influence also suggest similar cultural traditions which were Christian in inspiration. Holy places in Cornwall associated with the early Celtic missionaries – churches, wells, crosses – were more fixed as cult-sites than those centred on saintly remains which were potentially peripatetic.[51] Reformed monasteries, in their greed for relics, did acquire them from the region as Anglo-Saxon power advanced west of the Tamar river. St Neot's remains were taken to Huntingdonshire. But perhaps because cults in Cornwall were less transportable, they did not generally spread to the rest of the kingdom. They remained tied to their local origins to lend a distinctive flavour to the religious practices of the region.[52]

Elsewhere in England, the assertion of monastic and royal control at an early date perhaps created a climate less favourably disposed to cult-sites emerging from the landscape – one which had once, after all, been pagan. But many such sites did survive and with the seal of ecclesiastical approval. The rock at Ebblesfleet which preserved St Mildrith's footprints was in the late eleventh century, according to Goscelin, the centre of a thaumaturgic cult. Twelve springs burst forth, wrote Abbo of Fleury, at the point on the Norfolk coast where St Edmund, on his way to martyrdom, had landed and knelt in prayer.[53] We have already met the 'superstitious rustics' crowding St Ivo's well. Perhaps in many of these cases churchmen were simply accepting a more 'popular' attitude or responding to a preexisting cult, adapting rather than inspiring it. Just as early conversion had required a syncretic approach to numinous sites in the landscape, so later churchmen, in a largely Christianized country, found it necessary to respond to pressures and religious needs outside their initial control or even approval.

The depth of this Christianization was clearly not uniform. It is more evident around the minsters of 'urban' areas, though penetration into the countryside may already have been significant. Clerical characterizations of countryfolk as 'superstitious rustics' might be read as rhetorical topoi rather than statements of fact. The process of conversion had inevitably been slow and had involved compromise. If we follow the account of Bede (who preferred to play down the importance of 'Celtic' missionaries at a local level), conversion had begun from the top and had relied on kingly and aristocratic power. Although by the year 1000 Christianity may have become firmly embedded in the soil, not least through the proliferation of church buildings, it was a soil fertilized by values which had roots in a warrior and pagan past. Kings and thegns exercised a stronghold over the monasteries they had built and over the monks, often members of their own kin, who populated them. Such were the links retained by monks with families outside cloister walls that it is no surprise to find them enjoying the scarcely Christianized tales of Beowulf and his warband.[54] The same kind of links were stronger still between priests and local lords in churches at a sub-minster level. But there were churchmen who complained at the baleful influences of too close a tie with the secular world. By the eleventh century some were challenging these connections with greater vigour than ever before, and in new ways: during the period of Gregorian reform (see Chapter 2) the concern was not to uproot lingering paganism but to eradicate values which had come to be seen as too 'profane'.

(vi) Conclusion

The 'crowds' which gather ever more frequently in hagiographical accounts may indeed reflect wider changes outside the cloister. Church reformers had not solely concerned themselves with the state of monastic institutions and their clergy but also with reform of the laity. Their pastoral ideals were monastic in tone: lay people were to be brought closer to monastic observance, or at the very least, they were to be brought into closer association with clerical institutions. Conversion and pastoral reform had been pursued largely through the establishment of monasteries or minsters, and the monopoly of these institutions was still being enforced (financially through control of tithes) in the eleventh century. The surviving wills of lay people and the statutes of guilds also suggest a strong spiritual monopoly: 'minsters' were the places in which secure burial and intercession were to be found. They were also the places where a wider group of laity might be brought in contact with the relics of saintly patrons.

The religion practised by lay people was not just 'cultic', focused merely on saints' relics and shrines of monastic houses. Pastoral emphasis on confession, penance and other observances had made a wider impact: the building of neighbourhood churches, the activity of guilds, the demand among some lay people for instructional literature, the shadowy presence of 'vowesses' occupying a penumbric space between secular and cloistered worlds, seem to suggest overall that the Christian message was being internalized by the laity, despite the (inevitable) lament of church reformers that the process had not gone far enough. The 'crowds' at shrines also reflect a wider involvement by lay people in all kinds of 'Christian' activity by the end of the first millennium.

But the influence of the Church on lay society was not one-way. High-minded churchmen may have wished to keep the 'corrupting' influences of the world at arm's length: tenth-century monastic reform had been one of several reforming initiatives which had sought, in some way, to detach clergy from laity and 'purify' clerical institutions. Clerical views had often been deeply ambivalent about the influences of lay society and had not always lent themselves to subservient support of social hierarchy. But strong ties with kings and great landowners during conversion at an early date had meant accommodation with lay power. Bishops and abbots were firmly tied in to a strongly hierarchical society, their homiletic writings studded with theocratic pronouncements on kingship and on the maintenance of the social order. The strength of kingly power in England over Church life and religion, whether in control of saints' cults or in demand for prayers, is a striking consequence of the precociously centralizing impetus of royal government. Perhaps this strength and impetus can be overestimated. Assertions of royal and ecclesiastical authority were particularly strident in the early eleventh century, a time not of confidence but of crisis and disruption. It is clear too that other groups in society affected the ecclesiastical structure and the character of religion at a local level. Despite the continued monopoly of 'minsters', the building of thegnly churches on manors, the appearance of neighbourhood churches in towns, and the activities of guilds suggest a monopoly already in the process of disintegration. Local people, perhaps even 'peasants', might seek their own cults and structure their own devotions to suit local needs. The control that the laity, at all social levels, exercised over local churches was to be challenged during the eleventh century, but it was a strongly established characteristic of religious practice, and despite later reforming ideals, it was to continue in the ensuing centuries along paths both new and old.

Chapter 2: The Universal Church and the Laity c.1050–1500

A fifteenth-century confessor, possibly from the north Midlands, wrote down the following advice for an unknown married man.[1] It might have seemed depressing. Like everyone else, he was a sinner: unlike the 'innocent dog', he continually provoked the Lord; as a lowly 'dog', not a man, he might presume to enter a church. But there was hope. He could ask for mercy: his tears, even if those of his heart alone, might wash the feet of Jesus on the cross. He was to hear mass reverently, and while the clerks were singing, look at the books of the church – especially the Gospel and the Legend of Saints. On weekdays, when returning home, he was to say the Psalter of the Virgin Mary, and at dinner silence was to be broken only by readings in the vernacular to edify his wife and children. Further meditation could continue with confessors until vespers; after supper – a light one, to avoid gobbling – he was to go up to his 'cell' to pray. When finally in bed, he was advised to search his heart for the evil and good he had done that day.

Such advice was not necessarily comfortable; and as its recipient drifted off to an uneasy sleep, he might have recalled its final words – that he was not certain to survive until morning. Yet this spiritual regimen offered a literate family-man, busy with the affairs of the world, a practical, albeit unheroic, model of Christian life and a means to salvation. Few of these texts survive, even for the later Middle Ages; and the household arrangements for this lay person, with rooms set aside for prayer and confessors on hand, were unusual. But by the fifteenth century, it was possible for such advice to be written for lay people, in a way that was impossible in the eleventh. Instructional advice for the laity had been available (at the highest social echelons) in late Anglo-Saxon England, and in some ways the pastoral concerns of the Church after this period were a continuation of these efforts. But the most assured means of salvation which churchmen could then offer laymen, was a regime pursued, for instance, by the nobleman Leofric who had led a heroic, semi-monastic existence. Yet, dating from this period, the outlook of churchmen towards the Church as an institution, towards its place in the world, and towards what it meant to be Christian, was to shift significantly.

(i) Gregorian Reform: Universal Church over Local Churches

The reforming movement which overtook clerical circles at the highest levels at the beginning of this period was backward-looking: it sought to return the Church to the days of the apostles. But it had revolutionary implications.[2] Its focus initially was on a concern to lift the clergy out of the corrupting influences of the world. All priests – not just monks – were to maintain celibacy and independence of office, and be set apart from the laity. Pope Gregory VII's assertion of universal papal authority, particularly over the investiture of bishops, provoked a collision with emperors and kings to whom bishops were still regarded as 'feudal' subordinates. The issue, which was to rumble on well into the twelfth century, resulted in symbolic victory for the papacy. Secular rulers (in England by 1107) recognized the exclusive right of the papacy to bestow the symbols of episcopal office (ring and staff) on local bishops.

The drive to a more uniform Church, independent of lay authority, was expressed in the systematizing of canon law and doctrine. The theoretical power of the clergy was clarified by the elaboration of universal doctrines in the schools of Northern France concerning the sacraments. The Fourth Lateran Council in 1215, under papal auspices, trenchantly asserted the doctrine of transubstantiation at the mass, a miracle which only the priest could perform. Tightening control of doctrine was matched by a tightening control of cult. The concentration of decision-making powers on the papal curia in Rome began to include a claim to an exclusive right to bestow the accolade of sainthood. Canonization became a papal monopoly, firmly taken out of local episcopal hands by the end of the twelfth century. It also became a laborious and testing procedure, intended to act as a brake on the uncontrolled proliferation of new saints. In 1215 the authentication of newly discovered relics was also made subject to papal licence.[3] Moreover, universal cults tended to be promoted over local ones.[4] Local churches, in particular Benedictine houses, had traditionally centred their devotion on local saintly patrons and on the physical remains of these saints. But from the late eleventh century, local saints, especially if they did not have Lives written in the best Latin, were treated with more suspicion by universally minded churchmen. By the mid-twelfth century popes began to claim universal authority not as successors of St Peter and guardians of his shrine, but from higher authority: Innocent III (1198–1216) adopted the title of 'vicar of Christ' (which he purloined from the Emperor). Devotion to the mother of Christ was also strengthened: new cults of the Virgin made inroads into local cults. The new international orders, particularly the Cistercians, dedicated exclusively to the Virgin Mary, did not encourage the cults of local saints within their individual houses; nor did they favour devotion to relics. Celebration of universal feasts tended (in theory) to place much less emphasis on relics. Newer cults, such as wonder-working crosses did not need corporeal relics to work miracles; Marian cults could be embodied in statues and images rather than relics; and later Eucharistic cults, like Corpus Christi which appeared by the thirteenth century, focused on the transubstantiated form of the physical body.

The emphasis on a universal Church was contained within western Christendom. Papal claims to universal authority were opposed by the Orthodox Church in the East, and they were not without opposition within the western Church. Moreover, universal doctrines were developed only in controversy; local churches clung tenaciously to local cults. Yet the drive to greater universality was a powerful one, bringing local churches towards a great uniformity in practice – and even spirituality. According to a number of churchmen, location and physical experience might be less important within a 'universal' Church: Guibert of Nogent, who criticized 'excess' in devotion to relics, sought 'an inward world where nothing is either high or low or localized, where there is neither time nor place'.[5]

(ii) The Search for Religious Perfection

Guibert's search for an 'inward world' was part of a more general experimentation with religious life which is also evident from the late eleventh century. In no period in the Middle Ages were so many, and so varied, monastic institutions founded as in the first two-thirds of the twelfth century. In England, the number of Benedictine (and Cluniac) houses increased, but more spectacular was the flourishing of new orders – Cistercians, Carthusians, Augustinians to name the most prominent.[6] More informal explorations of religious life, within and outside the cloister, were undertaken by hermits and wandering preachers.[7] The charismatic preacher Gilbert of Sempringham set up his own order (a distinctively English experiment in double monasticism): according to his hagiographer, while Gilbert was a priest and lodging with a local family (until he saw himself in a dream fondling the breasts of his host's daughter), he was inspired to build a cell next to the local church in 1131, for a group of women.[8] By the mid-twelfth century some seventeen Gilbertine houses, for men and for women, had been founded in Lincolnshire and Yorkshire.

The search for religious perfection was not confined solely, or even primarily, to the outward performance of the religious life.[9] The emphasis on monastic ideals had developed by the mid-twelfth century into a preoccupation with the nature of the inner religious life and personal perfection. The Cistercians in particular – notably Ailred of Rievaulx (d.1167) in Yorkshire – encouraged a piety which placed great weight on the inner life, the acquisition of self-knowledge, above all through contemplation of the humanity and sufferings of Christ. In the thirteenth century, St Francis took the ideal of poverty and an affective devotion to the life of Christ still further.[10]

The cultivation of the inner life is evident in changing models of sanctity.[11] To some extent, older criteria of sainthood remained and were even encouraged with the assertion of papal control over canonization. Officially approved new saints continued to have aristocratic and clerical backgrounds, not least because potential saints often required powerful patrons, from the same milieu, to carry them through the gruelling process of canonization. However, there were some changes. In the twelfth century, an increasing number of men who had led an eremitical life (preferably within a community) were canonized. In the thirteenth century, individuals who had led a mendicant life of poverty in imitation of Christ began to infiltrate ecclesiastical calendars.

The search for the interior life of religious perfection was sharpened by changes in the moral theology of sin and repentance, developed in the schools during the twelfth century. The earlier penitential model had tended to focus on the objective nature of the sinful act and on the

elaboration of essentially arbitrary penalties and tariffs to achieve satisfaction. But a newer model placed greater emphasis on intention behind
the sinful act, satisfaction for which would take account of the circumstances relevant to the particular penitent's guilt. It was a model which
was more individually orientated, placing more weight on the individual
conscience and on a sense of personal responsibility in the process of
salvation.[12]

These changes had implications for the laity too. In the eleventh
century, the search for religious perfection had still seemed beyond their
reach. The ideal life had traditionally been monastic: a cloistered life
nourishing the soul was far preferable to a worldly life indulging the
body. Archbishop Anselm of Canterbury (d.1109) had these words of
advice for the nun who had wished to exchange her cloister for the
charms of a lover, since deceased: 'Go now sister; put yourself with him
in the bed where he now lies; collect his worms in your bosom; embrace
his corpse; kiss closely his naked teeth, for his lips are already consumed
with putrefaction ...' Contempt for worldly things remained a powerful
strain of thought. Orderic Vitalis rejoiced in the spectacle (in 1087) of
William the Conqueror's bloated corpse bursting out from a coffin which
had been made too small. The dead body of his son Henry I (d.1135) was
similarly uncooperative: it oozed, according to Henry of Huntingdon,
a 'dreadful black fluid' through the many hides in which it had been
wrapped.[13] A life lived in the world, particularly by laymen, was unlikely
to lead to a good end.

Yet there were strategies through which lay people, in association with
religious houses, might partake of the religious life and achieve a good
death. In the eleventh century, the most effective way was to assume the
habit of a monk, even if this were done only as death approached. But
by the twelfth century, a good death was achievable by other kinds of
association with the religious life.[14] Around 1110 Nigel d'Aubigny, lying
ill in bed, was advised by the bishop and monks of Durham that the
return of two manors snatched from the monks might enable him to
avoid everlasting Hell.[15] Henry of Huntingdon in his essay 'Contempt
for the World', has a hapless Robert of Meulan, close to death (1118),
advised by his confessors that it was more important to restore stolen
lands to their rightful owners, with penitential tears, than to pass his
inheritance on intact to his sons.[16]

The cultivation of the inner life, moreover, did not have to be confined
to the cloister. The monastic ideal had never meant a full retreat from
the world, and in the twelfth century, churchmen like St Bernard of

Clairvaux, the most illustrious of the Cistercians, began to focus more profoundly on how the life of contemplation might be applied to a life of action. In any case, if the virtues of a monk were indeed inner virtues, it might be possible for a layman to possess and develop them. By the end of the eleventh century, it was already considered appropriate for lay people to pursue a religious life beyond monastic walls. In 'estates' theory, the order of 'those who fought' was increasingly given a quasi-sacral status.[17] The knight who protected the Church – particularly against the infidel – might be deemed a pilgrim or a monk with a shield around his neck. The first crusade, triggered by Pope Urban II's sermon at the council of Clérmont in 1096, crystallized a conviction that a certain kind of activity, to which the lay knight was best suited, might be a route to salvation. A few early chroniclers of the crusades spoke of the crusading armies marching as though on an armed pilgrimage or even as a monastic community on the move. Yet a century later, it was possible for some churchmen to speak not just of crusaders but the entire body of the faithful as 'monks'.[18] The experimentation with religious life spread out of the cloister, not just to those laymen closely associated with monastic houses (in military orders, and as lay brothers and sisters) but to those more closely entangled with the affairs of the world. A lay life of activity could yet have its value, and in the thirteenth century the friars encouraged this view by allowing lay people a close association with them as 'tertiaries' in their orders.

The multiplying paths to salvation were open not just to the few, but also to the many. Crucial in this process, was the development in the second half of the twelfth century, ratified and still further refined in the thirteenth, of a worked-out system of penance and redemption, integrated with a more precise doctrine of Purgatory.[19] The emphasis on individual intention and responsibility was accompanied by other theological refinements in the mechanics of expiation which made the effective remission of sin a more manageable process, even for the laity. Whereas Pope Urban had promised crusaders in 1096 complete remission from sin and its consequences, twelfth-century theologians began to distinguish 'guilt' and 'punishment' due from sin. The result was that it became necessary no longer to undergo protracted penitential effort (possible only for monk or anchorite) or to make huge benefactions during life (possible only for the great landowner) to gain both forgiveness of sin and remission from punishment. Lighter punishments (possible for all) might be performed after guilt had been confessed; penance that remained incomplete at death might now be expiated in Purgatory.

Purgatory differed little, according to some, from the unpleasantness of Hell, and the worldly might reasonably expect a longer sojourn than the cloistered in its cleansing flames. But there was carrot as well as stick. The 'third place', for all its pains, was none the less the antechamber of Heaven, a staging post for the truly penitent on the road to salvation. The penitential strategies available to the laity were thus made more manageable. The incentive to perform the penances which had been traditionally required (saying prayers, giving alms to the poor, building churches, going on pilgrimage) was boosted by the evident efficacy and accessibility of all such good works in the process of salvation.[20] The austere regimes of the monk or the anchorite did not have to be copied in full; a connection with a religious house was no longer as necessary. Whereas Archbishop Anselm in the late eleventh century might gloomily doubt whether any would be saved with the exception perhaps of a few monks, St Hugh of Lincoln, a century later, was confident that the kingdom of God 'was not confined to monks, hermits and anchorites'.[21]

The gradual coalescence of a coherent idea of Purgatory had one other profound implication. The sense of responsibility of the living for the dead was made much stronger. From the eleventh century the dead had become ever more demanding, sometimes audibly so: monastic sources refer more frequently to the appearance of ghosts who demand suffrages of monks.[22] What these ghosts were and where they came from could still be a matter of disquieting uncertainty. In the later twelfth century William of Newburgh reckoned that some were vampires; but others were certainly wrongdoers in life, whose appearance could be explained by their need for penance. The dead father of a Northumbrian knight returned to seek absolution for tithes withheld, explaining that his absolution was now possible through God's grace and also through the alms of the faithful. For Walter Map this was a 'novel' case worthy of theological attention.[23] But by the thirteenth century, sermons make it quite clear that ghosts were returning from Purgatory, invariably seeking prayers and masses from the living. Moreover, souls did not need to return as ghosts to voice their demands. The traffic between living and dead was two-way and visionary journeys into the 'other world' had long revealed the needs of the dead; but from the end of the twelfth century, these also made explicit the importance of the living in providing relief for the dead in Purgatory, as a monk from Eynsham discovered on his other-worldly trip in 1196.

Such stories and visions served as graphic and didactic illustrations of a shift in doctrine which strengthened the ties between the living and the dead – with far-reaching implications for the penitential strategies of the laity. The process of expiating punishment due from sin could be continued beyond the grave: prayers, 'alms of the faithful' and especially the mass, as good works of penance, were also useful to souls in Purgatory. Moreover, by the thirteenth century it was also much clearer that those seeking such penitential suffrages did not have to turn to religious houses alone to provide them.

(iii) Pastoral Reform 1100–1300: the Parish

The search for religious perfection, resulting in an opening out of the cloistered life to the world, is evident also in the wider pastoral efforts of the Church. In a sense pastoral concerns had been part of the reforming currents during the eleventh century, and had also involved the religious. The monastic tradition had always contained a pastoral dimension. To Archbishop Anselm, reform of society still began with the monasteries: the direct connections of monks with their aristocratic patrons might be activated, who in turn might influence their dependents.[24] Reform might spread outwards from the monastic centre, in a series of concentric circles, like a pebble dropped into a pond.

In other ways, however, reliance on the 'feudal' hierarchy was becoming unacceptable. The concern of Gregorian reformers to limit dependence on great landowners made unpalatable any direct lay control over priests and over the income that supported them. The effort to reduce such control and purify the Church also involved the religious. Lay people were encouraged to give up income from tithes and donate them to the proliferating number of monastic houses. Bishop Herbert of Norwich, for instance, secured the 'patronage of holy places' by giving monks the possession of churches.[25] The prospect of spiritual reward was the promised return on investment – a return made all the more realizable, no doubt, by the developing doctrine of Purgatory.

Religious houses were also involved more directly in pastoral efforts. A greater emphasis on preaching began in the twelfth century. Monasteries continued to be important in the production of sermon material, and monks continued to preach. Gilbert of Sempringham, besides founding a new order for women, was so charismatic a preacher that he reputedly turned the local people away from indulging in 'feasts and spectacles' towards the 'monastic life'.[26] Yet enclosed monastic houses were not ideally suited for a proselitizing role, and individualistic efforts like

Gilbert's were to give way in the thirteenth century to still newer religious orders, the friars, whose primary purpose was to spread the gospel.

In any case, by the twelfth century, religious houses were not the main engines of pastoral reform. A more systematic effort was pursued through the expansion of episcopal government.[27] The diocesan structure had long been instrumental in the process of conversion, but the administrative capacity of bishops, already strong in England, was extended still further in scale and scope. This was part of a general expansion of government, including secular authority (see Chapter 3: ii), but it was also a consequence of the Gregorian effort to achieve independence from worldly corruption: in claiming universal jurisdiction over the affairs of Christendom, the pope required a bureaucracy to accommodate those who sought his ruling, and a system of government which could transmit doctrines and legislation from the centre and implement them at a local level. More Church councils conveyed orders to bishops who in turn filtered legislation down to their dioceses. An ecclesiastical council at Windsor in 1070 was already ordering bishops to appoint archdeacons.[28] By the late twelfth century, diocesan government had multiplied: archdeacons were holding assemblies of clergy; rural chapters were organized to which local clergy were summoned; separate church courts, generating their own business, had been clearly established. Eleventh-century bishops, like Bishop Wulfstan of Worcester, might have been praised for heroic perambulations of their dioceses; their late twelfth-century counterparts perambulated less perhaps, but had greater pastoral influence through the more mundane channels of episcopal administration.

In this governmental structure greater weight began to be placed on the parish. Episcopal government set out to ensure the presence of a properly equipped clergy at a local level. The 1070 Windsor council required archdeacons to ensure that churches kept a careful stock of vessels, and that priests knew how to celebrate mass properly. The instruction of the laity required not just an educated clergy but also a resident one. It was no longer enough to send out priests from a central church to administer the sacraments, sometimes irregularly, in outlying areas. The older 'minster system' had long been fragmenting, but it was now out of date from the ecclesiastical point of view, and its fragmentation could even be encouraged. Bishop Herbert of Norwich, for instance, in the early twelfth century established a resident priest in a chapel at Yarmouth to serve the pastoral needs of the local herring fishermen.[29]

Gradually the duties of the laity to the parish also came to be more clearly defined. Episcopal acta of the twelfth century sought to strengthen the ties between parishioners and the cathedral church of the diocese: the bishop of Exeter sent a mandate to his archdeacons to enforce the custom of 'Pentecostal' processions and oblations, and ensure that every chaplain kept a roll of contributing parishioners by manor.[30] Yet the primary duty of the laity was increasingly seen to lie in the support of local churches. The archbishop of York in the early twelfth century allowed the men of Nottinghamshire to process to the church of St Mary at Southwell, rather than to York, so that the building of the church there might be achieved more easily 'for the remission of their sins'.[31] Above all, the tithe became a customary demand because it was essential for the support of a locally resident priesthood. Gilbert of Sempringham's improvement of the morals of local people included the regular payment of tithe. A recalcitrant parishioner who had not paid was made publicly to measure out his corn: the amount due for tithe was piled up in the street and ostentatiously burned.[32] The definition of the parish as a territorial unit, with a parish priest dependent on regular tithes, was increasingly established and fixed.

The apparent emphasis (in extant records) on financial arrangements belies the importance of pastoral motives. The parish was becoming defined as the central focus of lay worship: in the twelfth century attendance of the Sunday sermon at the parish church was increasingly regarded as important. The gathering pace of systematic pastoral reform became enshrined in the decrees of the Fourth Lateran Council in 1215. The 'government of souls', it decreed, was the 'art of arts': unprecedented weight was placed on the priest, at a local level, instructing the laity. Indeed the thirteenth century witnessed a great expansion in the production of manuals designed to equip the clergy in his role as confessor and preacher.[33] For the 'safely sealed ear' of the priest had to be specially trained. What sins should he look for? What penances should he prescribe? There was uncertainty. Robert of Flamborough in the early thirteenth century, in discussing 'remissions which consist in the building of churches or of bridges or in other matters', considered that 'different men have different opinions as to how much value they have and for whom'.[34] In line with the newer ideas of schoolmen on sin and repentance, the confessor was taught how best he might draw out from the penitent the nature of his sinful acts, and prescribe penance most appropriate to his situation.

Emphasis on confession and preaching explains the need for the friars who were particularly suited to the role. Indeed they were important, though not exclusive, contributors to the growing body of penitential literature. But some manuals insisted on the monopoly of the parish and diocesan structure in the confessional and disciplinary process (sometimes in opposition to the friars by the late thirteenth century);[35] and it may be that the relative strength of this structure explains why the influence of the friars never became as great in England as in parts of continental Europe, notably the great towns of northern Italy. In any case the Fourth Lateran Council, by emphasizing the need for regular annual confession, had also set great store on the importance of the local parish priest and the dependence on him of the laity. For the first time, a minimum requirement to confess sins once a year before reception of the Eucharist at Easter was imposed, and in England it was taken up with some vigour. Synods brought conciliar decrees down to the diocesan level and expanded upon them still further: Bishop Poore of Salisbury in 1217 was even requiring parishioners to confess not once but three times a year.[36] Other synodal decrees spelled out the necessity of celebrating the seven sacraments in every parish: the laity were to be bound to their parish churches from baptism to last rites, from cradle to grave. The obligations of parishioners to maintain the ornaments and the fabric of their church were gradually expanded upon. English synodal decrees by the later thirteenth century are fulsome in their detail over what ornaments, books and parts of the church (the nave above all) that parishioners were supposed to administer.[37]

The performance of parochial duties required of clergy and laity began to be monitored in a new system of visitation. In the twelfth century there had been occasional summonings of local clergy and laity to undergo episcopal visitation, although even in the early thirteenth century the rare records of visitation suggest that inquiries were restricted to state of the local clergy alone. But beginning with Bishop Grosseteste of Lincoln's visitation of his diocese in 1238–39, the scope and frequency of the visitation was widened. Both clergy and laity were summoned to answer questions of a more general nature.[38] By the fourteenth century visitation records begin to show laymen being asked a wide range of questions on the satisfactory conduct of their fellow parishioners – and of their local clergy. Thus the penitential strategies of the laity and the disciplinary framework which enforced them were to be focused on local parish churches.

(iv) Pastoral Reform c.1100–1300: Books, Images and Religious Knowledge

The emphasis on the 'government of souls' required more of the laity than outward conformity. The deepening obligations placed upon the laity were part of a more general pastoral and theological concern to charge individuals with a more personal responsibility for their own salvation. Such a responsibility was to be encouraged by preaching, especially by resident clergy, but it was also promoted in texts which the laity might read for themselves. Anglo-Saxon churchmen had produced homiletic literature in the vernacular for noblemen, for the purpose of private prayer; but from the twelfth century, the range of material available to lay people was increasing. The prayers and meditational texts of Archbishop Anselm were collected in monastic circles and began to find their way outside the cloister. From the late twelfth century a monk at Beaulieu could write down a sermon for a local lady who lived five miles from the monastery. Other kinds of texts also show the importance of links between religious houses and their lay patrons in the process of transmission. Psalters (with their psalms, prayers and biblical paraphrases) began to be written and illuminated for noble patrons in the late twelfth century; by the mid-thirteenth so were books of hours (containing the canonical hours as well as psalms and other devotional texts).[39]

The language to be used in such texts presented problems: the primacy accorded to Latin by a reforming clerical elite cast suspicion on the use of the vernacular, and in England Anglo-Saxon was downgraded as the primary vernacular language after the arrival in 1066 of a new Norman elite (see Chapters 3: i; 6: iii). At any rate, what the material in these texts offered their lay patrons was a spirituality which had long been familiar within the monastic tradition. The psalms had been a prime source of religious reflection; the Beaulieu sermon (in Anglo-Norman), warning of worldly temptations and advising confession and true repentance to wash away sin, gave its lay owner access to a monastic topos. Psalters offered lay readers monastic meditations on death too. Sir Geoffrey Luttrell's lavish psalter, produced in the 1330s (probably influenced by contact with the local religious house at Sempringham) contained reflections (in Latin) on confession, extreme unction and the ultimate fate of the soul: beside the gloomy words from Psalm 87 ('For my soul is filled with evils; and my life hath drawn night unto Hell') Sir Geoffrey would have gazed at the figure of a man in the margin, staring at Hell's mouth, next to an open coffin.[40]

In the thirteenth century, the meditative and confessional tone in much religious literature was deepened still further. The increasing production of manuals designed for confessors was matched by a corresponding increase in texts designed to instruct the penitent in preparation for confession. *Handlyng Sin* (1313), produced by Robert Mannyng at Sempringham, for instance, was one of many texts which advised readers to examine their own conscience. Moreover, homiletic literature of all kinds was increasingly available to the laity, and in Middle English. Sermon collections (like the Northern Homily Cycle) appear more frequently. Collections of saints' Lives (like the South England Legendary) offered models of saintly behaviour to the laity. The *Ancrene Wisse*, written in the early thirteenth century, was designed for an audience of anchoresses, yet it attracted a wider readership: its focus on the inner purity of the heart was a model that could be applied to the laity. The friars were also influential in disseminating an affective piety, focused on the life and Passion of Christ (for instance in the thirteenth-century text *Meditationes Vitae Christi*), which was designed to nourish the inner life and lead the reader to penitential contrition.

Such literature was generally concentrated on inculcating certain virtues and avoiding certain vices. But it also presupposed a certain knowledge of doctrine. Church councils and synods in the thirteenth century began to define more explicitly what the laity needed to know. The need for the laity to adopt a more credal Christianity was asserted. The basic requirement to learn the Lord's Prayer and the Creed (which had appeared in early eleventh-century laws) was extended. Bishop Grosseteste in around 1239 devised a comprehensive pastoral syllabus, requiring the parish priest to teach his flock the Ten Commandments and the sacraments; Archbishop Pecham's syllabus in 1281 was more extensive still, requiring knowledge of the fourteen articles of faith, the seven works of mercy and the seven deadly sins. These were to be learned 'in the vulgar tongue' so that they might be better understood. Moreover, compendia of religious knowledge in the vernacular began to be produced, such as the poem *Orrmulum* (*c.*1200) which 'gladly' wished 'that all English people with ear should listen to it'.[41]

Most lay people were 'illiterate' (at least in the fullest sense of the term – see Chapter 6: iii). Traditionally, the image was the layman's book; and visual symbols were undoubtedly used to teach or encourage contemplation. The laity might find these in monastic houses; but their local parish church was becoming a place of more elaborate visual instruction. An early wall painting of Purgatory is found at Chaldon (*c.*1200); and by the early fourteenth century, parishioners at Widford (Oxfordshire), might have gazed at another *memento mori* which had once been an exclusively monastic topos – the image of three kings and noblemen suddenly confronted by three skeletons and told to amend their ways.[42] Oral and visual instruction could combine in drama, and during the twelfth century there are a growing number of references to plays centred on the liturgy and even on saints' Lives which were performed in monasteries before audiences of lay people, but also in more local churches. The range, scope and opportunity for the religious instruction of the laity had increased substantially.

(v) Pastoral Care and Spirituality in the Late Medieval Church 1300–1500

By the fourteenth century, a system of ecclesiastical government, reaching into local society, was able (in theory) to regulate the religious life of the laity with an intensity scarcely possible at the beginning of our period. Pastoral reform in the previous two centuries had created a system which was capable of instructing lay people, more often and in more detail, as to the formal obligations required, and the inner spiritual paths that might be followed in order to achieve salvation. Until recently, however, the late medieval Church has been seen as rather less dynamic. To turn from the twelfth century to the fourteenth century, was to turn from a period of religious liveliness to one of spiritual ossification. The great period of religious experimentation, it seemed, was at an end, and although new orders continued to be founded in the thirteenth century, the Fourth Lateran Council (1215) had already discouraged foundation 'lest an excessive diversity of religions should introduce serious confusion into the church of God'.

A centralized bureaucratic structure did make reform more difficult. Late medieval bishops seem caught up in ecclesiastical (and secular) government, and more remote from their flocks. Few were cast in the heroic mould of Bishop Grosseteste who had been not only innovative in practices of pastoral care, but also so worried by papal government, that he had journeyed to Rome in 1250 to fulminate before the supreme pontiff himself.[43] In the fourteenth century he would have found this task more difficult still. The period of the Avignon papacy (1305–77) saw the financial and judicial powers of popes multiply; and after 1378, a Grosseteste might have been unsure whether to take his complaints to Avignon or Rome. A papal schism meant that two popes now claimed universal authority. So where did the ultimate authority within the Church lie? What indeed was the nature of the true Church? Such questions deeply worried theologians and churchmen, and continued to do so after 1417 even when a council at Constance was able to reestablish one pope in Rome as the universal head of Christendom.

Nevertheless, in certain respects the ideals of a universal Church continued to be strongly emphasized. Universal cults were still promoted over local ones (although these continued to prosper, as we shall see – Chapter 3: i). New feast days papally endorsed in the later Middle Ages were often Marian or Christocentric: Corpus Christi, the Compassion of the Virgin, the Transfiguration, the Five Wounds or the Holy Name of Jesus were all feast days which did not depend on particular relics associated with particular locations.[44] The desire to detach saints from a particular locality was encouraged by the spread of images. By the fifteenth century, the diffusion of images of saints had become much more widespread: images were tending to replace relics as the focus of hagiolatry.[45]

A similar concern to reduce the emphasis on place and physicality is evident in the process of canonization. There was a shift in emphasis in what papal investigators required as proof of sanctity. Miracles remained essential proof, and even in the thirteenth century most of the miracles appearing in canonization processes were ones that occurred as close as possible to the relics of the would-be saint.[46] Such was the case with all the miracles of Bishop Osmund which were first presented (unsuccessfully) at the papal curia by the canons of Salisbury cathedral in 1228. But when another list of thirty-three miracles was compiled in 1424, in a second push for canonization, only six were recorded as taking place at the shrine itself. The majority had occurred well away from the tomb and for petitioners who had simply invoked Osmund's name.[47] Moreover, although miracles remained important proof of sanctity, they were of diminishing importance in late medieval cases of canonization: more emphasis began to be placed on the actual life of the saint than on his posthumous career of miracle working. In other miracle collections, in particular those adaptable for preaching, miracles also became more removed from a localized space and time. Cures in miracles also decreased in the fourteenth century, and preachers who used miracle collections in their sermons tended to concentrate on miracles more as models of spiritual life than as examples of the healing power of God's grace.[48]

A similar pattern of thought was encouraged by some churchmen in attitudes towards pilgrimage.[49] The physical act of pilgrimage to a particular shrine in possession of relics continued to be regarded as a meritorious practice – and thrived perhaps as never before in the later Middle Ages. Pilgrimage to the Holy Land remained the most meritorious of all. Other international shrines also received papal endorsement (notably St James at Compostela which first began to attract the English pilgrims in the early twelfth century). The merit to be gained by pilgrimage was more precisely codified with the emergence of clearer definitions of sin and penance. Remissions of punishment due from sin were formalized in grants of indulgence to holy sites: these did not necessarily have to possess saintly relics. Indeed by the late thirteenth century pilgrims might be attracted to a place as much by the prospect of indulgences as by the chance of contact with relics. Bishops still retained the power to grant indulgences, but papal indulgences were particularly valuable, and popes could use them to strengthen their universal authority: Boniface VIII in 1300 proclaimed the first of what became a series of Roman jubilees which enticed pilgrims from all over Christendom to Rome with the prospect of plenary indulgences.[50]

In some clerical circles the importance of journeys to holy places, even the Holy Land, had never been great: pilgrimage had meant a more interior search for heavenly Jerusalem. A twelfth-century sermon included in the 'Book of St James' of Compostela considered pilgrimage to the shrine worthless without the moral reform of the pilgrim. Church reformers of the late fourteenth century were more deeply preoccupied by the fear that the inner self could be neglected in the outward performance of ritual observance, pilgrimage included. The idea of the interior pilgrimage was encouraged. To one anonymous English author, writing after the Roman Jubilee of 1423, the daily repetition of ten Pater Nosters was of greater value than a journey of ten leagues a day to Rome. For some late medieval churchmen, pilgrimages might be journeys not of the body but of the soul alone. The interior life was asserted over the exterior, the universal over the local.

The attempt to enrich the interior life of the laity was also taken further. The pastoral ideals of earlier reformers were continued, even though from the mid-fourteenth century, pastoral efforts were severely hampered by the effects of the Black Death. From a practical point of view, the immediate problem for bishops after the plague first struck was a severe shortage of priests to fill vacant benefices. English bishops' registers in the late fourteenth century show a vigorous effort to recruit clergy and also to improve standards of clerical and lay education.[51] Instruction of the laity was also developed further.[52] Archbishop Thoresby of York expanded upon the brief guidelines set out by Archbishop

Pecham, and upon early fourteenth-century texts (particularly William of Pagula's *Oculus Sacerdotium*), to produce a catechism for the instruction of clergy and laity. His *Lay Folks' Catechism* in 1357 provided a comprehensive guide to belief and practice structured around the Creed, Ten Commandments, the seven works of mercy, seven virtues, vices and sacraments – and in verse so that they might be better committed to memory. A large quantity of such literature in the vernacular was produced throughout the fourteenth and fifteenth centuries. John Mirk's late fourteenth-century *Instructions for the Parish Priest* spelled out the duties of the priest in the confessional as well as the pulpit; his *Festial* provided a compilation of homilies appropriate for Sundays and Feast days throughout the liturgical year. Instruction was also more widely available in the expanding number of plays based on the liturgical year or on saints' Lives.

These plays and texts did not expect the laity to take a purely passive role. Beyond the rote-learning of basic doctrine was a continued emphasis on the examination of conscience: the would-be penitent needed to be aware of the perils of temptation and prepare carefully for the confessional. Sin might be satisfied by outward action, yet was worthless without inner reflection on guilt. In *Dives and Pauper*, an early fifteenth-century exposition of the Ten Commandments, 'Pauper' reminds a complacent 'Dives' that God takes more heed of a man's heart than his fine gifts to churches.[53] Monastic instruction on dying well, which had appeared in psalters, was available for an even wider audience by the fifteenth century. *The Book of the Craft of Dying* first appeared around 1414 and was soon translated into English. It survives in some 200 manuscripts. The tone is introspective: everyone must confront his own death. Woodcut editions depict the deathbed scene, the soul leaving the body, threatened by demons, but protected by the intercession of Christ on the Cross and by the priest administering extreme unction. The message of self-examination was accessible too through plays such as 'Everyman' presenting the lonely pilgrimage of death. Everyman is deserted by friends and family, but confession and charitable deeds offer relief from despair, while his own Good Works go with him to his grave.[54]

The inner devotional life of the clergy and the laity was a concern to which theological literature paid increasing attention from the fourteenth century. Manuals of instruction overlapped with devotional texts.[55] Even the *Oculus Sacerdotium*, mostly catechetical in content, included a meditative section on Christ and his wounds. Meditation, in an ever greater variety of religious contexts, was encouraged of the laity in instructive literature, often written in English. The *Lay Folks' Mass Book*

offered advice as to how best to prepare mentally for receiving the
Eucharist. But from the mid-fourteenth century texts also began to appear
which had a stronger affective dimension. Richard Rolle (d.1349), himself
a hermit, wrote his *Judica Me* within the traditions of the *Ancrene Wisse* and
of confessional texts for the priesthood. He wrote for a local anchoress,
but his words were addressed to a wider audience and there was much
more emphasis on inner mediation within it. Some late fourteenth-century
works were exploratory or visionary rather than didactic. The *Revelations of
Dame Julian of Norwich* are the personalized visions of an anchoress; the
Vision of Piers Plowman by Langland is a complex exploration of contemporary society and values, within a search (a rather inconclusive one) for the
best spiritual life. More prescriptive was Nicholas Love's 'best-selling'
Myrrour of the blessed lyf of Jesu Christ (a translation of a thirteenth-century
Franciscan text) which encouraged meditation around the life of Christ.

Such concerns had origins rooted in the monastic past. There is little
in the spirituality of such texts that cannot be found in the more mystical
writings produced, for instance, by the Cistercians in the twelfth century.
Some of the monastic orders of late medieval England, particularly the
Carthusians (of which Nicholas Love was one) continued to be active
in the promotion of this kind of devotional literature. But the context
of these concerns is now clearly different. By the fifteenth century, more
than ever before, such spirituality is no longer confined to the cloister.
In the first place, monastic life might be lived in the mind. A fifteenth-
century text like the *Abbey of the Holy Ghost* encouraged the reader to
construct his own mental monastery of prayer and contemplation. It
proclaimed itself to be a 'book of the religion of the heart': 'penance
shall make the chapter-house' it stated, '...contemplation the dormi-
tory'.[56] Moreover, a kind of monastic life could also be lived in the world
itself. The *Epistle on the Mixed Life* by Walter Hilton (d.1396) sought to
marry a contemplative life with an active one. Examination of the issue
was not new, but it was one which received much greater attention, all
over Europe, from the mid-fourteenth century. Indeed *The Abbey of the
Holy Ghost* and *The Book of the Craft of Dying* were based on translations
from French texts. The 'mixed life' found expression in a variety of forms
on the Continent – in the religious houses of the Brethren of the
Common Life, inspired by Gerard Groote (d.1374), which lay people
might enter; or in the more diffuse *Devotio Moderna*, of which Thomas
Kempis's *Imitation of Christ* was the most famous exposition. In a variety of
ways, a lay person might find the spiritual means to merge a busy life in
the world with contemplation of the other-worldly.

(vi) Universal Church and Clerical Power: Limitations

The 'Instructions' for the fifteenth-century townsman were, thus, the product of four centuries of ongoing change in which the laity were offered multiplying and more precise paths towards salvation. In a sense they provided opportunities that had not been available to lay people in the eleventh century: a spirituality which had once been contained within the cloister was open to a much wider society. To put it in contemporary terms, lives of contemplation and action had traditionally been discerned and distinguished in the biblical figures, respectively, of Mary and Martha; but increasingly the life of the former (once exclusively monastic) was seen as adaptable for the laity, while the life of the latter (usually seen as inferior) was increasingly valued for its spiritual possibilities.[57]

Yet there were limits. Lay access to 'monastic' spirituality was never total. The changing ideals both of the religious life and of sanctity did not entirely accommodate the life of the lay person lived in the world: the 'mixed life' was second best; very few lay people were ever canonized. Moreover, the 'Instructions' reveal other changes too. Spiritual self-help went only so far: in the penitential regime of the fifteenth-century townsman, the priestly confessor looms inescapably large. Instruction certainly implies control. The ideals and spirituality which the laity were encouraged to adopt had not entered the world by some vague osmosis, but by a process which had involved human agency and clerical structures of power. Ecclesiastical government, increasingly bureaucratic and centralized, had sought to regulate and impose doctrines and duties on the laity and contain them within the framework of the parish. The priesthood had been elevated above the laity and was underpinned by the payment of tithe. Newer doctrines of sin and penance supported priestly authority. The perils of refusal to pay tithe had been made quite plain in visions of Purgatory by the early thirteenth century: the English peasant who was taken on a visionary tour of the afterlife, in Roger of Wendover's account, caught a glimpse of the cleansing flames of Purgatory, as well as a whiff of the infernal stench of Hell because he had thus far not paid his tithe.[58] The discourse of penitential literature, moreover, in a sense encouraged the internalization of a system of regulation which placed the priestly confessor as the essential mediator between God and Man.

Clerical authority had indeed been greatly bolstered since the days of Gregorian reform. The corporate sense of identity within the clergy had been developed, while the vertical lines of authority from the Pope down to the parish priest had been strengthened. By the later Middle Ages

local churches were part of a universal Church in a way that they had not
been in Anglo-Saxon England. The clergy (theoretically) were detached
from the proprietary hold of lay people and might expect to regulate lay
spirituality and behaviour as never before. It would be a crude distortion
to interpret this extension of clerical authority as a cynical effort to
increase power alone: pastoral reform was a genuine motive. But whatever the motive, structures and discourses of ecclesiastical power had
been put in place which both prescribed and limited lay activity and
spirituality.

Moreover, prescription also meant proscription. The process of creating a more universal Church, where definitions of orthodox doctrine
were tightened and enforced by a new professional class of literate clerks,
also sharpened definitions of what was unacceptable. By the end of
the twelfth century, rules on the enclosure of women, for instance, were
becoming more tightly defined.[59] By then too, variety in religious opinion, especially if it were of a critical kind, was less tolerable. Persecution
and the charge of 'heresy' was a more likely weapon to be used against
nonconformist behaviour of all kinds (see Chapter 6: iv).

Thus the universal power of the Church over the laity had certainly
been extended. The paths to salvation open to the laity became more
numerous, but they were also more strictly defined and patrolled.
Nevertheless, it is important not to see even a universal Church as a homogeneous unit imposing a single will upon the laity. Significant ambiguities
remained, and interpretation of ideals, doctrines and practices was never
uniform or clear-cut. Ecclesiastical opinion, even on so central a topic as
the Eucharist, was certainly not undivided.[60] Doctrines had often been
formed and modified in the midst of controversy. There remained uncertainties as to the access permitted for lay people to religious knowledge.
The multiplication of preaching and religious texts, and the prescription
of different forms of religious life for the laity, were encouraged by
pastoral reformers, but they also encountered a strong current of clerical reluctance to offer unmediated doctrinal, and especially scriptural,
knowledge to a wider lay audience.

More fundamentally, the call to reform the Church was an inherently
unstable idea. The wider reforming movements of which Gregorian
reform had been a part, were also potentially subversive of papal and
ecclesiastical authority. The desire to return to primitive ideals and
the Church of the apostles had been embraced but not wholly contained
by the papacy. The hard-line idealism of Gregorian reform could not be
sustained to the satisfaction of idealists, and by the mid-twelfth century

the call for reform was being used against the institutional Church. Indeed, the success of the Gregorian reform in building an institution more financially independent of secular rulers, and in asserting universal papal authority over cult and doctrine, appeared to widen the gulf between the contemporary Church and its apostolic progenitor (see Chapter 6: iv).

Throughout the period, reforming ideals and morality had a way of slipping beyond any simple function (whether unconscious or otherwise) of exerting clerical authority. New institutions which sought to capture and stabilize the reforming currents, like the Cistercians or Franciscans, were hoist with the petard of their own idealism: as their orders expanded, so their their ascetic values were turned against them (see Chapter 5: ii). Attacks on institutional failures to live up to ideals of apostolic poverty were largely contained within clerical circles but they became part of a rhetoric of reform and renewal which was potentially open to more subversive application (see Chapter 6). Moreover, the contrast between ideal and reality was drawn in many other contexts. A monastic contempt for the vanity of worldly things flavoured criticism of religious practices throughout the period, and while there were churchmen who encouraged visual representations of biblical or doctrinal truths, there were others (like the Cistercians) who warned against the distractions of 'superfluous beauty'. The bodily performance of pilgrimage might be compared unfavourably with pilgrimage of a more spiritual kind. The perception of contrast between outer practice and inner idealism was also made more acute by other developments in doctrine and attitude. The demand for outward satisfaction of sin and for internal contrition were supposed to operate in harmony, but they could also pull in different directions. Confessional manuals encouraged an examination of conscience with a rhetoric which emphasized the danger and falseness of outer things: confessor and penitent were urged to look behind the activities and behaviour which masked sin. Even the 'good works' of penance might be the outward signs of inner depravity. Lavish gifts to church building, vestments or bells, or even gifts to the poor, were worthless if born of pride: so warns the puritanical 'Pauper' in *Dives and Pauper*.[61] Thus, new doctrines of penance and Purgatory encouraged the performance of outward 'good works', but their proliferation (especially in the later Middle Ages) did not always appear, to the critical eye, to sit comfortably with the stress on inner contrition.

Homiletic literature was also a potential source for the criticism of the clergy. From the early thirteenth century, manuals for confessors had encouraged the examination of penitents according to social status and occupation, the better to understand the motives of the sinner. The clergy, like all other groups, were portrayed as having their own characteristic sins.[62] Pastoral efforts to improve clerical standards encouraged a rhetorical discourse – in sermons, instructional manuals and in episcopal statutes – which highlighted, sometimes in excoriating detail, the perceived failings of the clergy. Once again, the ideal of reform behind the drive to a universal Church was potentially subversive of clerical power within it. Although the structures of ecclesiastical power had steadily increased, discourse on those structures did not tend unambiguously to the strengthening of clerical authority over the laity. The uncertainties in the nature of clerical authority were only deepened from the late fourteenth century. The spectacle of Schism opened new debate on the nature of the Church, sharpening as never before a sense of possible disjuncture between the visible outer church and the true inner church of the saved.

This chapter has concentrated on the Church as agent, directing the religious life of the laity and controlling social behaviour. In England, episcopal government was stronger than in most other regions in Christendom, and its strength may partly explain why the parish framework became particularly well established as the primary unit of pastoral care.[63] But the Church, in England as elsewhere, was also acted upon: clergy and clerical institutions were caught up in social changes they sought to direct and alter. Prescriptive instruction of the laity did not operate in a social vacuum. It might seek to control lay behaviour, yet it also internalized social norms, conditioned by, rather than conditioning, social change. In manuals for confessors, although the traditional division of the three orders was generally adhered to, increasingly close attention was paid to social detail and the existence of an expanding range of social groups. Social diversification was even reflected in penitential doctrine. A more complex society, Le Goff argues, demanded a more complex afterlife; economic change and specialization meant that new categories of sins and sinners had to be dealt with.[64] Purgatory spared from Hell those sinners whose very calling could endanger their souls: knights who spilled blood, butchers or tanners who dealt with polluted goods, merchants who handled money. New social needs projected themselves on to changes in the formulation of the afterlife.

Prescriptive instruction might also reinforce social and patriarchal hierarchy (see Introduction: iii). In the fifteenth-century 'Instructions', the patriarchal authority of the layman over his wife and children is assumed. As we shall see, the penitential regimes and devotional habits required of men and women could differ along gendered, if not misogynistic, lines. Moreover, in the later Middle Ages, the context of profound social upheaval places the 'Instructions' in a different light: its prescriptive and patriarchal certainties perhaps reflect anxieties towards change. The desire to assert authority spilled over into religious tracts (see Chapter 6: viii). Yet here too there were ambiguities. Religion did not automatically support social hierarchy. The whole thrust of pastoral reform and homiletic instruction had been towards a moral regeneration of society and the exposure of vice at all social levels. Confessional advice emphasized the responsibilities and failings of those in authority towards their social inferiors; the weakest in society – including women – might, by their distance from the corruptive influence of wealth and power, expose the ungodliness of those in authority, clerical and lay. In the years after the papal Schism, these impulses are particularly evident. Churchmen from the very heart of the establishment, like Jean Gerson, Chancellor of the University of Paris, looked behind institutional facades to locate sources of renewal. He supported – not without grave reservations – the canonization of the female mystic Bridget of Sweden (d.1373) who, like many others, had raised a prophetic voice against perceived corruption.[65] The very emphasis on the ideals of a universal Church in this period begins to look like the product of crisis;[66] and the search for spiritual renewal within it could cut right across hierarchy, both lay and ecclesiastical.

As the following chapters will show, the limitations of the universality of the Church and of clerical power in England were many. Papal and ecclesiastical control over the local clergy and churches, over sanctity and over forms of devotional life was far from complete. It was limited, at the highest levels, by kings who retained effective control of ecclesiastical appointments, and who sought to control saints' cults and even forms of devotional life (see Chapter 3). Certainly by the later Middle Ages there existed notions of a 'Church of England' within the more universal Church.[67] At a lower social level, ecclesiastical control was limited by the demands of wider groups of lay people. Pastoral reform was as much a response to demand as an imposition of a clerical vision. The growth and character of a system of parish churches was conditioned by local circumstances and shaped by local parishioners (see Chapters 4 and 5). The growing number of homiletic and devotional texts was a response to demands from an increasingly literate laity; and in the later Middle Ages the diffuse and uncertain provenance of many texts illustrates how the forms of devotional life that they advocated were not the product of some centralized clerical diktat (see Chapter 6). Moreover, just as the meaning of prescribed devotions and religious practices was prone to varieties of interpretation even within clerical circles, so among the laity and within different social contexts, interpretation and practice were various. The nature of the universal Church was fundamentally shaped by the laity.

Chapter 3: Saints, Cults and the Holy

In 1386, disturbing news reached the ears of the bishop of Lincoln. In the fields of Rippingdale, near the high road, people had made for themselves a statue known as Jurdan Cross. The statue had worked miracles. Bells were being rung, processions held and sermons preached. To the bishop, the statue was fake, the miracles false and the processions used only for profits which were being appropriated by laymen for their own use. But in 1392 the pope came to a different verdict, apparently impressed by the cult's popularity and antiquity to which the bishop had made no reference: the cross, it was now said, had stood for almost a hundred years and the miracles had attracted pilgrims from all over England. A chapel was to be permitted at the site.[1]

Contact with the holy, particularly through the saints, their relics and miracles, had been an essential aspect of Christianity at an early date. Control of its manifestations had long been of concern to the Church, in part because of the need to supplant and eradicate pagan beliefs. Conversion in Anglo-Saxon England had required a process of appropriating and Christianizing holy but pagan places of worship. The Rippingdale case may show how successful the pastoral efforts of the Church had been since the days of conversion. Even the bishop tacitly assumed that the cult was 'Christian' – that it was a cult venerating Christ rather than one venerating an object or location. Indeed, by the later Middle Ages the spontaneous appearance of new cults was not unusual. Perhaps they were already occurring in Anglo-Saxon England; what is so striking about the later period is their frequency and their ready appearance outside the narrow confines of religious houses. The penetrating programme of pastoral reform had contributed to a familiarity and close contact with saints among the laity at large: the proliferation of relics and pilgrim 'souvenirs', the multiplication of images in parish church altars and on windows and walls, the growing output of saints' lives and legendaries, were but a few of the contexts in which saints had become readily accessible features of public and even domestic life. Pastoral reform had also sensitized lay people, at all levels of society, to miraculous events and to a large variety of objects – such as crosses, relics, images or the Host – through which they might be worked. Attachments to new cults and saints were the side effects of pastoral effort within a universal Church.

What troubled the bishop in the Rippingdale case, however, was the apparent control that locals had exercised by initiating and controlling the cult. Even in the days of the early Church, a more fundamental concern than paganism was that direct access to the divine at holy places or through holy objects, however Christianized they might be, posed an inherent challenge to the Church's role as sole mediator between God and Man. From the twelfth century, the requirements of a universal Church had demanded a still tighter control of the holy in all its forms: a more centralized monitoring of sainthood, a greater uniformity of cult, a closer inspection of miracles, and an emphasis on the Eucharist as a ritually repeated clerical miracle. The Rippingdale case shows the universal Church in practice, an obscure corner of Christendom suddenly illuminated under the papal spotlight of scrutiny. It also shows the practical difficulties in any ecclesiastical attempt to regulate sudden appearances of the miraculous. Churchmen might not agree as to what was holy, and ironically here it is the local bishop who appears more hostile than the pope to the establishment of a new local cult.

The ideals of a universal Church were powerful and increasingly pervasive in Christendom. But however much ecclesiastical procedures for authentication were tightened, who and what might be deemed holy, and by whom, remained troubling questions, all the more so by the end of the fourteenth century. The clergy of local churches might have local attachments and agendas which cut across universal ideals. The laity, from the king downwards, had other agendas. Moreover, the different social contexts in which cults manifested themselves meant a diversity in function and interpretation which churchmen could not control or dictate with any ease.

(i) Local Churches and Local Saints

The ecclesiastical hierarchy in Anglo-Saxon England had developed strong attachments to local customs and saints: these had become part of an English sense of identity. Part of this identity (as Bede had strongly emphasized) was also 'Roman': within monastic houses, many of the saints who served as their holy protectors were recognized as part of an established Roman tradition. But many too were little known beyond the locality, let alone beyond English shores. The Gregorian papacy's assertion of universal papal authority over the local churches of Christendom cast doubts on home-grown saints whose claims to sanctity were not grounded in Lives written in the best Latin. The proliferation of saints' Lives written in England from the late eleventh century was one result of the pressure resulting from changing ecclesiastical standards.

There was pressure from other directions. The Norman conquest in some respects brought about great change: the Anglo-Saxon aristocracy was virtually wiped out, and in taking over land and churches, the incoming Norman hierarchy was confronted by a large number of saints, like Alphege of Canterbury or Ecgwine of Evesham, whose obscure names did not trip easily off Gallic lips. 'Who is this Etheldreda about whom you prate?', demanded the new Norman sheriff in Cambridgeshire of the monks of Ely.[2] Some cults became identified with resistance to the Normans. St Cuthbert apparently saved Durham from a punitive expedition by the Conqueror, by shrouding the city in a dense fog. Earl Waltheof was executed for rebellion in 1076: his 'incorrupt' body became the centre of a cult at Crowland Abbey, and in the wake of miracles in the early twelfth century, Englishmen apparently flocked to his tomb.[3]

Revisionist historiography has tended to play down the actual threat to Anglo-Saxon saints in the aftermath of the Conquest.[4] Normans, like the sheriff in Cambridgeshire, expressed scorn not so much because English saints were obscure but because they were loathe to recognize saintly ownership over land which they, as conquerors, wished to appropriate. Yet English monks and nuns certainly felt threatened: eviction from their houses was a distinct possibility, just as their aristocratic kin had been swept from their lands. Some did not help their own cause. Abbot Wulfketel of Crowland was deposed in 1085 'because he was English' and because he was 'hated by the Normans'.[5] Subtle forms of resistance were possible. The credentials of native saints could be made more evident. In the 1070s and 1080s a large number of saints' Lives (complete with the posthumous history of their relics) were addressed to Norman prelates who were clearly thought hostile to these saints and to the custodians of their remains. The message of these texts is apparent: usurpers of saintly lands could expect reprisals (in the case of St Ecgwine, of a surprisingly murderous kind[6]); in any case royal and even papal approval had long been extended to these cults, and their prosperity signified continuing divine approval for their English custodians.

The Norman ecclesiastical hierarchy was increasingly affected by Gregorian reform which could also strengthen hostility to local saints. Yet attitudes to Anglo-Saxon saints, certainly by the time Anselm was appointed archbishop of Canterbury in 1093, were actually softening. Norman colonists had begun to adopt many of the Anglo-Saxon saints as their own. A later abbot of Crowland, the Norman Geoffrey of Orleans (1109–24), can be found speaking out against a Norman monk who had denounced Waltheof as a traitor. By the early twelfth century there were still English fears that the Anglo-Saxon past, and its saints, were being lost to memory; but William of Malmesbury, himself of mixed Norman and English descent, wrote many histories and saints' Lives in which an integrated view of the Conquest and of the Anglo-Saxon past was presented.[7] By the 1140s there was enough assimilation between conqueror and conquered for surviving Anglo-Saxon saints to be threatened no longer.

There were, in any case, strong incentives for clerics of Norman origin to adopt the saints of Anglo-Saxon England. Norman archbishops of Canterbury might find in their local saints powerful patrons of their claims to primacy. Colonizing monks who took over an Anglo-Saxon house could adopt its saints as a statement of their legitimacy: divine approval for the refoundation of Much Wenlock nunnery as a Cluniac cell for foreign monks in 1079, for example, was 'proved' with discovery of the remains of St Milburga (d.715).[8]

Later religious communities continued to preserve local cults. Guibert of Nogent wrote that it was customary for monks to raise money by carrying around the feretories and relics of saints; and he described the popular fervour stirred up by the fund-raising tour around southern England in 1113 of the relics of Laon cathedral.[9] In many parts of Christendom cults of relics in the eleventh and twelfth centuries were becoming public spectacles as never before.[10] The liturgical veneration of saints was enriched with new texts and newly built churches, and was coordinated with feasts and the rising number of markets or fairs. Feast days and market days tended to coincide. St Ivo's cult at Slepe was boosted by the abbot and convent through the creation of a new town at Slepe, and the grant of an Easter fair in 1110.[11] There was also a tendency to widen the catchment area of would-be pilgrims: miracle stories increasingly emphasize the arrival of outsiders, beyond the locality, at saintly shrines. Stories of relic translations stress the presence of crowds and mass pilgrimages. At the translation of St Cuthbert's relics in 1104 'men of all ranks, ages and professions', according to Simeon of Durham, '... hastened to be present'.[12]

Such vigorous promotion of local saints and their relics by religious houses cut directly across the path to a more universal Church. English bishops too, despite a stronger attachment after Gregorian reform to papal authority, might do the same. They could indeed promote universal saints or new universal feasts, but they often retained an insular perspective sometimes at odds with Roman universalism. Even archbishops like Anselm, or Thomas Becket martyred in 1170, were as much interested in championing the rights of Canterbury (a primacy of which popes never particularly approved) as they were in defending the 'liberties of the Church' as a whole.[13] Bishops were not always enthusiastic about local cults generated by monastic houses, but they could promote public cycles of local saints. Bishop Grandisson of Exeter considered veneration of new saints illegal before proper papal canonization, yet he assiduously promoted the production in his diocese of Lives of Cornish saints whose cults had never been papally ratified.[14]

The claims to sanctity of long-dead native saints continued to be advanced, sometimes against new competitors. The martyrdom of Thomas Becket created a cult at Canterbury which became the dominant pilgrimage centre in England. Other shrines responded: soon after 1170, at a time when Thomas's shrine had already started to turn pilgrim heads, a previously austere St Cuthbert began to adopt a more accommodating attitude towards petitioners for his cures at Durham.[15] The translation of St Thomas's relics in 1220 prompted concerted efforts in other dioceses to assert the sanctity of local saints. Following a vision, the canons at Dorchester claimed discovery of the tomb of St Birinus (former apostle to the West Saxons), despite the bishop of Winchester's objection, based on the authority of Bede, that the body had long been located in Winchester.[16]

Despite attachment to pre-Conquest saints, bishops did also promote new candidates for sainthood, submitting them before the papal curia. The process could be taxing: it took two attempts, separated by more than two hundred years, for the bishops and canons of Salisbury Cathedral to win canonization in 1457 for their own (Norman) bishop Osmund (d.1099).[17] Thus candidates put forward for canonization mostly reflected the background and concerns of patrons who had the necessary power, wealth and influence to persevere: these candidates unsurprisingly reflecting the localized and elitist concerns of the ecclesiastical hierarchy in England. Some of these would-be saints were certainly admired, by lay people as well as the clergy, for the austerity of their lives: Gilbert of Sempringham (d.1189) established a reputation for holiness by virtue of his eremitical life lived in a local community. But Gilbert was no wandering hermit or subversive preacher. He enjoyed the support of his local bishop, became head of a monastic order and was canonized in 1202. Most of the holy men officially promoted in England for canonization were bishops or heads of male religious houses.[18] Most too were expected to have some noble background – Gilbert's biographer felt that his subject's 'worldly origin' and his mother's 'inferior rank' were defects which had to be overcome.[19] Bishop Osmund of Salisbury was promoted by the cathedral canons as one of their own, a sober administrator and promoter of the Sarum liturgical rite.

With regard to the candidature for canonization, an aristocratic and clerical view of sainthood prevailed in England throughout the medieval period, one which reflected the relative strength of the ecclesiastical hierarchy. In other parts of Europe – especially in Northern Italy, where society was more heavily urbanized, less hierarchically structured and where political authority was more fragmented – new saints were more likely to spring up unchecked by episcopal authority.[20] There too, under the more powerful influence of the mendicant orders, new saints were less likely to possess an aristocratic or clerical background and more likely to base their pretensions to sainthood on a dedication to 'poverty' and an enthusiastic devotion to the sufferings of Christ.[21] In England, where bishops remained powerful figures, stricter monitoring of cults and sainthood continued. Nevertheless, there were significant limits to such control even in England. For one thing, authoritarian control did not come from bishops alone. In Anglo-Saxon England secular and ecclesiastical hierarchies had been inextricably intertwined; and although after the eleventh century some of these ties had unravelled, in other ways they remained, changed and even strengthened. These ties continued to affect the presence and nature of saints and cults in England.

(ii) Cults, Saints and Royal Power

Long after the Conquest, the monarchy in England retained a strong grip over the Church in England. However much Gregorian reform had threatened royal power, in theory detaching the clergy from its 'feudal' ties to royal authority, in practice ideological assertion gave way to practical politics. Despite the occasional clash between king and archbishop (even the spectacular martyrdom of Thomas Becket in 1170 at the hands of Henry II's henchmen), the relationship between 'regnum' and 'sacerdotium' in the twelfth century was one of compromise. Becket's high idealism against royal encroachment on 'the liberties of the Church', struck a shrill and discordant note in a climate which, if not entirely harmonious, tended towards accommodation. In any case when churchmen reflected on the relationship between Church and king, the dominant theme was its symbiotic and hierocratic nature: as Archbishop Pecham affirmed in 1281, it was the Church's task to affirm and support the king to meet his divinely imposed responsibilities towards his Christian realm.[22]

The reality of royal power made compromise all the more necessary. The expansion of ecclesiastical government in the twelfth century was matched by a corresponding extension of royal bureaucracy in a country where traditions of centralized government were already strong. Royal government remained heavily dependent on clerical personnel, and it was not until the mid-fifteenth century that laymen (trained in civil law) came to dominate the lower ranks of royal bureaucracy. But as civil servants, clerics (including bishops) could be called upon to serve royal interests; and royal need for money – more voracious still from Edward I's reign – made it increasingly difficult for English clergymen to withstand demands for taxation on clerical wealth. Moreover, especially from the late thirteenth century, notions of royal sovereignty, fed by interest in Roman law, were given material expression in royal statutes which proclaimed limits to papal rights of universal jurisdiction over the clergy and Church property.[23]

However, other developments had shifted the ground on which royal power might be based. Gregorian reform had elevated the clergy to the position of sole mediators with the divine, effectively stripping kings of much of their sacrality. No late medieval king (with the possible exception of Richard II) claimed authority directly from God. Moreover, the broadening range of royal government over matters temporal conversely attenuated royal links with the other-worldly. The expansion of bureaucratic government and legal procedures reduced the need for recourse to supernatural agency in the ordering of society.[24] Yet the predatory nature of royal government, especially under the Angevins in the twelfth century, left its kings exposed to criticism against their secular rule. Perhaps it was a sense of insecurity that prompted Henry II, for instance, to consort with hermits whose asceticism confirmed proof of a link with the divine.[25] Later kings continued to seek out 'holy men' to assure themselves of divine approval for their actions.[26] Yet assurance could also be found elsewhere. Despite Gregorian reform, vestiges of sacral authority survived, not least in the ability of an (anointed) king to heal scrofula with the 'royal touch'. It may be that kings of England were initially less successful than the Capetians in developing the sacred aspects of their kingship. But the more predatory of them seem particularly anxious to demonstrate their powers: Edward I revived the sacral pretentions of English kingship and managed to unearth and bless some 2000 diseased persons in one year.[27]

A more systematic way in which kings, all over Europe, began to compensate for the decline in sacral kingship was through the cultivation of dynastic cults of saints. In some ways the Norman conquest inhibited the easy continuation of native cults by a new foreign dynasty. William I and his son preferred burial in ancestral monastic houses on the continent; so for the most part did their Norman and Angevin successors. Those laid to rest in England (like Henry I at Reading) had no real equivalent to the royal mausoleum in France, enjoyed by their Capetian rivals, under the protection of St Denis. But Anglo-Saxon kings had provided a precocious precedent in the use (and provision) of royal saints, and the Normans had partly rested their claim to rule on the authority of Edward the Confessor whose early reputation for piety finally received papal endorsement, at Angevin request, with his canonization in 1161. Under Henry III, the cult of St Edward at Westminster attracted greater royal attention, and later kings turned the saint into an integral part of their kingship: Edward's ring (and the slippers of St Edmund, former king of East Anglia martyred in 869) were used as part of the coronation regalia. Kings with higher-flown ideals of kingship made particular efforts to exploit the cult. Richard II wished his supporters close to him in death as well as life: burial of important curialists near his intended tomb at the abbey threw the cloak of sanctity beyond the royal person and over his entourage too.[28]

Royal interest in other Anglo-Saxon saints had also quickened in the thirteenth century – perhaps also a sense that sanctity could be a commodity transmitted by inheritance. Henry III and Edward I were diligent in attending translations of relics of their saintly predecessors within England: perhaps they felt that the sanctity of distant ancestors might be transferred to them. Richard II visited sites associated with the royal martyrs Ethelbert and Edward; Henry V made a pilgrimage tour in 1421 (as did Henry VI in 1449) of East Anglian shrines where Anglo-Saxon royal remains were particularly clustered.[29] Some late medieval kings contrived to discover in their royal ancestors saintly qualities which had hitherto escaped detection: Henry VI sought the canonization of King Alfred whom he referred to as the 'first king of England'.[30]

Behind much of this interest (aside from the devotional preferences of particular kings) lay a shift in royal dynastic ambition. The continental ambitions of Angevin kings gave way, certainly under Edward I, to attempts to impose an imperial hegemony over the British Isles, and to efforts, from Edward III's reign, to prosecute a war in France which could be presented as a patriotic venture. Grafted on to a growing sense of English identity, Anglo-Saxon saints enjoyed posthumous careers of a lively and sometimes xenophobic kind. St Wulfstan assisted Edward I in his Welsh campaigns, St Cuthbert in his war in Scotland in 1296.[31] Edward III purposefully visited shrines of northern saints during his Scottish wars in 1330s to elicit divine support. He also offered to put his own sacral powers to the test in the prosecution of his claim to the French throne, challenging the Valois king to prove his right to the throne by touching for scrofula.[32]

Saints and cults of a more universal kind also submitted to royal appropriation. Papally canonized saints were exploited. Thomas Becket was quickly turned from victim of royal oppression to instrument of dynastic ambition: Henry II's success against William the Lion of Scotland in 1174 was attributed to Thomas's intervention.[33] Phials of Christ's blood and fragments of the True Cross were gathered into an expanding royal relic collection. Henry III had a relic of the Holy Blood ceremoniously installed in Westminster abbey as though in sanctification of his rule.[34] In the fourteenth century St George was beginning his transfiguration from universal saint into honorary Englishman, and by 1418 he was formally deemed 'protector of the English nation'.[35] The cult of the Virgin Mary (with whom St George was connected) had also begun to serve national interests. The Wilton Diptych (probably painted in the late 1390s) showed, next to the Virgin, a red-cross banner surmounted by an orb depicting an island. It may represent Richard II's dedication of Britain to St George and Mary herself as protectors of an imperial realm.[36]

Association with particular saints and cults helped clothe the bodies of late medieval kings in a vicarious aura of sanctity, or even infuse their veins with sainted blood inherited from saintly progenitors. Ideas of kingship were also developing in ways which lifted kings out of the mundane and secular. By the fourteenth century a clear distinction had emerged between the office of kingship and the person who held it; yet at the same time the king as person was increasingly surrounded by institutions and ceremonies which mediated his power in a more impersonal manner.

Royal courts and households were expanding in personnel whose status within them was determined by a carefully calibrated hierarchy. The ceremonial display of royal power increased, not least in the growing detail surrounding coronation orders and funeral processions.[37] Outside the court, the programmes of entry ceremonies into towns consciously linked royal with divine power. Richard II's entry into London in 1392 equated royal headship of the country with Christ's headship of the Church. During the entry ceremony following his victory at Agincourt in 1415, Henry V was greeted by St George and by 'twelve kings of the English succession, martyrs and confessors' who presented the king with bread and wine as though at communion.[38]

Under Henry V in particular there was a concerted effort, in conjunction with the ecclesiastical hierarchy, to promote common public worship. Heretical opinions were suppressed; appropriate models of spiritual behaviour were devised (see Chapter 6: vii). Henry's foundation of a Carthusian house at Sheen and a house of Brigittine nuns at Syon engaged the spirituality of two orders, renowned for their austerity, in a permanent round of prayer for the Lancastrian dynasty. Anglo-Saxon saints like St Chad at Canterbury, previously of local significance, were promoted by Archbishop Chichele as worthy of national devotion, while the feast day of the 'universal' St George was promoted to the rank of double feast.[39] Under Henry V it is possible to speak of a national Church under the tight control of the king. His delegation to the Council of Constance announced England's unity under the Lancastrian monarch: Thomas Polton asserted that English kings had the longest association with Christianity of any European ruling dynasty.[40] Such pretensions were not unique within Christendom during the period of Papal Schism, when notions of quasi 'national' churches and cults under the close supervision of their rulers began to reassert themselves. But in England these notions had long traditions, reaching back to Bede's construction of Anglo-Saxon kingship. Royal control of saints and cults drew on deep roots.

By the later Middle Ages, then, kings had developed the aura of kingship in several ways. If they could no longer be priestly, they had been able to preserve and extend aspects of sacral kingship, to draw connections with an Anglo-Saxon heritage of saintly kings, to associate their rule with other long-dead and even 'living' saints, and to elaborate upon the mystique of royal ceremony. Yet for all this, there were significant limitations to their ability to harness the 'holy' to secular purposes. No late medieval English king was canonized; saints (as we shall see) could attract anti-royal followings; royally favoured cults did not always become popular. The dismal failure of Henry III's Holy Blood relic at Westminster to attract widespread pilgrimage, despite the impressive accumulation of indulgences, is testimony to Henry's own inadequacies as ruler, but at a deeper level it shows that royal control of the sacred could not be guaranteed. Ceremony too might serve purposes other than sanctification of royal rule: London had its own agenda in the Entry ceremonies provided for its kings. Moreover, local saints retained local identities despite attempts to turn them into agents of royal rule. In the north of England, St Cuthbert may on occasion have been drafted into royal service, but he also emerged in a fifteenth-century Life with a specifically northern identity: the Life was proudly written in 'language of the North in lede / That can non other Inglis rede'. Anglo-Saxon saints did not all become aligned with royal or national identities; and not in all regions were they dominant. Cornwall preserved memories of its pre-Anglo-Saxon heritage: there was a larger than average survival within the region, in church dedications and guild foundations, of saints with a British, Cornish or Breton past.[41]

In the end, there were significant limits to the extent of any kind of authoritarian control. Notwithstanding official efforts to promote saints and other cults, at a local level new 'saints', never officially promoted, still less canonized, continued to appear. The establishment of a papal monopoly of canonization afforded the papacy control neither over the beginnings of a cult nor over the criteria of sanctity. Canonization was generally a process of adjudication on the validity of a cult which had already begun: the 'reputation' of the would-be saint had already been established outside the papal curia.[42] In England too, kings and bishops were faced with new cults of saints who had not been officially promoted. In fact the vast majority of people who acquired saintly reputations were not put forward to the papal curia. Neither tightening papal procedures nor strong ecclesiastical (and secular) government in England had much effect in dictating who was recognized as holy at a local level.

(iii) Unofficial Saints

The appearance of holy men or women was not necessarily a problem for those in authority. On occasion local holy men, usually hermits, performed functions which served rulers as much as the ruled. A significant number of them in the twelfth century – Wulfric of Haselbury (d.1155) for instance – were of English or Anglo-Danish descent, mediating between the native population and their Norman or Anglo-Norman masters in the first few generations after the Norman Conquest. Cut off from the normal bonds of society, but close to the heart of the local community in his cell by the side of the parish church, Wulfric earned a reputation for austerity and for mediation between locals and a wider society, including Norman lords.[43] In the opinion of one exasperated local priest (to whom the hermit had not given the power to speak French in front of his Norman archdeacon) Wulfric's mediation did not go far enough; notwithstanding, both priest and hermit were apparently on excellent terms, Wulfric on occasion contributing to the financial welfare of the parish church.[44] A would-be saint in the twelfth century who respected the rights of the parish might well have appealed to bishops concerned to tighten the parochial structure (see Chapter 2: iii).

In general, English bishops were relatively successful in regulating the religious life of the laity, certainly before the appearance of Lollardy in the late fourteenth century (see Chapter 6: v). Yet they were continually troubled by the sudden and sometimes disturbing appearance of individuals locally recognized as 'saints'.[45] During the charged atmosphere of recruitment for the third crusade in 1190, a man was murdered at Northampton, and his body was thrown over the city walls. His death was blamed on the Jews. His tomb attracted pilgrims; miracles were reported. The bishop – the saintly Hugh of Lincoln no less – tried to suppress the cult. A riot followed, quelled only by the bishop's charismatic presence. Another cult appeared in London in 1196: there, a preacher, William FitzOsbern, was executed for rabble-rousing, and acquired the status of a martyr; the archbishop was forced to break up the crowd gathering at the spot where he had been hanged.[46] Violent death could also make martyrs out of unlikely candidates. The bishop of Worcester could not bring himself to endorse the admiration among people in Bristol for a man, murdered by sanctuary violators in 1279, who had spent long stretches in prison.[47] The bishop of Lincoln was equally dismissive of the cult in 1313 surrounding Laurence of Oxford, 'hung on account of his evil crimes'. In 1440, despite being burned as a lapsed heretic at Tower Hill in 1440, Richard Wyche worked miracles at his grave site, to the alarm of the bishop and aldermen of London.[48]

Many of these unofficial new 'saints', even if apparently 'orthodox', failed to conform to the type of candidate which English bishops wished to promote for canonization at the papal curia. In the fourteenth and early fifteenth centuries a number of humbler priests acquired local recognition as miracle workers, and roused episcopal suspicion. The obscure Richard Bovyle (d.1359), rector of Whitstone church (Cornwall), who also seems to have died a violent death, worked miracles, and his body was moved from the cemetery into the church. The bishop of Exeter was prompted to investigate the cult in 1361.[49]

Martyrdom could have political implications. Waltheof's miracles attracted a patriotic following which the Council of Westminster (apparently) tried to suppress in 1102.[50] Later opponents of royal authority could also acquire the status of martyr.[51] Simon de Montfort died in defiance of Henry III at the battle of Evesham in 1265. A well sprang up at the spot where he fell. Miracles were worked and pilgrims, aristocratic and peasant, were attracted.[52] In June 1405 another rebel, Archbishop Scrope of York, was beheaded for treason in a field outside York. Miracles occurred both there and at his burial place in York Minster.[53]

In some ways such cults may point paradoxically to the strength of royal power in England. The relatively large number of 'political saints' which appeared in England compared with other countries testifies to the close and traditional identification there of kingly with saintly authority: whether royalist or anti-royal, these cults are part of the same discourse. Moreover, kings were to some extent able to harness culted rebels. In the more reconciliatory atmosphere of Henry V's reign, Scrope's cult was permitted, and its potentially subversive nature was neutralized. Nevertheless, such cults showed that connections between royal and saintly authority might be turned against individual kings; they showed too that royal power to suppress them was limited. Waltheof's miracles continued despite official denunciation; de Montfort's continued in defiance of royal prohibition until at least 1279. Henry V compromised over Scrope's cult partly because his father's efforts to prohibit pilgrimage to York Minster had failed. New saints' cults had a tendency to develop momentums of their own, slipping beyond the control of royal and ecclesiastical authority.

In the later Middle Ages, threats to authority of all kinds fed anxieties over new cults. In England Lancastrian usurpation in 1399 may well have injected a new instability into the dynastic authority of kings, an instability which Henry V's victories could only temporarily efface (see Chapter 6: v). The shoring up of royal power within the bulwarks of saintly and religious authority was as much a mark of anxiety as of institutional strength. There were wider concerns about the nature of sanctity and authority, and about authentication of the holy. Papal Schism had also created new uncertainties and a renewed urgency about the reform of Church and society, in which the judgment of other-worldly authority had a part to play (see Chapter 2: v and vi).

These concerns are reflected in *The Book of Margery Kempe*. It purports to be the spiritual autobiography of a woman from King's Lynn, dictated to scribes and written down between 1436 and 1438 ('purports' because function and authorship of the text are keenly debated – see Chapter 6: ix).[54] At one level the text is about the problem of authenticating the holy life, perhaps too about the nature of sanctity. Margery's spiritual journey takes her on physical pilgrimages to shrines in England and all over Christendom, and to holy men and women in search of confession and reassurance about her own life. But her mobility, as a 'single' woman, invites hostile reaction from secular and ecclesiastical authorities, and her own search for spiritual reform leads her into outspoken and contentious criticism of those same authorities. The Book suggests exemplary models for her behaviour, authenticating her life on previous saints and would-be saints – including Bridget of Sweden whose prophetic denunciation of clerical corruption at the time of the Schism had enjoyed a mixed reception. The authentication of spiritual authority transmitted through the female body and voice was particularly fraught and traditionally required careful monitoring; but it is no accident that, in the context of anxiety about the nature of the Church from the late fourteenth century onwards, reforming voices from outside the mainstream of ecclesiastical life, and from the margins of patriarchal society, were listened to.

There is also something in Margery's experiences which reflects English conditions. Most of the Book is taken up with her early and troubled travels between 1414 and 1417 – during the effort to heal the Schism at the Council of Constance, but also at a time when Lancastrian legitimacy was still being intensively asserted as well as threatened. The Margery of the Book also seeks authentication for her spiritual life from episcopal authority: the bishops and archbishops she meets are always presented as on her side. At times too she seeks assurance from royal centres of spiritual power: her final return to King's Lynn takes her into the Lancastrian foundation at Syon.[55] The Book reflects the strong presence of royal and ecclesiastical power in England, but it is deeply ambivalent about any necessary equation of sanctity with established authority.

(iv) Unofficial Cults: Superstition and Paganism?

The charismatic and saintly authority attributed to men and women was not the only manifestation of the holy. Other kinds of cults continued to spring up with alarming speed, and in places which bishops condemned as 'profane'. By 1296 a private chapel erected by Edmund of Cornwall at his manor of Hambledon, but unlicensed for public worship, had become a place of pilgrimage, and of miracles which the bishop of Lincoln dismissed as 'pretended'.[56] Other such pilgrimage sites were wells or springs rather than chapels, and throughout the later Middle Ages bishops were kept busy investigating sudden manifestations of their miraculous powers. Great numbers were flocking to a well in a field at North Crawley (Bucks) in 1299; an 'immense concourse of people' within a matter of days in 1464 gathered at a well at Wembdon (Somerset) which had suddenly begun to work cures.[57]

Wells were not the most frequent generators of miracles in the later Middle Ages. Bishops investigated more cases of miracle-working images – particularly those of the Virgin Mary. In the late thirteenth century, one Thomas de Poynton brought a statue of the Virgin from Scotland to his local chapel of Fraisthorpe where it stood, widely venerated, until his death in 1299. His widow sold the statue to the rector of Foston-on-the-Wolds, where it continued to attract pilgrims and offerings. Archbishop Greenfield of York ordered inquiries, and for a while in 1313 prohibited veneration to the image.[58] His contemporary, Bishop Baldock of London, had been investigating a case in 1306 of an image at Ashingdon church with a reputation of such miraculous virtue that crowds daily crawled up the hill on their knees to visit it.[59]

Perhaps such cults of images are testimony to the growth of a more universal Church, where cults did not have to be tied to a particular locality. Yet the spontaneous appearance of cults, often in rural areas, frequently provoked a knee-jerk response by those in authority. One reason for this may have been a continuing fear of paganism. Certainly such fear was still evident in the twelfth and even thirteenth centuries. Bishop Hugh of Lincoln struggled to stop veneration of springs at Berkhamsted (Hertfordshire) and High Wycombe (Buckinghamshire).[60] The Bishop of Winchester in 1295 deemed it necessary (as several previous synods had done) to condemn the worship of stones, wood, trees and wells.[61] Thereafter worries that paganism might lurk behind such devotion virtually never appear in episcopal investigations. Occasionally, later bishops did condemn unauthorized veneration as 'pagan': Bishop Grandisson of Exeter considered that some miracles were inspired by the Devil and led to idolatry; and in 1351 he denounced devotion to an image of the Virgin Mary at Frithelstock, in a remote part of Devon, as little more than worship of an idol, perhaps to Diana. Yet his denunciation looks more like defamatory rhetoric, used to suppress the cult, than impartial observation of actual belief. The fact that the chapel and its new attraction also undermined the integrity of an existing parish church probably served to sharpen the hostility of a bishop who on other occasions condemned as 'degenerate' those who presumed to set up unlicensed places of worship. The bishop had the chapel demolished.[62] In other cases, the rhetoric of denunciation was not employed even when an alleged connection with paganism might have been easy to make. An investigation into miracles at a well near Bisham in 1385 by Bishop Erghum of Salisbury resulted in the removal of an adjacent tree on which a remarkably tame bird had perched.[63] It may be significant that the bishop did not feel the need to condemn devotion there as a pagan well- or tree-cult.

Moreover, episcopal investigations seem to reveal not pagan survival but practices which, if once pagan, had been thoroughly Christianized. In the later Middle Ages, wells approved by bishops were ones which had become deobjectified and personalized – treated not as places holy in themselves but as places associated with a particular saint, preferably of a kind approved by churchmen. Bishop Sutton of Lincoln in 1290 found the well at Oxford to be connected with St Edmund (canonized in 1247); another well at Hambledon in 1296 was the birthplace of St Thomas Cantelupe and was producing miracles in advance of his canonization (1320).[64] The cathedral clergy of Lichfield could process to a holy well, associated with its patron saint Chad.[65] Such wells might be perfectly acceptable. Even spontaneous cults, when sufficiently monitored, might be applauded rather than condemned. Some time before 1452 at Old Cleeve, rain and flooding had caused a landslip to engulf the local chapel. Its images and altars, however, had been marvellously preserved, and it was through these, in the favourable assessment of Bishop Bekynton of Exeter, that 'Jesus and the Virgin Mary had deigned to work signs of miracles and numberless recoveries of health'. The bishop granted an indulgence to encourage others to visit the site.[66]

In any case late medieval bishops were more likely to dismiss cults as 'superstitious' rather than 'pagan'. Sometimes little distinction is drawn between the two terms: Bishop Grandisson could associate superstition with pagan idolatry. But others categorized superstition with mere credulity. Bishop Erghum also scoffed at the stupidity of people at the Bisham well who believed that a cure of a man with an inflamed eye had been anything more than the result of 'the wholesome application of cold water'. Even more telling is the frequency with which bishops linked credulity with more artful deceit. Miraculous events encouraged pilgrims – and their offerings. 'It is our experience,' Bishop Grandisson remarked, 'that [the people] are frequently led on by cupidity as well [as superstition]'.[67] Warmth of attachment to the cult at Frithelstock had been stoked by the local Augustinian priory: the miraculous image had lain in the canons' chapel. It was the unseemly squabble between the prior of Bridlington and the rectors of Carnaby and Foston over pilgrim offerings which drew Archbishop Greenfield's attention to the miraculous image originally set up in Fraisthorpe chapel. The image at Ashingdon church was in the possession of the rector; the Bisham well was owned by the local Augustinian priory. In these cases, local clergy or monastic institutions were at one with local lay people in adherence to these cults.

Episcopal investigations of these cults give a partial view of beliefs behind them. The condemnation of a cult as 'pagan', 'superstitious' or fuelled by greed, seems more rhetorical than descriptive. Undoubtedly, bishops also had to tackle fraud: mobile pardoners with their relics of 'pigges bones' were part of the late medieval scene. But the unscrupulous were only exploiting a more genuine enthusiasm for cults. It is hard to be sure of what the people caught up in these cults really believed. In any case, the boundary between appropriate and inappropriate belief was sometimes unclear. Faith in holy objects was not always of a sort which met the strictest ecclesiastical standards of devotion. To many lay people, the talismanic properties attributed to a wide range of objects (for instance, the Host, biblical text written on parchment, or 'secondary' relics like pilgrim souvenirs) may have been what mattered most. Such attributions could seem uncomfortably close to paganism in the minds of some churchmen. Yet a belief in the innate power of sacred things was perfectly respectable: in the ceremony of exorcism, salt and water, suitably blessed, had an objective and coercive power, though one created by virtue of the Church's own power.[68] Interest in charms was not restricted to the 'unlettered': the fifteenth-century yeoman Robert Reynes copied charms against fever into his common-place book.[69] The clerical author of *Dives and Pauper* was against the hanging of written charms around necks to ward off sickness, *unless* these were the words of the Pater Noster, the Creed or Holy Writ.[70]

What concerned these late medieval bishops most when faced with miraculous phenomena was not the nature of beliefs behind them, which were generally accepted to be 'Christian', but the context in which they had emerged. Outside a carefully monitored shrine (preferably at the heart of the episcopal see) and particularly in sites reckoned disruptive of the disciplinary framework of the parish, reported miracles had to be treated warily. But the anxieties of late medieval churchmen over new thaumaturgical cults may also reflect other concerns. The author of *Dives and Pauper* was particularly disturbed that charms might be used in the 'fiend's' service.[71] In the fifteenth century, once again partly as a consequence of Schism, the particular concern felt about the disjuncture between outer and inner lives sharpened a fear that outward practices might well hide more satanic influences. The use of supernatural power was made the subject of greater scrutiny: the stronger association of sorcery and witchcraft with the work of the devil made the Church hierarchy more wary still of practices that used holy objects to control the forces of nature.[72]

(v) Saints, Cults and Social Context

However strong the will of bishops to control the 'holy', the frequent sprouting of cults in unapproved places or through unofficial 'saints' exposed the limits of episcopal efforts to contain the initiatives of local lay people (and clergy) in deciding what or who should be deemed holy. It exposed too the practical limits to ideals of a universal Church. The papal monopoly of canonization did not prevent recognition at a local level of certain people as 'saintly', and whose qualities of sanctity did not fully match papal criteria. Moreover, the assertion of papal authority over local churches and of a spirituality which prized inner reflection above outer devotion focused on a particular location, were evidently ideals not universally shared. Location mattered in local cults: they were centred on place, where waters welled or springs gushed; and even the more movable objects such as relics and images tended to become fixed in location and venerated where they were situated.

Universal cults too, Marian or Christological, acquired strong localized attachments among the clergy and laity, becoming subsumed into the fabric of communities who adopted them. Even the Cistercians, who did not favour local saints, treated the images and cults they promoted as possessions which would attract pilgrims to their own houses. In the early fourteenth century Meaux abbey was the destination of local pilgrims through its possession of a miracle-working cross, which had been carefully carved by a carpenter esteemed for his austere lifestyle.[73] Proliferating images of the Virgin became objects of physical pilgrimage – which troubled many churchmen, including Archbishop Fitzralph of

Armagh who felt the need to insist in 1356 that 'St Mary the Mother of God is in heaven, and never in those places ... on earth'.[74] Moreover, the ascension of Christ and the assumption of his Mother into heaven could not apparently remove all trace of their physical appearance on earth. Relics associated with Christ, including his blood (notwithstanding theological doubts concerning the validity of such relics), were avidly acquired by religious houses – especially after the sack of Constantinople in 1204 by crusaders who emptied the city of its vast collections of relics. The Cistercian Hailes Abbey boasted its own Holy Blood relic, and in contrast to the beleaguered relic at Westminster it attracted pilgrims in numbers which Henry III might have envied.[75]

Perhaps what attracted most lay people to cults was the ability of saints, relics or other holy objects to work cures. Throughout the later Middle Ages, this remained the essential hallmark of new local cults, whether surrounding holy objects or people. The fame of John Shorne (d. *c*.1315) at New Marston rested on his skill in tackling gout, ague, toothache and blindness, as well as on memories that he had caused a holy well to flow during a drought (and that he had conjured the devil into a boot).[76] It was its power to cure infertility that brought women on their knees to the Ashingdon image. Moreover, an essential component too of these cults was a devotion experienced through the senses and focused on the visual and tangible. The mass-manufacture of pilgrim badges at major shrines from at least the end of the thirteenth century was a response to consumer demand.[77] Physical contact of these 'souvenirs' with the holy objects they represented allowed some of them to acquire vicarious miraculous powers in their own right. Moreover, enthusiasm surrounding holy people was not generated by contemplation of their inner spirituality. It was the prospect of contact with the burned heretic Richard Wyche which pulled in the crowds, their fervency stirred by the sweet odour of his ashes – a mark of sanctity fraudulently manufactured for profit by the local vicar, it was alleged, who had furtively poked spices into the heretic's smouldering remains. To discourage the pious collection of Wyche's ashes, the London authorities chose an action equally intended to impact upon the olfactory senses: they had the site turned into a dunghill.

None of these devotional practices in themselves could be condemned by the Church. Miracles of healing and saintly relics recognizable by their sweet odour remained respectable in the eyes of the highest ranking of churchmen. Many universal saints in the later Middle Ages had acquired specialized skills. John Shorne's expertise with toothache was matched by the specific talents attributed to more widely venerated saints. The Lives of saints (particularly the Golden Legend) were trawled for incidents which might link them with particular afflictions: Margaret of Antioch's dramatic reemergence from the bowels of a dragon identified her as a patron saint of childbirth (even though the author of the Golden Legend had dismissed the dragon story as apocryphal).[78] The growth of specialist saints was no doubt powerfully stimulated by the importance placed in popular veneration on miracles of healing. Such views were not necessarily discouraged by the Church, even if some churchmen worried about or satirized their excesses. After all, by their curative powers, saints were given an immediacy as heavenly intercessors, bringing them down to earth into a direct and intimate contact with the sufferings of ordinary people. It was a matter of emphasis and degree. Fixation on healing powers might distract from inner reflection; for papal investigators of new cults, thaumaturgical miracles were of diminishing importance. Yet other clerics, notably the local priests and monks, welcomed – perhaps with genuine piety – the emergence of cults in their neighbourhood.

Attitudes to pilgrimage were subject to similar uncertainty of interpretation. Even amongst churchmen, opinion remained divided as to its exact merits. Popes encouraged pilgrims to Rome with plenary indulgences after 1300; yet other theologians had strongly emphasized that physical pilgrimage did not matter besides the importance of an inner pilgrimage of contrition. How lay people viewed the shrines they visited may well have differed from how the custodians viewed those same shrines.[79] Despite some clerical efforts to stress the spiritual nature of the journey, the miracles recorded at major shrines show the continued desire for cures among the lay people who went on pilgrimage. Perhaps the women who travelled to hill-top chapels dedicated to St Katherine (as at Milton Abbas, Dorset) did so in mental substitute for pilgrimage to Mount Sinai where St Katherine was buried – or perhaps they went (as later folkloricists claim) to ask the saint to find them a husband.[80] Escape from her husband perhaps motivated Margery Kempe's more extensive travels in the early fifteenth century, or at least escape from a worldly marriage which had come to constrain her own search for religious perfection.[81] But like other pilgrims she was lured to many places, including Rome (at the time of a jubilee), by the prospect of indulgences too. The motivation of lay people undertaking pilgrimages, and the meaning invested in them, were multiple and complex and did not always meet the exacting standards of some churchmen. Margery Kempe's pilgrimages in one sense appear as the models for the emphasis on inner reflection: arrival at her destinations was often accompanied by intense visionary experiences. But her travels also invited criticism. General concern at all forms of mobility, bodily and social, in the later fourteenth century bred suspicion of pilgrims; and particular concern with the mobility of women meant that the pilgrimages of Margery Kempe, as a 'single' woman, generated gendered complaint.[82]

Saints and cults served many other functions in local society besides the intercessory. Meanings attached to them were also subject to change. When the laity adopted new cults, their significance might alter with circumstance and context. Corpus Christi was a feast day which received final papal approval in 1317 to celebrate the miracle of transubstantiation and the unity of the Church as one body. But at a local level its adoption spawned a plethora of other associations. Certainly it was attributed with talismanic or healing powers: timely display of the Host at key moments could quell riots and disturbances (see Chapter 4: vii). But there were many others meanings that developed, especially around formal processions of the Host on the feast day itself.[83] At first these processions were undertaken by ecclesiastical bodies, but by the end of the century the processions had moved into a more public and secular arena. Perhaps under the pressures of social upheaval in the wake of plague (see Introduction: iv and Chapter 5: viii) civic authorities in a number of towns (such as York and Coventry) had adopted the cult, and constructed around it an idealized ordering of civic society which confirmed their authority around the unifying presence of Christ's body.

However, such was the symbolic power of the Eucharist that it also generated associations and meanings which could not be contained by those in authority, secular or ecclesiastical. Civic authorities had neither a stranglehold on power nor a monopoly of the meaning of the procession (see Chapter 5: viii). In any case, the body of Christ itself was a symbol which might serve to undermine, as much as preserve, the social order. Sermons preached on Corpus Christi day proclaimed a message of Christian liberation from the Fall. Perhaps the rebellious peasants in 1381 who made a point of meeting, according to one chronicler, on Corpus Christi day before converging upon London, had 'read' a more social message into sermons of Christian liberation.[84] Within different social contexts and groups, religious symbols were open to a variety of interpretations.

The meaning invested in saints was also open to divergent opinion. The specialized attributes of 'universal' saints might be officially recognized but their meaning and purpose could alter with local circumstance or audience. St Margaret was popularly venerated because of her skills with women in labour, but to a monastic audience she remained a role model for the struggle against temptations of the flesh.[85] St Anne, as the mother of the Virgin Mary, was very much a 'universal' saint, but interpretations of her role were far from uniform. As patron of a well at Buxton, St Anne was a curer of ailments. Within the pages of a personalized Life written by Osbern Bockenham (1440s) for Katherine Denston, a Suffolk gentlewoman, St Anne seems to appear as the mothering saint and talisman in Katherine's own hopes and fears for childbirth. In the verse life written for the parish guild of St Anne at Acle, and copied into the commonplace book of Robert Reynes, a well-to-do 'yeoman', Anne and her husband Joachim are appropriate role models for the guild members – scions of respectability ('right rich folk') carefully located in the poem within their family and kin.[86] As we shall see (Chapter 6), 'official' models of the holy life were also altered and reinterpreted to suit audience and social context.

Attitudes to local saints underwent changes too. The survival of Anglo-Saxon saints did not mean unbroken continuation of function and meaning; nor did it depend on official promotion alone. In Norfolk, the obscure (if not mythical) Walstan of Bawburgh was admired as the result neither of official canonization nor of royal promotion as an English saint.[87] According to legend, he had lived in the eleventh century as a farm hand, and in death his intercession was sought for a good harvest and the curing of sick cattle. The offerings to his shrine in the parish church were so large in 1309 that they apparently funded the rebuilding of the chancel. Like most other saints, his continuing (or revived) appeal was partly the result of a traditional belief in his wonder-working powers. But he may have had another appeal, in the later Middle Ages, to those in authority. The Lives give him a royal background, despite his humble life; and he is shown satisfying a local landowner by his dedication to hard work – a quality felt, by employers and moralists, to be in dangerously short supply in the later fourteenth century. There is a specific social context to the popularity of Walstan's late medieval cult which reflects contemporary anxieties.

(vi) Conclusion

The proliferation of cults and saints may indeed be testimony to the success of pastoral reform. As part of the effort to instruct the laity with the rudiments (and even finer points) of the Christian faith, a deeper acquaintance with the significance, mysteries and miracles of the 'special dead' had undoubtedly been developed. Cults of saints were no longer centred chiefly around monastic houses as they had been in Anglo-Saxon England. Familiarity and contact with saints by the later Middle Ages meant that devotion to them could appear at every social level. There is no obvious fault line, in this sense, between a 'popular' and 'elite' religion, between supposedly semi-pagan 'peasants' on the one hand, and a clerical hierarchy or high-ranking laity on the other. Rural communities seem to be at one with local religious houses and clergy in the cultivation of new saints; belief in the talismanic and thaumaturgical properties of relics seems to cut across all social boundaries.

Yet there were differences of attitude to saints, even if these differences were only occasionally aligned with particular groups in society. At a rhetorical level, these differences could be stressed. The perception that 'rustics' were superstitious or pagan influenced the episcopal elite in their characterization of 'popular' practices, and became a tool wielded to control and reform devotional 'excess'. Elitist ideals of a universal Church and an emphasis of inner spirituality provoked some churchmen (and even some lay people) into criticism of devotional practices which focused too much on particular locations and on the physical experience of miracles. Such differences of view could be divisive, and may have reflected other kinds of social division still to be discussed, not least differences in levels of literacy (see Chapter 6: iii).

The main focus of this chapter has been on the difficulty of imposing any standard models of sanctity and holiness on 'the community of the faithful'. The ideals of a universal Church and a greater uniformity of cult could only be partially realized. Papal control of sainthood and new cults was limited. Even canonization proceedings were responses to demand rather than initiators of cults. Papal control was not constrained simply because of the inevitable limitations of the machinery of papal government, but also because concerns and loyalties at a local level, and among both clergy and laity, constantly worked against any vision of universality. Even 'universal' saints or cults acquired associations to suit the local requirements of religious houses or lay people who adopted them.

In England royal and episcopal authority had a marked effect on the presence, nature and spread of cults of saints. Anglo-Saxon saints as well as new 'universal' cults were subjected to royal needs. English ecclesiastical calendars in the twelfth and thirteenth centuries are remarkably conservative in their choice of feast days, while legendaries and saints' lives are remarkably archaic in their choice of subjects. The newly canonized saints from England in the later Middle Ages were those who came from the upper echelons of the ecclesiastical hierarchy. Yet even in a country where centralized government was strong, unapproved cults could emerge. Bishops were not over-worried about the survival of pagan beliefs behind cults; their concern was focused on the authenticity of these cults. The charismatic qualities of martyrs or the miraculous powers of images were not easy to assess, still less to harness. In the later Middle Ages, social disturbance, dynastic upheaval and Papal Schism intensified anxieties about the miraculous and holy, what their appearance might mean and how they might be contained.

The ideals of sanctity and the meanings of cults were in any case slippery in nature. Local audiences – whether monastic house, aristocratic household, urban or peasant community – might choose to interpret the lives and miracles of even the most 'universal' saints in very different lights. Social context and change around the object of devotion, social status and gender of the devotee, altered interpretations of cults. Lay people at all social levels appropriated cults to suit both pious and social needs. Even in so closely governed a country as England, secular and ecclesiastical authorities at the highest levels had only limited control over the appearance and interpretation of the holy.

Sudden manifestations of the miraculous were not the only aspects of religious life over which such control was qualified. The more collective and structured activities of lay people were also prone to stray from any centralized control, and the following two chapters will look at other ways in which the laity tailored religious practice to local requirements.

Chapter 4: Corporate Religion: Structures and Practices

The church of Wimborne Minster (Dorset) had an illustrious past.[1] It was founded as a nunnery and double monastery in the early eighth century on royal estates; its founder Cuthberga, daughter of the king of the West Saxons, was soon revered as a saint. By the tenth century it was no longer a nunnery, but it was certainly a 'minster', probably supplying priests for the outlying areas of a wide 'parish'. By the twelfth century it had been refounded as a royal collegiate chapel. Yet its 'minster' origins cast a long shadow over the structure of the parish it continued to serve. It remained a 'wide and populous parish' which troubled one of its fourteenth-century deans; and in 1545, 1700 people were claimed to be communicants at Easter. Outlying settlements continued to recognize its jurisdiction: villagers from Hampreston, although with their own chapel, were still required to make a two-mile, flood-threatened journey to Wimborne Minster to bury their dead. The royal origins of the church also continued to loom large throughout the Middle Ages: the cult of Henry VI (d.1471) was promoted there; the mother of Henry VII, Margaret Beaufort (d.1509), made elaborate provision for her soul at the church. But long before then, the church had become much more than a refuge for royalty. Its churchwardens' accounts, which survive from 1403, reveal how much the parish had become the focus of considerable collective activity on the part of the laity. They show parishioners accumulating rents, managing offerings and collections to pay for feast days, church ornaments, and from 1448 rebuilding work on the church tower. The royal cults had even become their own. They collected small offerings made to 'Saint' Henry and much larger ones to St Cuthberga.

When in 1538 the cult of saints was first threatened by royal decree, they petitioned the dean to be allowed to keep the silver around the head of the image they had adorned.

The adoption of the cult and shrine of St Cuthberga by lay parishioners, and its assimilation into parish worship, is a reminder again of the adaptability of saints' cults to particular social contexts. Moreover, the history of this one church is a microcosm of the main themes of this chapter. Medieval religion was strongly corporate in expression, and the collective activity of lay people, especially by the later Middle Ages, was most obviously expressed in the parish. Indeed ecclesiastical initiatives had made the parish the central focus of corporate lay worship, prescribing the religious practices which were to take place within them. Were these standards adopted by the laity? The simple answer is that they were, but very much on the laity's own terms. The formation of the parish structure was not just the result of clerical initiative or compulsion, and attempts to impose even a limited kind of uniformity were belied by the considerable variety in parish structures and practices. Some had complex or unusual features, in the case of Wimborne Minster through its preservation of royal and minster origins; the collective activities and devotional interests of late medieval parishioners were common in kind but not in particulars. Moreover, the parish was not the only focus of lay corporate activity: guilds and households were two other structures (though less formalized than the parish) on which devotional or other interests were concentrated. The diversity of such structures and the activism of lay people within them are the most striking features of corporate religion at a local level.

(i) Corporate Structures: the Parish

The parish structure was created out of the fragmentation of the 'minster system' whose wider 'parochia' became subdivided into smaller parish units.[2] Such a process was already taking place in the eleventh century, and by the thirteenth it was all but complete, with some 9000 churches enjoying full parochial rights. Bishops had encouraged these developments in the interests of pastoral reform: Bishop Wulfstan of Worcester (1062–95) built churches on his manors and encouraged others to do the same, no doubt to ensure that more vills and neighbourhoods had their own resident priests.[3] In thirteenth-century synodal decrees, bishops made clear what the parish was: a territorial unit, supporting a resident priest who supplied the sacramental needs of the parishioners within. Ideally the parish church was thus the central focus of lay corporate worship. But the reality was more complex because the process of its formation had not been uniformly directed by episcopal decree. The consecration of a growing number of churches with parish rights was the result of reaction more than initiative: bishops were responding to demand. Like many other landowners, the lord of East Carlton (sometime after 1109) requested that the bishop of Lincoln should consecrate the chapel of East Carlton with a cemetery and make it independent of the former mother church of Cottingham.[4] Such chapels were statements of manorial power which was advancing further in a period of colonization and land clearance. Following the enlargement of his vill, the manorial lord of Depyng acquired full parochial rights for his chapel of St Guthlac. The Crowland chronicler preferred to coat this acquisition with devotional gloss: by improving the fertility of the soil, this lord had created a 'garden of Eden' from a 'swamp'.[5] Here, the manorial church served the settlement around it, and in some parts of England more than others the strong hand of lordship in creating the parish structure is evident.[6] In the Midlands especially (less so in Cornwall or the east of England, in the former Danelaw where the proportion of 'free men' was higher), the large number of small parishes with single settlements within them was partly a measure of how effective local lords had been in concentrating settlement around the manorial centre, and in exploiting the profits from land – and from ownership of the local church.

Powerful though it was, lordship was not the only influence at work. The parochial structure was also shaped by groups of people, lower down the social hierarchy, who were able to act collectively in other contexts. The local vill was a focus of corporate activity in law: it had long been required to send representatives to hundred courts. Angevin royal reform in the twelfth century was to make these and other administrative functions more important. By the thirteenth century the capacity of local peasantry to act as a 'community of the vill' is quite evident (see Introduction). Land might also be held corporately (even though formal privileges were not granted for this purpose as they were in parts of continental Europe). Although the parish was not recognized as a corporation in law, even in the later Middle Ages, habits of collective activity in the vill translated readily into a parish context (most obviously when boundaries of the manor or vill were coterminous with those of the parish).[7] Churches could be founded collectively, and examples of peasant endowment of churches may be found in the twelfth century.[8] Even a manorial chapel may have been the product of wider pressure.[9]

From the episcopal point of view, the proliferation of churches was desirable in one sense, for it brought the Church's ministry closer to the people. But it also brought other problems. Resident priests had to be funded from tithes, and the erection of new churches might infringe on the financial basis of an existing church. From the twelfth century, bishops were reluctant to grant parochial status – the full rights of baptism and burial in particular – to new chapels. The episcopal acta of the late twelfth century show attempts to prevent 'unlawful' foundations of chapels within existing parishes. By then canon law had begun to 'lay its cold hand on the parishes of Europe' and freeze the pattern which in many places has existed ever since.[10]

There were other vested interests in keeping the parish structure more inflexible. The fragmentation of minster 'parochia' into smaller parish units was neither uniform nor complete. Those minsters which evolved into parish churches, like Wimborne Minster, continued to serve outlying vills in areas which were once within their larger 'parochia'. More frequently they clung to financial rights due from nearby chapelries. As a result some late medieval parishes were complicated structures, with mother churches still holding on to several chapels in various degrees of dependence. Moreover, monastic houses (some of which were former minster churches) held tithes intended to support the local resident priest. This was a process which bishops had encouraged in the twelfth century to loosen the 'polluted' grip of laymen on spiritual revenues: churches could no longer remain the private property of a local lord. By 1200 a quarter of all local churches in England were in the possession of religious houses. The effect of this change did not always have desirable pastoral consequences, even though bishops sought to ensure that religious houses appointed and supported parish priests within their care through a system of vicarages.[11] It also meant that institutions holding tithes were reluctant to encourage further fragmentation of parochial rights and possible loss of revenue from tithe.

Here again, however, vested interest and episcopal stricture might go unregarded by lay people. Demand for the marks of parochial status continued throughout the later Middle Ages. In some instances we find groups of lay people resenting the restrictions of canon law. The attempt to 'freeze' the parish structure did not make allowance for shifts in population and the growth of new settlements whose inhabitants might demand their own chapel and additional parochial rights. Yet the parish structure was not inflexible: if bishops were reluctant to see new parishes founded, they were ready, nevertheless, to allow chapels to acquire parochial rights if these did not undermine the existing parish church. In any case, severe depopulation in the wake of the Black Death meant that after 1348 there was more pressure to combine parishes than to found new ones.[12]

Problems certainly remained. Where fixed parish boundaries covered a wide area, locals in outlying settlements, far from the mother church, could legitimately make their case for concessions before the bishop or even the pope.[13] The cemetery was the parochial right which gave rise to the most demand and conflict. In 1407, the inhabitants of Great Ocle (Lincolnshire), petitioned the pope for a cemetery to be added to their chapel, and evidently hoped to strengthen their case by appealing to the sensitivity of papal nostrils: because of the distance from the mother church, bodies left unburied for too long had begun producing a 'horrible and perilous smell'.[14] Some claims stretched the truth: the inhabitants of Kingsbridge (Devon) in 1414 shamelessly described the gentle two-mile incline to the mother church of Churchstow as a 'dangerous and difficult ascent'.[15] Exaggerated or not, such demands are a measure of the collective capacity and awareness of parishioners: the acquisition of parochial rights for their local church was a matter of corporate pride. Indeed, it was not just bishops or clerical institutions who protected the rights of mother churches. *The Book of Margery Kempe* recounts how tenaciously the parishioners of St Margaret's in King's Lynn fought to preserve the 'worship' of their church and prevent a group of rich merchants in 1432 from acquiring the right of baptism for the chapel of St Nicholas within the same parish.[16]

From the thirteenth century onwards, then, a parish system was essentially in place, forming an important focus of collective activity. But such activity was likely to differ from parish to parish: the various pressures which had brought about the replacement of the 'minster system' meant that the resulting parish structure was a complex one, and as at Lynn, did not command uniform attachment. Lordship, settlement and vested interest had created very different kinds of parishes: at one extreme large parishes with scattered hamlets and chapels acting virtually as separate parishes (especially for instance in the north of England), and at the other, small ones with a single settlement which closely followed the manorial boundary. Over this great variety, bishops could only struggle to impose some kind of coherence.

(ii) Fabric Fund and Churchwarden

Tithes were intended to support the parish priest; Gregorian reform had required them to be removed from lay control. In the twelfth century, moreover, payment of tithes were enforced as never before: the expanding pastoral aims required an ever greater expenditure, not least in equipping the resident priest with the ornaments, vestments and building now deemed suitable for his high calling. But sometimes 'polluted' lay hands were involved in the process. At Doddington, in around 1177, parishioners were acting with the parish priest to apportion tithe revenue on the church fabric, books and vestments.[17] Moreover there are already signs of additional forms of revenue being accumulated through collective effort. By the end of the twelfth century, altar lights within churches could be supported by funds managed by individual parishioners.[18] Perhaps too, parishioners were already electing their own representatives. By 1235 it seemed unremarkable for parishioners, as at Edington (Wiltshire), to be expected to elect 'a trustworthy man or two' to manage an endowment which funded altar lights and distributions to the poor.[19]

Episcopal approval for fabric funds, supporting long lists of clerical paraphernalia and managed by elected parish representatives, is quite evident in synodal decrees by the late thirteenth century. The development of these funds had been the result in part of pastoral reform. But it had also been a response to growing lay initiative, and the wish of parishioners to assume control over funds which supported the responsibilities required of them. Perhaps clerics had initially resisted this change. Decrees early in the thirteenth century occasionally mutter disparagingly about lay control of church goods.[20] The vicar of Saltwood complained in 1252 that the laity at a chapel in his parish were presuming to possess a miracle-working cross with relics, and offerings from pilgrims, 'as if they were the clergy'.[21] In the late thirteenth and early fourteenth centuries, disputes did occur between vicar or rector and parishioners over collecting boxes and allocation of funds.[22] Perhaps this lay initiative was also a reaction to inadequacies in the parish system, particularly in the wake of appropriation of tithe to monastic institutions.[23] Direct evidence for this is flimsy; and the occasional disputes over funds look more like the teething problems in a system still in the process of development in some parishes, rather than lay distrust of clerical provision or clerical antipathy to lay control. On balance, the formal investment of parishioners with powers over church funds, separate from tithes, seems like episcopal regularizing and encouragement of practices which lay people, already sensitized by the pastoral effort of the Church, were also developing on their own initiative.

It is also clear that the formal duties required of parishioners by synodal decree were not unwelcome burdens. Visitations of parishes reveal occasional shirking of responsibility; yet it did not need clerical enforcement to call delinquents to account. The task was fulfilled by parishioners themselves; indeed, in other respects, they went much further than the passive fulfilment of formal duties. Inventories, particularly in the wealthier parishes, show stocks of equipment which far exceed the skeletal list set down in synodal decree. Churchwardens' accounts (surviving from the mid-fourteenth century) begin to show regular mechanisms for raising revenue (rents, church ales, offerings on feast days) none of which were explicitly required by ecclesiastical legislation.

There were other external pressures on the development of parish finances. The financial requirement of the English crown gave royal government an interest in the parish as a potential unit of taxation as early as the twelfth century.[24] Moreover, the funds which some parishes had accumulated by the end of the fifteenth century were large, surpassing collections for secular taxes. The elected parish representative – the churchwarden – became a powerful local figure; and as the corporate muscle of parishes developed, more came to be required of him. The parish began to replace the vill as the local unit of royal taxation during the fourteenth century; by the end of the fifteenth century some parishes were already administering poor relief, which later Tudor legislation was to make universal.

Yet the secular requirements of the king were largely reactive to developments taking place at a local level; and they had little bearing on the methods used by local parishioners. The great variety of fund raising was adapted to local circumstances, economies and landscapes.[25] No two parishes employed quite the same methods. The more rural areas (as is already apparent in visitations of parishes belonging to St Paul's Cathedral in 1290) rented out 'stocks' of sheep or cattle. Late medieval fabric funds at Halesowen (Worcestershire) profited from offerings to relics; churchwardens at Morebath (Devon) collected rent from beehives.[26] Church ales were often the most productive form of fund-raising in rural areas; in larger towns there was an increasing tendency to rely on rents from property (often given by benefactors in return for services for the dead – see Chapter 5: iii). Specific parish projects might require special efforts: the rebuilding of the church tower at Wimborne Minster after 1448 was preceded by several years of meagre spending, vigorous collection at church ales, and the cultivation of support from local gentry. Such diversity reflects not grudging performance of duty but collective initiative, and a willingness to manage funds over which local parishioners exercised direct and flexible control.

(iii) Parish Church Building

The appearance of the building in and around which these developments were taking place, was also changing.[27] Most obvious is the shift, by the end of the eleventh century, from smaller wooden churches to larger ones built of stone. Relatively few churches in Anglo-Saxon England (probably only those which had enjoyed minster status) had been stone built, but from the eleventh century an increasing number were, including those that had begun as 'private' chapels of local landowners. Moreover, in the twelfth century, beginning with the larger churches (often those which had once been minsters, or those with important patrons), and increasingly with lesser ones, aisles began to be added on to naves. During the thirteenth century different parts of the church, especially chancel and nave, began to be rebuilt in different ways. In larger churches cruciform in shape, chancels tended to be extended eastwards after c.1200. Smaller churches too, ones originally built as simple box-like structures, show a clearer division between chancel and nave.

Once again these developments are explained partly by the pastoral concerns of clerics. William of Malmesbury c.1125 saw 'in every village, town and city churches and monasteries rising in a new style of architecture', and attributed the trend to the arrival of the Normans who 'breathed new life into religious standards'.[28] The standards which the Norman ecclesiastical hierarchy were beginning to implement, at least by the end of the eleventh century, were those set by the wider reforming movements within Christendom. Emphasis on the elevated role of the priest, not least in celebration of the Eucharist, might well explain architectural attention to the east end of church buildings. The chancel was becoming the clear preserve of the priest. Lay access to the chancel was restricted. Within it, space was needed for the elaboration of liturgy associated with the mass: after c.1200 more chancels came to be equipped with fittings such as the double piscina (for washing both the priest's hands and the vessels after mass) or a more elaborate stone Easter sepulchre.[29]

Priestly requirements did not by themselves determine changes in church architecture. In referring to the Norman Conquest, William of Malmesbury might have linked church building more explicitly with secular power. The monumental architecture of some of the great churches and monasteries in England after 1066 speaks of a triumphalist colonial attitude.[30] At a more local level, the continuing foundation of 'private' chapels, and increasingly in stone, bears the stamp of local lords who wished to demonstrate their manorial power in the churches, as well as the manors, that they possessed. The addition of aisles, first appearing on churches with important patrons, may reflect the same architectural trend which produced more aisled halls in manor houses at much the same date.[31]

Late medieval churches continued to bear the mark of seigneurial power. Tombs, coats of arms and plaques commemorating benefaction, in chapels, aisles and on towers, all tell of a strong lordly or gentry presence in a large number of churches (see Chapter 5: v). But if such a presence could still be overwhelming in some churches, it is diluted in most. A much wider group of parishioners had come to dictate the shape of the building. Arguably, population pressure (until the beginning of the fourteenth century) meant a greater need for space: the addition of aisles, which could serve to widen access around the nave, might also reflect the pressure of numbers.[32] But demographic pressure is not the primary explanation for expansion. Church interiors provided for much more than congregational space. The growth in the number of larger stone churches partly reflects the investment in an institution which, as we have seen, was passing from private to more public hands. The thirteenth-century synodal decrees enshrined the parish as the focus of public worship: collective investment in a permanent structure for worship reflected a sense of corporate parochial status.

The use of space within parish churches was also subject to sharper definition. In line with the 'religious standards' to which William of Malmesbury refers, but under pressure too from lay demand, former minster churches (or 'monasteries' with parochial functions) altered and clarified their arrangements with parish congregations. Within them, arrangements for lay corporate worship might differ from other parish churches with single resident priests. Those minsters that became parish churches might preserve an echo of their minster past by retaining a larger staff of resident clergy. Some minsters evolved into more 'respectable' Benedictine houses; others into Augustinian priories; still others into collegiate churches. But in many cases these too continued to perform parochial functions, retaining chapels within them for lay use. Such arrangements did not always bring peace. In 1298 the bishop of Lincoln suppressed the parochial chapel within St Frideswide's (Augustinian) priory, Oxford, because it disturbed the canons in their choir.[33] The Benedictine abbey of St Albans retained a chapel attached to the north nave aisle for lay use; but here, lay influence seems gradually to have extended into the nave, the paintings executed between c.1230 and 1310 on the north nave piers apparently serving as altars for lay devotion.[34]

The clearest division in the use of space, in all churches, was between chancel and nave. In former minster churches with large bodies of clerical personnel, the chancel area had probably always been the exclusive preserve of the clergy. However, ecclesiastical legislation in England (more so than in continental Europe) began to mark out for all churches a clearer division between chancel and nave, not just in terms of access, but also in terms of responsibility. From the 1220s, the upkeep of the nave became the duty of the laity – thus making the development of communal funds all the more necessary. The division was not absolute: there are later disputes over the exact point where responsibility ended. In some smaller chapels, the laity can be found (willingly, it seems) maintaining the chancel too. Even so, in the later Middle Ages, it is no accident that the architectural history of chancel and nave tends to diverge. After 1350, eastward extensions to the chancel came to an end for the most part; rebuilding centred chiefly on the nave. Churchwardens' accounts frequently reveal a corporate will in the effort to rebuild. The best-known example is the spectacular effort made by the parishioners of Bodmin (Cornwall) who shared their church with an Augustinian priory, and who rebuilt the nave at a cost of £270 between 1469 and 1472. The names of 460 individuals are recorded as contributors.[35] Collective responsibility, if not pride, is on display; perhaps too a willingness to go beyond the duties 'imposed' on the laity by canon law, for the parishioners of Bodmin rebuilt the chancel as well as the nave.

There were certainly local and regional differences. Churches show regional traits in terms of their shape and development over time. Monumental towers abound in late medieval Somerset but not in Lincolnshire; clerestories are absent in Cornish churches but are plentiful in Suffolk ones. Few large scale rebuildings occur in York after 1450, yet in Suffolk a peak in rebuilding occurs in the late fifteenth century and in Somerset during the early sixteenth. Differences in wealth played their part – Somerset and Suffolk were among several regions which profited from the wealth of the late medieval cloth trade. Late medieval churches in poorer regions were more likely to retain their earlier structure untouched.[36] But the correlation between wealth and rebuilding is not an automatic one; and the presence of a single benefactor could make a crucial difference. Moreover, a sense of corporate responsibility can only in part explain late medieval rebuilding. The type of work is significant. In general this took the form of additions – of aisles, chapels or towers – rather than complete rebuildings, and part of the explanation must be sought in the liturgical and devotional needs that these extensions served (not least the penitential requirements of the dead – see Chapter 5: iii). Wealth explains capacity but not motive.

Nevertheless, late medieval work on the nave, as opposed to the chancel, is explained best by the duty and capacity of lay parishioners to rebuild the part of the church that had become their own. It was a kind of ownership which was more acceptable to the new standards of churchmen in the wake of Gregorian reform. Churches which served parochial functions were (in a formal sense) no longer the private property of secular landowners, but public edifices, built of stone. Yet in formally stripping the lay patron of most of his powers, and investing a wider group of parishioners with responsibilities, churchmen were replacing one kind of ownership with another. Over areas where responsibility existed, a sense of collective lay ownership grew up. At Roseland (Cornwall) in 1396, the parishioners demonstrated a territorial attitude towards their nave in a dispute with their vicar: during a service at Epiphany, the vicar claimed that his parishioners would have chased him out of his chancel by the window, and not let him pass through the body of the church 'because that belonged to the parishioners not to him'.[37]

(iv) Priest and Parishioner

Elevated above the laity, removed from the congregation in the chancel, with exclusive powers over the sacraments, the parish priest was set apart from his flock. His distance from the laity had been increased theoretically by Gregorian reform which had placed strong emphasis on priestly status. The expectations of the priesthood had risen within the Church itself. Gregorian reformers hoped to eradicate clerical marriage, and had occasionally cast doubt on the validity of sacraments performed by unworthy priests. Although later canonists were generally adamant that the efficacy of the sacraments was unaffected by the morality of the performer, the sense that a priest should live up to standards higher than those expected from the laity remained powerful. The fourteenth-century chancellor of Oxford, William de Rymyngton reminded his clerical listeners in one sermon that their daily consecration and consumption of the body of Christ meant that they were 'far more bound to observe the stainlessness of chastity' than the laity were.[38] The efforts from the twelfth century to raise the educational standards of priests also demanded new levels of clerical expertise and discipline.

In rising higher, the priest had further to fall. A gap did open up between high clerical expectation and reality on the ground. Even into the thirteenth century, church reformers had found it impossible to break ingrained habits of clerical concubinage. Archbishop Pecham in 1281 bemoaned the woeful ignorance of the priesthood. Moreover, uniform pastoral provision was difficult to achieve. Appropriation of tithes into the hands of the religious houses meant reliance on monastic abilities and their willingness to provide a suitable vicar. The irregular formation of the parish structure sometimes left pastoral coverage inadequate in large parishes.[39] Pastoral provision in the later Middle Ages was made all the more difficult by the Black Death. The massive shortage of priests prompted rapid recruitment of clergy who did not always meet the highest of clerical standards. The problems faced by the priesthood ultimately meant that the lofty ideals envisaged by the reformer could never be achieved uniformly.

Recent research, however, is inclined to reverse the traditional image of priestly failure. The pastoral efforts of the church – even in the later Middle Ages – were in the circumstances relatively successful. But the gap between expectation and reality remained, and it was a gap which did not tax the minds of churchmen alone. Provision of churches with resident priests had brought the church's ministry closer to the laity: by the thirteenth century more lay people, more regularly, were able to observe the activities of priests at first hand, as well as criticize them during the visitations of bishops or their officials.

By the later Middle Ages the complaints of lay people at priestly inadequacy are heard more frequently. Whether these complaints amount to widespread 'anticlericalism' is open to doubt.[40] Too often the term has been used to cover a disparate variety of complaints, some of which had been actively elicited by the Church hierarchy. The growing importance of visitation in the thirteenth century had widened pastoral inquiry into parish life, and had also brought in lay people to enforce standards, including those of their parish priest. Late medieval visitations show that parishioners did not necessarily hold their local priest in awe. The vicar of Great Faringdon was accused in 1405 of adultery, drunkenness, withholding sacraments, engaging in farming and worldly labour, and failing to preach the 'articles of the faith' to his parishioners 'so endangering their souls'.[41] Such complaints were perhaps not so much 'anti-' as 'pro-clerical' – parishioners apparently anxious to enforce standards set by the Church hierarchy, including the obligation to preach.

In other cases, charges brought against clergy are not as clear-cut as they might seem. It is difficult to know what the ordinary parishioner wanted from their local priests. Were parishioners eager to enforce clerical standards or, on occasion, employing charges to cause trouble for an unpopular priest with the visiting archdeacon? The vicar of Highworth was accused of rape in 1405 before the dean of Salisbury's officials; but in 1410 the same dean granted the vicar a life pension in consideration of his 'long and diligent ministry' and 'owing to age, infirmity and blindness'.[42] Decanal amnesia or the rapid physical deterioration of the vicar seem more unlikely explanations for the apparent discrepancy than a false accusation in the first place. Did the laity want more sermons? The charge of inadequate preaching rarely appears in visitation records. Parishioners perhaps expected a higher standard of sexual morality of their priests, but they may have been more relaxed in their attitude to clerical concubinage than the ecclesiastical hierarchy. Charges of delinquency in visitations show a greater sensitivity to priestly familiarity with parishioners' wives than to the possible presence of a mistress in the vicarage. On the other hand, lay familiarity with local priests could breed reverence rather than contempt: a number of the men locally recognized as 'saintly' in the later Middle Ages (and without episcopal approval) were members of the secular clergy (see Chapter 3: iii). In the end, the local priest, despite the occasional lapse, might be accepted into local society as someone closer to his fellow parishioners in education and behaviour than to the bishop and his officials. .

Furthermore, in some ways, especially by the later Middle Ages, the gap between local priest and laity was smaller in practice than in theory. Gregorian reform may have deprived the local lord of his proprietary right over the priest, but his influence could still be felt. Proprietorial control lingered in the right of advowson – the right to present a priest to a benefice. A local lay patron continued to enjoy rights of burial and even seating in the chancel. Lay control also developed in other more collective forms. The sense of ownership over communal funds and over parts of the church building which began to develop in the thirteenth century, is evident in attitudes to the local priesthood. In Germany this process has been called 'communalization', and seems to have extended further there than in England (or France).[43] In English parishes too there is a good deal of evidence, albeit sporadic, for the exercise of 'communal' powers over the local priest, and for the preference that he should be resident. Occasionally the local priest might be elected by parishioners;[44] some chapelries seem to have 'hired' their own chaplains. Where clerical response to a vacancy was not swift enough, parishioners might take matters into their own hands.[45] Greater control was exercised over the lesser clergy, like the parish clerk, who might be paid for from lay funds. The parishioners of Navestock (Essex) in 1458 had particular expectations of their sacristan: they wished one Robert Tympayn to occupy the post because he was able to sing.[46]

The ability of lay people to exercise control over the local clergy was not limited to occasional parochial arrangements. Regular, systematic and direct control was exercised, as we shall see, in the growing number of guilds and chantry services. In practice, the relationship between local priest and layman could be close; and it is the variety of lay influence over local priests which best explains why there was no widespread 'anticlericalism' even in the later Middle Ages. Yet the theoretical distance and implicit tension in the relationship between clergy and laity remained; lay expectations of the clergy had been raised by ecclesiastical ideals which were always going to be difficult to realize. By the later Middle Ages, parishioners themselves could adopt the admonishing voice which had once been the property of Gregorian reformers. One of the complaints at Great Faringdon was that the vicar had not sufficiently detached himself from worldly behaviour. The elevated status of the priest was accepted, but it was a standard before which lay people could call the clergy to account.

(v) Guilds

The parish formed an important focus and framework of collective activity, but it was by no means all-embracing. Lay people had long formed associations of guilds or fraternities with explicitly religious services and obligations. These were perhaps already common in Anglo-Saxon England, and more common in the eleventh and twelfth centuries than surviving evidence would suggest. By the end of the thirteenth century, references to guilds began to appear in greater profusion; the fourteenth and fifteenth centuries have been called their 'golden age'. Tens of thousands must have been in existence at any one time, and in forms even more diverse than those of the parish. They are found in almost every social context, from the village to the royal court (though more at the 'middling' level of society), and in every size, from guilds with a handful of members, to those which numbered many hundreds.[47]

In some ways the activities and growing abundance of these guilds were the expression of the kind of piety that churchmen had increasingly encouraged of laypeople. For a time there were continued fears that guilds harboured practices which, if not pre-Christian, were potentially un-Christian. Walter Map in the late twelfth century made passing and contemptuous reference to the 'drinking house' which went by the name of 'ghildhus'.[48] But clerical criticism of guilds disappeared soon after; local clergy can often be found as members. In any case, guilds had long expressed aims which had fuller clerical approval. The moralizing injunction on guild members, expressed in many guild statutes, to live in 'peace and charity' with each other, echoes the voice of churchmen who sought the moral reform of lay society. Perhaps too, guilds were a lay expression of the search for religious perfection beyond the cloister. Membership of a fraternity might allow a member to accommodate devotional needs with life lived in the world: living in 'peace and charity' was one way to follow the example of Christ.

However, the duties that many guilds imposed on their members were often limited. Some guilds required their members to go on pilgrimage; but by the fifteenth century these active requirements are less apparent, and even attendance at guild feasts or at other services might not be compulsory.[49] In fact, the popularity of guilds is best attributed to the specific services that they offered. From the eleventh to the fifteenth century, one element common to virtually all guilds was commemoration and suffrage for the souls of their members – a concern sharpened with the shift in theological thinking on penance and Purgatory (see Chapter 5: iii). The stimulus of pastoral reform is evident in other aspects of guild activity. The funding of lights, vestments, extra masses, said and sung, of lights before images – all forms of activity (even if varied in scale and scope) typical of late medieval guilds – was perhaps stimulated by thirteenth-century synodal decrees which, although framed within the context of the parish, emphasized lay responsibility to provide altar lights, ornaments and other liturgical goods. In other ways, guilds might be agents of the kind of religious instruction promoted by pastoral reformers: some guilds funded religious drama based on saints' lives or biblical stories;

others (like the Pater Noster guild at York) encouraged the repetition of basic prayers which reforming bishops had required the laity to learn.[50]

However, the stimulus of pastoral reform was only one influence on guild activity. Ecclesiastical decree did not explicitly encourage guild foundation, preferring to direct lay devotional attention towards the parish. And just as parishes were formed by pressures that were much wider than the impulse of pastoral care, so guilds were the expression of many other forms of lay activity. Patterns of local trade are evident in guilds which accommodated the exigencies of daily economic life: a guild at Thetford by 1289 provided mass services for those coming to the town on market days; conversely a guild at Boston in 1260 provided dawn masses for those who had to leave town early.[51] It is no surprise to find guild foundations particularly abundant in areas of dense population or more intense economic activity.[52] The pressures which bound groups of lay people into crafts of a similar trade to protect their interests, especially from the thirteenth century, were reflected in the religious services with which these crafts usually provided their members.[53]

The structure of a religious guild formed around other social and political associations. The growth in corporate identity of towns, especially from the twelfth century, was given a spiritual dimension in guilds which were exclusive to the civic elite. In places which did not acquire borough privileges (often in towns dominated by an ecclesiastical landlord), the structure of the religious guild acted as a surrogate town council.[54] Membership might reflect a local political agenda. The inclusion of local gentry from outside the town in the St George guild of Norwich in the fifteenth century reflects an urban wish to cultivate the support of a wider political elite.[55]

Guilds were flexible and voluntary associations, forming quickly (and disappearing) in response to the social and religious needs of the moment. By the end of the thirteenth century, such a flexible response was less possible within the 'frozen' parish structure which could not give ready expression either to the ties which bound individuals across many parishes or to the appearance of new groupings (a new settlement, for instance) within an existing parish. There are strong grounds for arguing that the proliferation of guilds from this period was also the result of a more rigid parish structure: guilds provided outlets for changing social and religious needs in ways which the parish could not.[56]

Qualifications to this generalization are required, not least because parish structures were so varied in size, and guilds so varied in the needs they met, that even a flexible parish structure would not have accommodated them all. Moreover, the late medieval parish structure was not entirely rigid; nor was guild foundation unrestricted, and from the late fourteenth century, royal government and civic authorities subjected guilds to more careful monitoring (see Chapter 5: viii). The relationship between parish and guild could be a complicated one. On the one hand, much guild activity seems complementary to parish worship.[57] The forty guilds contributing to the rebuilding of Bodmin church 1469–72 seem to function thereby as supplements to parochial worship: their 'voluntary' membership was another way for parishioners to fulfil their 'obligatory' duties owed to the parish.[58] In this sense, such guilds formed part of a continuum of collective activity within parishes which lay people, in a variety of ways, ran and funded themselves. On the other hand, larger guilds with wider membership could diminish the loyalty (and flow of funds) of its members towards their parishes; smaller ones could operate almost independently of parish officials and even take over activities (such as funding of altar lights) which in other parishes were the remit of churchwardens.[59] So various were guilds in function and structure, that they defy generalized definition. They were neither the agents of ecclesiastical reform alone nor simply the adjuncts of parochial worship, but expressions of collective activity, religious, social and economic, forming when need arose.

(vi) Households and Domestic Chapels

Although, in ecclesiastical eyes, the parish had become the primary framework of pastoral care, the domestic household was also recognized as a unit of worship and as a place of religious instruction. Richard Ullerston in the early fifteenth century followed a long tradition, reaching back to the New Testament and the letters of St Paul, when he described the home as an environment where fathers and mothers would teach children the basics of religious faith.[60]

At the highest levels of society, households were equipped with their own chapels. Although, by the thirteenth century, these chapels were carefully licensed so that they did not infringe on the financial rights and sacramental dominance of the parish church, they were in many ways the continuation of the 'private' churches which landowners had founded (in part) as monuments to their manorial power. Occasionally such chapels might still be licensed to serve a wider community than the immediate household.[61] In the later Middle Ages, all great aristocratic households might expect to have chapels, their chance of permanence improved, especially after 1350, when more of them came to be built of stone.[62] Besides the nobility, knights and gentry also began to attach chapels to their manor houses by the thirteenth century; by the early fourteenth, they were regularly petitioning bishops for 'oratories'. By the end of that century, a growing number of wealthy townsmen were acting similarly.[63] In the fifteenth century there is evidence for certain town dwellers and yeomen in the countryside using rooms within their houses as chapels. The yeoman farmer Robert Munton used a room in his small household as a chapel.[64]

The kind of religious environment that these households created varied greatly. Aristocratic households were able to run a structured liturgical life which echoed the monastic observation of daily mass and of the liturgy; and their dispensing of other sacraments, from christening to burial, turned them into virtual parish churches. Unusual household regimes followed the monastic model more closely, as was the case with Cicely, duchess of York (d.1495), who in widowhood apparently followed a punishing schedule of daily prayer and devotional observance. Other late medieval widows, lower down the social hierarchy (and very occasionally married couples) might also heighten the sanctity of their domestic life by taking a vow of chastity.[65]

It was rare to maintain such strict religious observance, and humbler households would not have enjoyed the luxury of confessors and priests to serve their needs. But an increasing number had books of religious instruction. We shall see in more detail (Chapter 6: iii) how books were increasingly available to a wider circle of people than the aristocracy: here we should note that although these might be the focus of individual and private devotion they also served the household and perhaps the wider family group. Thomas Boyton, a bowyer of Salisbury, was licensed to have an oratory for his wife and family in 1389, and in 1400 he willed that the son of a kinsman be given his black psalter once the boy had reached the age of seven.[66] Books which purported to provide instruction to sons or daughters show how the family home might educate children (and servants) in social and religious respectability. Perhaps some families regularly listened to edifying words at mealtime: the 'Instructions' for the Northern townsman suggested that the task might be carried out by his children as soon as they could read. In late medieval England, gatherings in private to absorb religious teaching are usually associated with Lollard heretics (see Chapter 6: vi), but they were perhaps a wider phenomenon. After all, it was during a fireside chat, and whilst engaged in sewing, that Joan Clyfand claimed in 1429 to have learned about the heretical activities of her neighbour Margery Baxter.[67] The 'godly household' existed long before Puritanism, and by the later Middle Ages it existed across the social spectrum.

The 'godly' household had social as well as religious responsibilities. During the later Middle Ages, the male 'householder' with his wife, children and servants was increasingly constructed, in the legislation of some towns, as an agent upholding wider civic ideals, social, sexual and moral.[68] The social dimension of an 'institution' which certain clerics valued as a unit of pastoral care will need further consideration (see Chapters 5: viii and 6: viii).

(vii) Communal Worship: the Mass

The great variety of religious structures which lay people controlled or participated in, was complemented by the richness of devotional experience within them.[69] Evidence for this is not abundant until the later Middle Ages, but by then celebration of the liturgy, whether in a parish church, guild or household chapel, had undoubtedly become more elaborate. The emphasis was communal. At the heart of the liturgy was the mass, and in its recreation of Christ's sacrifice the promised redemption of the world to all believers, without distinction, was renewed. Its performance demanded harmony amongst those present at the service.

Potentially it emphasized division between priest and laity, for transubstantiation was a miracle that only the priest could perform, and (for most lay people) consumption of Christ's body was restricted to Easter. Vision of the elevated Host in the chancel, although more frequent at the Sunday service, was usually possible only at a distance from the nave. Yet such distance does not seem to have alienated the laity from the mass. There is anecdotal suggestion of regular attendance at the Sunday service in the twelfth century;[70] by the later Middle Ages, evidence for the desire to have mass celebrated, in all kinds of settings, seems much stronger than evidence for its avoidance. Visitation records do not suggest large numbers of absentees from church services; and if sermons sometimes give the impression of clerical despair at noise during mass, it is not a complaint that many priests levelled against their parishioners. Some Lollard heretics in the fifteenth century seem to suggest that church-going was so high in their parishes that they were forced to attend in order to avoid detection.[71] Perhaps parishioners were themselves keen to maintain distance from the mass celebrated in the chancel. The sense of holiness and drama that surrounded the whole performance was deliberately heightened: one of the most distinctive features of late medieval churches, even the smaller ones by the fourteenth century, were the rood screens that separated nave from chancel. These were paid for by parishioners themselves.[72]

However, seeing the elevated Host was clearly desirable. It is apparent in so many contexts: in the 'squints' constructed in some churches to allow parishioners sight of the high altar from side aisles in the nave; in the dismay of one Lollard preacher in 1407 that his audience at Shrewsbury had scurried away from his sermon at the sound from a neighbouring church of the sacring bell, signalling the elevation; in the annoyance of parishioners at Grayingham (Lincolnshire), in the early fifteenth century, when their priest positioned an image such that it obscured their view of the Host at divine service; in the timely display of the Host to break up a lynch mob in Salisbury about to set upon Sir Robert Hungerford in June 1449; in the physical embellishment of the mass paid for by lay people, such as the Hull alderman who bequeathed £10 in 1502 to make angels, 'like those at King's Lynn', which would ascend and descend from the roof of his parish church at the elevation of the Host.[73]

Quite apparent too is the widespread effort by lay people to increase the occasions on which mass might be celebrated. Already in the thirteenth century, some guilds were founded expressly to provide additional masses outside the normal times of the parish mass. In 1454 parishioners in Hull secured papal permission to have mass celebrated before daybreak because they had often been forced to put to sea in great haste without hearing mass.[74] The proliferation of side altars in aisles and chapels, especially in wealthier parishes, is one of the most distinctive and ubiquitous spatial developments in late medieval church interiors. Here again activity of smaller groups (in guilds) or individuals (founding chantries) within the parish is clear. At these altars, mangaged by lay people, access to the officiating priest was much closer than it was at the high altar. By the later Middle Ages access to the mass was more frequent, and it was a service which lay people could pay for and time to their requirements.

The centrality of the mass in religious life strongly suggests to some historians a culture, especially in the later Middle Ages, which was commonly shared and understood, with a communal sense of unity as its highest ideal. Such historians are little swayed by arguments that interpretations of the mass, and the body of Christ, could be very different depending on context; that the desire to see the elevated Host did not necessarily come from the full internalization of theological niceties; that some churchmen worried about 'superstitious' attitudes, and that others, not least John Wyclif in the late fourteenth century, denounced devotion to the Host as too cultic. Such historians would regard it as a distortion to reduce the communal ideals of the mass, as a Marxist might, to an expression simply of social conflict and hierarchy, or to stretch the range of possible interpretations, as a post-structuralist might, so as to render the mass empty of core meaning for contemporaries. By the fifteenth century, surely, a layman who attended a Sunday service, whatever his walk of life, would have understood about the saving powers of the mass, and would have found the form and content of the service similar in any church in England, if not in Christendom as a whole. And yet the growing homogeneity of late medieval religion cannot be divorced from its social context – one in which communal ideals seemed threatened as never before. The social dimension of the mass, in all its settings, will need further investigation. But before that, the mass needs to be placed within its liturgical context.

(viii) The Liturgy

In a formal sense, the seasonal cycle of the Christian year, and the celebration of the liturgical year from Advent to Whitsun, was of universal significance for all Christians: it took the parishioner through the essential meaning of the faith, from Incarnation to Redemption. Overlaid on the pattern of feast days which culminated at Easter (and which were confined essentially to the period from November to June), were anniversaries of saints' days, and special feast days which took place throughout the year. The liturgical calendar (although conservative in England) was not static: new saints were officially created, and new universal feasts instituted, often filling the relatively unoccupied summer months. There was also some variation in liturgical rites, even in a more universal Church, although in fifteenth-century England the Sarum rite was becoming more widely used.

Ecclesiastical requirements were certainly not the only forces which shaped liturgical celebration. There were political pressures too. Just as English kings had become interested in using the parish as a unit of taxation, so they also attempted to use parish worship for political ends. Prayers and processions were demanded of the people against the enemies of England. Nationalistic feeling was actively marshalled through the Church at a local level, especially from the fourteenth century onwards. On occasion, Edward III instructed the parish clergy to raise alarm against the Scottish invasions or against 'gallic machinations' in his war with France. More systematically in each year from 1415 to 1419 Archbishop Chichele ordered every parish church in England to celebrate special masses for Henry V's campaigns in France.[75] The effort to establish more uniform public worship (see Chapter 3: ii) is evident in Chichele's promotion of the Sarum rite, and of royally adopted saints (like St George) as worthy of national use.

The success of this programme can be overrated. Chichele was already troubled in 1417 that parochial effort in support of royal campaigns had begun to flag. The cult of St George did become more popular, a popularity expressed in the foundation of guilds dedicated to the saint (such as the elitist guilds embracing town councillors in Norwich or Salisbury). But these guilds, in adopting a royally approved saint, were also doing so for their own local purposes. Other officially promoted saints, such as the royal 'Saint' Henry under the early Tudors, enjoyed shortlived popularity. By the 1490s the collecting box for 'Saint' Henry at Wimborne Minster, despite the church's strong Tudor links, could annually expect no more than a paltry penny or two. Parishioners there preferred to celebrate St Cuthberga's feast day on 31 August with much greater vigour. Late medieval evidence indicates the degree to which celebration was a matter of choice for the parishioners themselves. It suited the churchwardens and parishioners of Kingstone (Somerset) in 1450 to shift the dedicatory feast of the church from the eve of Purification to the first Sunday in October 'so that it may be observed with more solemnity and devotion'.[76] There was a great deal of variation at a local level as to which feast days were particularly celebrated and with what kind of investment. Parishes in larger towns tended to be more lavish in their outlay on spectacle and perhaps more responsive to the newer feasts. But even in a small village, parishioners themselves might take steps to ensure that the great Christian feast days were enhanced by extra lighting.

The kind of beliefs which lay behind communal investment in celebrations is harder to ascertain. Lay practices on feast days did not always meet with ecclesiastical approval, and as with devotion to saints' cults (see Chapter 3: iv), charges of 'superstition' and even 'paganism' were levelled against them. After all, the Christian calendar had been grafted on to the seasons of the year and practices on certain feast days appear to have more to do with seasonal requirements than exposition of the Christian message.[77] Protection of the crops from sowing to harvest time was of immediate concern: the clerical author of *Dives and Pauper* condemned the 'superstition' of 'leading the plough about the fire' in January to ensure 'a good beginning of the year'.[78] Midsummer fires and watches seemed to echo pre-Christian rites to protect crops before harvest. Yet we should be cautious in dismissing the 'Christian' element in such beliefs. The marking of significant seasonal moments with Christian celebration could be appropriate even for high-minded bishops. Liturgical books encouraged prayers at Rogationtide for the safe gathering of the harvest crop. What concerned churchmen most was the excessively secular and distracting nature of seasonal celebrations, rather than 'pagan' belief. May Day games, so the Dominican John Bromyard argued in the fourteenth century, were excuses for 'wanton frolicking', devices sent by the devil to recapture souls after Lenten abstinence.[79] The parishioners of Freckenham (Suffolk) in 1331 incurred the bishop of Rochester's displeasure by drinking beer after the Easter communion. Occasionally, the local clergy expressed outrage at the activities of their parishioners: in 1437 the vicar of St Helen's in Abingdon complained to the bishop of Salisbury that his parishioners were carrying a 'carnal and diabolic effigy' in procession on the feast of the Holy Cross. But he did not imply that the effigy was a throwback to a pagan past.[80] Moreover, such complaints generally came from the upper echelons of the Church hierarchy – and might be directed at the local priest as much as at lay people: bishops, at least in thirteenth and early fourteenth centuries, can be found warning parish clergy against indulging in ales and holding them in their churches.

In any case, by the fifteenth century such warnings are rarer. The ubiquity of ales and other forms of collective festivity in churchwardens' accounts seem to have clerical approval. The bishop of Worcester's denunciation of Hocktide festivities in 1450 as 'disgraceful sport' was not echoed by others, as popularity for the event (at least in southern England) seems to have spread.[81] In any case, expenditure from these sources – on processions, plays, candles and lights – was clearly directed towards increasing the solemnity of the relevant feast day. A large number of feast days on which attention was lavished – Easter week above all – have no obvious link with the changing of the seasons. Whether the laity as a whole had been fully able to internalize the message of the liturgical year may be empathetic guesswork: we have yet to explore fully the social dimension of communal celebration. But the processions, plays and special lighting that many parishioners paid for and experienced as part of the Easter week celebrations might, at the very least, indicate a desire to enrich the devotional experience of the occasion. There is also no reason to assume that, by the later Middle Ages, former pagan practices were overlaid with a veneer of Christianity, even if beliefs among the laity did not always match the theological sophistication of certain churchmen.

Furthermore, communal celebrations within the 'ritual year' appear to be on the increase in many parishes from the late fourteenth century.[82] Several explanations may be sought, not least the changing social context (see Chapter 5: vii); but at one level, the accumulation of collective festivities marks no more than the continuation of a longer term development of the parish as a focus of communal organization. These festivities allowed the articulation of a communal identity which had been growing in most parishes since at least the thirteenth century. But how communal was the parish 'community'?

(ix) Community and Hierarchy

It is possible to regard late medieval communal religion through a haze of nostalgia. Roger Martyn did so in the 1580s.[83] He recalled the state of his church of Long Melford (Suffolk) as it had existed in his childhood, before the Reformation. The communal processions held on Palm Sunday, Corpus Christi day, St Mark's day, Rogation and St James's day are remembered with affection; the bonfires held on the eves of St James, Midsummer, Sts Peter and Paul and St Thomas are scenes of neighbourly good cheer. The references to furnishings in the aisles and chapels, to the affective images of the Crucifixion and Our Lady of Pity, seem to point to the richness of devotional experience, available to all parishioners, within a wealthy rural parish.[84]

Roger Martyn's recollections conjure up an image of cosy communality – and lend weight to the image of late medieval religion as a holistic culture, in which all social ranks shared. Yet they also suggest something quite other. Roger Martyn's nostalgia for his parish is also an unashamed trumpeting of his own family's high profile within it. The elevated place once occupied by his own and other gentry families is quite evident from the very beginning. His description of the church interior moves swiftly from the high altar to 'my ile' (a chapel completed in 1484), later passing to an aisle and a chapel which had been built by the Cloptons, another local gentry family. The communal celebrations seem designed to mark out the social contours of the parish. The two processions on Palm Sunday ended up at the door of Clopton's aisle or at the east end of the lady chapel. The canopy of the holy sacrament was carried by four 'yeomen'. Roger casually mentions the mass held in St James's chapel on St James's day as 'maintained by my ancestors'; and it is at gentry manors that the drinkings on feast days are held. On St Thomas's eve, the Martyns had deigned to provide the poor of the parish with mutton pie, peaspods and ale, although they had apparently been unable to countenance more than a few 'of the honest and more civil poor neighbours' actually inside their house.

The extent and type of participation within parish life was partly determined by social position. There were ways in which the landowning elite were distanced from the parish 'community'. Great aristocrats, with lands in many parishes, were generally not attached to any one parish. As we have seen, their households, certainly from the mid-fourteenth century, began to serve as the primary focuses of their pastoral care: licensed with their chapels, portable altars and personal confessors they were, in effect, exempt from the synodal obligations towards a parish church. Their involvement in the corporate religious life of the majority of the population, therefore, was minimal. As patrons of parish churches, aristocratic families might condescend to act when petitioned; but they had no need to invest in parishes or guilds for their collective salvation.

Such investment was perhaps more important for the lesser landowner. By the thirteenth century, knights or 'gentry' had become a more clearly defined social group, settled in their own manorial house and increasingly independent of the 'feudal' honour. In the later Middle Ages, the greater 'gentry' too might have their own household chapels. The lesser gentry were not so distanced from local parish churches. The Martyns of Long Melford were clearly involved in the parish life. But it is an involvement of a particular kind. In a sense, their dominance represents a continuation – in changed circumstances – of the territorial attitude of local thegns in the Anglo-Saxon period who had once founded their own property churches. By the thirteenth century it was no longer possible to 'own' a parish church: private churches had tended to become public, while the development of fabric funds and churchwardens meant that the corporate strength of other parishioners had increased. A need to exercise control over lesser tenants in a locality remained, which inevitably meant involvement – of a socially distinctive kind – in parish life.[85]

The collective activity of the parish also allowed expression of other kinds of hierarchy. However 'communal', the organization and management of the parish were run by the more prominent members of local society. There is little reason to believe parochial decisions were regularly, if ever, taken in council meetings which included everyone. Decisions or accounts drawn up 'with the assent of the community' were a convenient fiction, a rhetoric justifying hierarchy, even though those involved might have to make concessions to wider interests within the parish. The eighteen villagers of Pleshey (Essex) may have agreed in 1394 to the removal and rebuilding of their parish church on a new site 'with the assent of all our neighbours, the lesser as well as the greater'. But such references are scarce (and for the Pleshey villagers it was an agreement probably forced upon them).[86] Churchwardens rarely came from gentry background, but neither were they from the humblest ranks. In larger towns, occupancy of the office was often a rite of passage to more elevated positions in town government. In more rural parishes the churchwarden was usually from the same social group (or might himself serve) as the reeve on manors or as the juror or chief pledge in courts.[87]

From the later fourteenth century social upheaval placed further pressure on communal identities. As we shall see, hierarchy and oligarchy tended to assert itself over structures of parish, guild and town (Chapter 5: v, viii). Within the parish the development of communal funds during the fifteenth century tended to concentrate power in church-wardens' hands, and by the end of the fifteenth century there is more evidence for the consolidation of oligarchy within the parish elite. The greater reliance on landed property to fund parish celebrations in the more urbanized parishes reduced reliance on communal fund-raising events like church ales: those parishioners excluded from parochial office had fewer occasions for regular inclusion in activities which supported communal funding. The appearance of fixed seating in some urban churches during the fifteenth century allowed hierarchy to be displayed.[88] The London parish of St Mary at Hill, at one point in the late fifteenth century, arranged the names of fifty-seven important parishioners in an elaborate pyramidal structure, tapering to an apex of churchwardens and aldermen, thus carefully calibrating their position in the local pecking order. The other parishioners were excluded altogether.[89]

Was the late medieval parish or town a 'community' at all? There is a case for avoiding the term completely.[90] It carries with it a connotation of harmony, an almost unconscious sense of shared values and belonging, which makes too many assumptions about the arena of social activity it is supposed to describe. At extreme ends of the social strata, the parish 'community' in operation was a force for social exclusion. Did the poor at the manor-house door feel quite so included in the 'communal' parish festivities of Long Melford? On the other hand, it would be cynical to dismiss the activities of prominent parishioners as devoid of a communal sense of responsibility, or at the very least a sense of the need for coop-eration rather than enforcement of social dominance. The office of churchwarden could place a heavy and financially unrewarding burden on its holder. The collective responsibilities and capabilities of late medieval parishioners created a kind of unit which, simply out of 'com-mon sense', one might call a 'community'. But such a description of the late medieval parish seems most viable if a definition of the term incor-porates the existence of hierarchy or even coercion.[91] More important, the emphasis on the term itself in the later Middle Ages is best explained by the sharpening of social divisions and of a feeling that consensus was more under threat.[92] And there were other possible fault lines in the parish 'community'. Did gender divide it too?

(x) Community and Gender

According to some contemporary assessments, female collective activity had distinctive qualities. In 1497 a Venetian ambassador marvelled at how the women in London devoted themselves to worship in their parish churches and to reciting their rosaries in public. In 1516 a heretic, Michael Gamare, described how it was the practice of the women in his parish (Wimborne St Giles, Dorset) to make offerings before an image of St Giles.[93] Two very different men make the similar assumption that gen-der determined the nature of piety. In town and country, and regardless of social status, we might even conclude, that women were more devoutly attached to parish religion than men.[94]

Ecclesiastical prescription and social custom certainly made it likely that women would experience and participate in corporate religious practices in ways which were gendered. The liturgy itself contained gen-dered distinctions: slightly varied arrangements for males and females were recommended at baptism and death; the ceremony of purification or 'churching' ultimately recalled the essential impurity of the female body (and was to be postponed longer after childbirth if the child were female).[95] Spatial boundaries within the church were potentially more restricting on women than men. The chancel was the preserve of the clergy, but it was also a place (under ancient canonical prescription) which was particularly to exclude women when mass was being celebrated – although perhaps some priests were more relaxed about prescription than others: in 1405 the vicar of Lyme Regis (Dorset) had to be reprimanded for allowing women to approach the high altar.[96] Gender distinctions were to some extent observed in seating arrangements: when fixed seating first becomes apparent in some churchwarden accounts in the early to mid-fifteenth century, it appears to have been made for women alone. In other ways the role of women within the parish was more limited: inevitably, few became wardens of guilds or altar lights, and very few ever became churchwardens. The more infrequent appearance of women in parish accounts or in wills as benefactors of the parish, reflects their more marginal economic status.

Restrictions did not, however, exclude women from participating positively in communal celebration. Their gift-giving was more limited, but it may have been discriminating in ways which were gendered. Women were encouraged to be charitable – the biblical figure of Martha was sometimes offered as a female model of merciful action – and analysis of their wills seems to suggest a greater propensity among women to give to the poor.[97] Female testators were also more likely to show a particular attachment to their parish churches: more frequently than men, they left bequests, often personalized items rather than money, to individually identified altar lights.[98]

Does this suggest a deeper devotion among women to the religious culture, especially the saints, of their parishes? Perhaps (always assuming, for instance, that the bequests of wives or widows do not also reflect the preferences of their husbands). But besides pious preference, patterns of bequests also reflect other constraints which were themselves gendered. The containment of women's bequests to their parish church reflects the more localized nature of female patterns of work: that men were more likely to leave bequests to churches outside their own parish reflects their greater economic mobility. Female attachment to the parish church was also socially proper: late medieval 'courtesy' texts prescribing correct behaviour placed greater stress on female attendance than male. Perhaps the Venetian ambassador in 1497 was describing nothing more spiritual in the behaviour of London women than a concern for 'bourgeois' respectability, nurtured at home, paraded in public, and reflecting male as well as female concerns (see Chapter 6: viii). On the other hand, the home might also be a spiritual unit, and married women were obliged to look after the welfare of the household, spiritual as well as social. Female attachment to the local parish church (and gifts of domestic goods to parish altars) was perhaps an extension of a more positive role that women could perform within a household, albeit within its generally patriarchal structure.

Women also participated collectively in parish life. In some parishes women played a significant role in fund-raising. Occasionally, churchwardens' accounts by the second half of the fifteenth century record the presence of guilds of women – 'wives' or 'maidens' – contributing to fabric funds.[99] At the same time, more references to Hocktide (shortly after Easter) appear, which seems to have involved women in a game of role-reversal, extracting money from men by tying them up.[100] It is a moot point whether these activities offered women new opportunities for active involvement in the parish. They were not annual in all the parishes that held them, nor did they take place in every parish; and if role-reversing suggests kinship with the potentially subversive world of carnival, it was of a very attenuated kind. Other activities which specifically involved women placed them in roles which reconfirmed rather than subverted domestic routine: after 1498 the wives of the 'town' in Wimborne Minster (Dorset) competed with the wives of 'the country' in selling cakes for the profit of the church.[101] In fact the appearance of Hocktide festivities occurs at a time when some parishes were developing or expanding a whole range of different fund-raising activities from different groups within the parish, some of which were defined by age as much as by gender. Croscombe parish (Somerset) by the later fifteenth century relied on the fund-raising activities of 'maidens', but also of 'younglings' or young men (and the more lucrative revels of Robin Hood). Some communal activities were more exclusive to men: 'hoggling' was a fund-raising activity in some parishes which apparently involved men, sometimes at New Year, collecting from door to door.[102]

At the very least, such activity meant that there were particular ways in which women (and men) might participate collectively within the parish. Was a sense of gender identity, of a positive kind, reinforced through involvement in this activity? For all the negative associations of 'churching', perhaps the women who gathered and progressed to church for Purification, had candles lit, psalms sung and blessings bestowed, saw themselves as following the path of the Virgin Mary through whose body (however innately impure) mankind was redeemed.[103]

But the activities of female parishioners also suggest that there was no single 'gender identity' for all women. 'Churching' was exclusive to those women who bore children. The gendered roles and activities within the parish included some women and excluded others – generally fund-raising or altar-light stocks involved women as wives or maidens. Type of parish affected the kind of activity available to women: the larger town parishes which increasingly relied on property to balance their books had less recourse than rural ones to the collective activities of women as well as of men. Social status or 'class' was perhaps an even greater determinant of female activity. The few women who did become churchwardens were more often of higher social status – wives and widows of important men – than their male counterparts. The wills of gentry women (as with men) do not show the same attachment to individual parishes and their altars. Fixed seating within the church, by the end of the fifteenth century, was more likely to be arranged along the lines of social rank than of gender. In town parishes the women who acquired seats were generally the wives of high-ranking burgesses.

Thus, there were ways in which the 'community' of the parish included distinctions and differences based on gender as well as social class. The more limited involvement of women in late medieval parish life reflected their more marginal economic position, and even if the post-Black-Death economy had provided women with more opportunities for work, anxieties about the nature of female work had increased by the end of the fifteenth century. Their involvement was gendered, but it is hard to discern a specifically 'feminine' kind of piety that determined the religious behaviour of all women within the parish. Involved as maidens or wives, their activities (more than those of men) were organized along the pattern of the life-cycle, on marital status and on their role in the household; as wives or widows of gentry and burgesses they might occupy a more prominent position within their parishes.

Contemporary assessments of a specifically 'female' piety need not be taken at face value. On the one hand, the Venetian ambassador was observing social mores rather than intensity of devotion. Courtesy texts of the later Middle Ages considered daily attendance at church a mark of female respectability. Such texts should also be set within a wider context of moralizing legislation in late medieval towns which sought to curb social disruption – in this case, perhaps, there was a perception that women migrating to towns and seeking work as servants were potentially disruptive (see Chapter 6: viii). On the other hand, characterizations of women as singularly devout had pejorative connotations. Michael Gamare was appealing to misogyny. By singling out women in his parish, and identifying practices as specifically female, he was presenting local parish worship in a negative light. Such female piety, he said, was 'a lewde thynge and a madde condition'.

(xi) Conclusion

The great variety in corporate religious practices by the later Middle Ages in one sense represents the successful realization of the Church's pastoral effort. The 'missionary' character of minster churches, with their bodies of clergy ministering to sometimes distant flocks, had disappeared, even if vestiges of the 'minster system' continued to influence the parochial structure. In their place was a much more intensive scattering of local churches, to which ordinary people had more immediate and regular access. The proprietorial control exercised by lords in such churches had also been diminished; in their place were churches of a more public kind in which a wider group of parishioners had been formally invested with responsibilities for corporate worship. But pastoral effort was only partly responsible for the corporate structures and celebrations that developed. The external demands of bishops (and the administrative requirements of the crown) had only in part shaped the parish as a fixed territorial unit. Much more important in the process were the demands of the laity themselves. The location of churches and their territorial boundaries had been responsive to local requirements, and even when the parish structure became more rigid new needs could still be met. Indeed the variety of corporate forms of religion, especially guilds, was a product of lay society and the manifold expressions within it of collective association. The control that lay people could exercise over corporate celebrations, over the funds that supported them, and over the clergy whether in the parish, guild or household, is one of the most striking features of late medieval religion.

The 'communal' nature of these celebrations and structures needs careful analysis. Divisions and tensions between different social groups projected themselves on to corporate religion. The celebration of the mass and liturgy might ultimately express aspirations of harmony and even equality, but in the context of social upheaval particularly from the later fourteenth century, such aspirations could take on other associations. As we shall see in the following two chapters, the desire for order often represented elitist fears of disruption: the growing expenditure on 'communal' celebrations in towns and parishes reflected a concern with disorder, while ceremonial expressions of order might attempt – often contentiously – to sanctify hierarchy. The moralizing in courtesy texts or urban legislation justified suppression of social disruption. None of this need imply that late medieval religion 'functioned' merely as a crude form of social repression, or that it was incapable of encouraging a devotional experience and spirituality which could transcend and even defy worldly pressures. But the structures in which it was developed took on the colour of their social setting, and its practices bore the stamp of social division.

Chapter 5: Corporate Religion: Death and the Afterlife

In his 'Pilgrimage of Human Life' (written in the 1330s), the French Cistercian Deguileville described a vision of life as a kind of pilgrimage on the road to the heavenly Jerusalem. During life on earth, it was a battle against sin in which the combatant was helped by proper instruction in the Church's doctrines, and by the performance of the sacraments which offered the hope of grace. Death came as a terrifying moment, but not so much for the body as for the soul. Satan scents victory. But judged on St Michael's scales of justice, a remorseful conscience rehearsing past sins, the soul is spared descent into Hell. Contrition and confession has been made, even if full satisfaction has yet to be carried out. The soul passes through Purgatory, its cleansing flames mitigated only by the continuing prayers, alms and masses performed by the living. For some it will be a long and painful wait: one soul remains chained to a coffer of money which his executors have neglected to discharge for him; another, who has indulged too freely in life's frivolities, is encased in a block of ice for what will seem to last for 100 years. At least they are spared the horrors of Hell. All await the Second Coming and Last Judgment, when souls are reunited with bodies and dispatched to their final destinations, heavenly or otherwise.[1]

Deguileville's vision is a reminder that the separation of 'life' from 'death' is misleading. The individual soul would have a journey which extended beyond the grave, and the corporate practices of the living had consequences for the dead – not least because, as the vision makes clear, penance performed in life affected the soul in the afterlife. Moreover, by the time this vision had been written, the geography of the afterlife had already been well explored and a safe passage through its difficult terrain clearly signposted (see Chapter 2: ii). The idea of Purgatory and the need for penance had been essentially worked out. What impact did these ideas have on the laity? The vision of Deguileville was known in English translation, to magnates of royal blood by the 1430s, and a second work, 'Pilgrimage of the Soul', was eventually printed by Caxton in the 1480s. But by then notions of Purgatory and of the need for penance were of greater currency, and although their impact is at first visible only at the highest echelons of lay society in contact with the monastic life, by the thirteenth century their influence, as we shall see, had reached far beyond the cloister to the church at a local level.

Deguileville wrote his second work in 1355: by then another event had occurred which may have given his visions added poignancy and interest. The catastrophic impact of the Black Death in 1348 and subsequent outbreaks (particularly the 'children's plague' in 1361), meant that there were additional reasons to contemplate and prepare for death. But the impact of plague on attitudes to death and on penitential strategies is not a straightforward one. It needs to be placed in the context of other social changes and within the longer history of attitudes and practices associated with the afterlife – not least because these had a social dimension. Deguileville's vision applied to Every Man; Death was the great leveller. But social division and hierarchy had a way of projecting themselves beyond the grave.

(i) Attitudes to Death

Medieval views on death have sometimes been characterized as morbid, a morbidity which deepened from the fourteenth century onwards. 'No other epoch has laid so much stress as the expiring Middle Ages on the thought of death': such was Johan Huizinga's famous and oft-repeated assessment.[2] There were certainly some uncomfortable reminders of mortality available to the laity, even before the later Middle Ages. The dialogue between the soul and a decomposing body had been known in Anglo-Saxon homilies, and was a theme widespread (in a Latin poem) by the thirteenth century. Disturbing sermons could be heard from the pulpit: 'Never was there carrion so loathe, As man when to his grave he goeth' was one of the texts suggested in a fourteenth-century preaching handbook. According to John Mirk's tract on sermons in the early fifteenth century, the corpse brought to the church, was a 'mirror for us all';[3] and such 'mirrors' took on material form in the sculpted skulls of Golgotha below a rood screen (such as at Cullompton, Devon), or in double tombs with a cadaver effigy (like Sir John Golafre's at Fyfield, Berkshire, from 1440), or in the Dance of Death (as at St Paul's by the 1440s). All these images were reminders that none but the saint could escape corporeal decomposition after death.

If death of the body were the end, these images might seem morbid indeed. But as Deguileville's vision made clear, the death of the body was only one minor, if uncongenial, process in the art of dying. Within the monastic tradition contemplation of death was simply a stimulus for reflection on the more extended pilgrimage of the soul; and in any case a far more important stimulus, especially from the twelfth century onwards, was meditation on the Passion of Christ. The image of Christ on the Cross certainly generated some distressing if not gruesome depictions; but in the end, this was not death at all, but victory over it; and it was a victory which ensured that the soul could not die. Death was only one stage in a pilgrimage which led ultimately to the Last Judgment.

The Last Judgment was distinct from the death and fate of an individual: it represented the apocalyptic fate of all mankind. There was a rich medieval tradition surrounding how it would come about. The Revelation of St John which spoke of the Apocalypse had long fuelled millennarian beliefs: those of Joachim of Fiore (d.1202) were particularly influential from the thirteenth century onwards, even after 1260 (the year in which Joachim predicted the appearance of the Antichrist) had passed without mishap. Illuminated manuscripts produced for a royal audience in the middle decades of the thirteenth century show a strong interest in the Apocalypse of St John. The 'Burckhardt-Wildt Apocalypse' produced at Lincoln or York c.1280 shows the Fourth Horseman, Death, as a cadaver. The experience for those still living in the Final Days was, then, unlikely to be particularly pleasant: the Apocalypse announced by the Four Horsemen, would herald the terrifying reign of the Antichrist. Throughout the period, radical preachers continued to echo this theme. The hermit Thomas Scrope apparently spent many years from 1425 in the diocese of Norwich preaching that the 'new Jerusalem, the bride of the Lamb, was about to come down from Heaven'.[4]

For the most part though, millennarian preaching was not as prevalent in England as in some of the more volatile parts of continental Europe (see Chapter 6: iv). Moreover, the Last Judgment was not always presented in apocalyptic terms. For those already dead – and ultimately for all those to be saved – there was the promise of ultimate redemption.

Christ would return. Souls would be judged and reunited with the body in the Resurrection (although theologians continued to be troubled about what form this would take). Some of the more grisly representations of death had precisely this message of hope in mind. In the dialogue between body and soul, the rotting corpse is promised eventual restoration to mint condition. The pristine effigy above the sculpted cadaver in late medieval double tombs may signify the same ultimate prospect. In the long scheme of things, death of the body meant little – which was why images of the Last Judgment were far more widespread than images of death itself. Cadaver tombs or paintings of the Dance of Death were uncommon in England. Wall paintings in parish churches had a much wider repertoire of Christian imagery, and images of death were contained within a broader eschatalogical context. On the north wall of Pickworth church (Lincolnshire) fourteenth-century parishioners may have been confronted by an image of the Three Living and Three Dead, yet facing the high altar, above the chancel arch, as in so many other churches, a painting of the Day of Doom held out the promise of resurrection.[5]

The inevitability of death and of the Last Judgment had one other consequence: it made careful preparation of the soul all the more imperative. Within the monastic tradition, entry into religious life, renouncing the world, was itself a preparation for dying. Instruction of this kind was increasingly available to the laity, notably in psalters available to the high-born. The dangers of worldly pleasure fill the pages of Sir Geoffrey Luttrell's psalter (penned in the 1330s). One illumination of a Christmas feast shows a banqueter, perhaps Sir Geoffrey himself, peering dolefully over his raised goblet. Well he might. The words above his head are taken from Psalm 115: 'The sorrows of death compassed me ...'[6] Such a message was delivered by the more widely disseminated texts on the 'Craft of Dying' in the fifteenth century.

By the later Middle Ages careful preparation for the soul had become all the more essential because of what lay between the death of the body and its ultimate resurrection. The once ill-defined and indeterminate period of waiting for the soul had come to assume a more definite form. By the thirteenth century, Purgatory, the middle place between Heaven and Hell, had become fully integrated into a system of penance and offered the laity strategies for salvation which made more manageable the shifting of the burden of sin. Salvation was not necessarily the more easy to come by: the urgency and difficulty of achieving a mental state of true contrition meant that there was no room for complacency. In any case, as Deguileville's vision displayed, and the occasional returning souls emphasized, Purgatory was not a place in which to tarry long. Like meditations on the Last Judgment, terrifying visions of Purgatory were intended to encourage contrition and good living in preparation for death.

But Purgatory was still a place which was infinitely less awful than a Hell from which there was no escape; and as with the Last Judgment, despite its travails, Purgatory's existence offered relief from the horrors of bodily death. It lay within reach of the average sinner as a half-way station on the road to ultimate salvation; and by the later Middle Ages its message was accessible far beyond the cloister. It lies behind the manuals for priests who were to instruct their parishioners on confession; it appears in the exempla of sermons for friars and parish priests; and visions of purgatory, once found only in monastic writings, are occasionally recorded by laymen. In 1465 Sir Edmund Leversedge, a Somerset gentleman, testified to a frightening vision of torment in Purgatory which forced him to turn from a life of idle luxury to one of penance.[7]

The influence of Purgatory, as we shall see, was profound. But in the end, it is worth emphasizing that it was only one stage in a much longer process which took body and soul on a pilgrimage from birth to Last Judgment. It was also a stage in a journey during which the essential emphasis was placed, by theologians, on the importance of confession and the state of mind of the sinner, over and above the good works which might eventually speed the soul through Purgatory. Perhaps this is partly why visual representations of Purgatory were never quite so common as those of the Last Judgment: the third place was a transitional phase only, and its pains merely a means to an end. Ultimately, gruesome depictions of death, Hell's torments and purgatorial pains were intended to stimulate self-examination in preparation for the Last Judgment; and ultimately too, this process of contrition, through the offices of the Church, held out the assurance of salvation.

Thus, even in the later Middle Ages, the more gruesome images of death need not be seen as essentially morbid. Those that appear, in any case, mark not so much a change of 'zeitgeist' as a transference to the laity of the kind of spiritual contemplation which had once been the province of the cloistered alone. The fourteenth-century handbook on preaching had drawn its text on 'carrion loathe' straight from the words of the Cistercian monk St Bernard. Themes which had once occupied the religious or high-ranking lay people were taken up by parishioners. A painting of the Dance of Death, displayed twice annually in the parish church of All Saints' Bristol, was the thoughtful gift of a layman in the mid-fifteenth century, to instruct his fellow parishioners that 'every man should remember his own death'.[8]

The broader impact of these ideas and doctrines on the beliefs of the laity are not easy to discern. Their spread is evident, orally and visually, in the texts and images of confessional manuals, penitential literature, or church paintings. Yet much of this evidence is prescriptive, even if it might indicate a receptive audience and even if it was sometimes produced by lay people themselves. Beliefs which (perhaps) owed something to a pagan past also persisted: it was possible for Walter Map in the twelfth century to accept the existence of 'succubi' or vampires plaguing the folk of the Welsh March lands; for a thirteenth-century Life of St Modwenna to describe shape-changing peasants returning from the dead; or for John Mirk in the fifteenth century to repeat the story of three men in Shrewsbury being bitten in the neck by an 'adyrcope' or 'vryn'.[9] The idea of Purgatory itself may also have incorporated folkloric tales of souls returning from another world. But there is much stronger evidence for the wider effect on lay people of fully Christanized ideas to do with penance and the purgatorial afterlife, and it is best gauged in the evidence for good works that were supposed to flow from the penitential impulse. By the later Middle Ages this kind of evidence is abundant – most obviously in the wills of lay people which survive in large numbers from the mid-fourteenth century onwards. Whether the good works that they requested flowed from a deep sense of contrition, as churchmen might hope, is hard to fathom. But at the very least, some trends in the pattern of pious giving 'for the soul' do emerge.

(ii) Religious Houses and Lay Society

In the eleventh century the task of caring for the dead and their afterlife was still the monopoly of the religious. It was also a task which the laity – or at least an aristocratic elite with the closest ties to monastic houses – recognized as best carried out by those who specialized in a liturgical round of prayer, masses and commemoration. The adoption of monastic habit was the ideal means for a lay person to secure association with a religious house. Ela, countess of Salisbury eventually became a nun in her own foundation of Lacock abbey in 1238.[10] But a more vicarious association was possible through entry into the 'confraternity' of a monastery. By the twelfth century, the confraternity list of Thorney abbey numbered some 2300 (mainly high-ranking) lay people. Hugh, earl of Chester, in 1090 expected that inclusion in such a list at Abingdon abbey would afford him commemoration 'like one of the brethren'.[11]

The huge expansion in the number and type of religious houses founded from the end of the eleventh century and well into the twelfth seems to demonstrate a stengthening of this penitential impulse. Another trend is evident too. Founders and benefactors began to expect more specific suffrages for their soul. By the end of the eleventh century, royal burials were accompanied by more individualized offices of the dead, trentals and anniversaries; and by the early twelfth century magnates could ask for more tailor-made observances. The monks of Thorney were asked specifically for a funeral and anniversary service from one Geoffrey de Trelly sometime between 1085 and 1112. Some inmates of religious houses could even be earmarked to perform particular intercessory functions: in return for the grant of two large churches, the earl of Warwick around 1124 required Kenilworth priory 'ever to have a canon in the priory' – implying that this canon would say mass for his soul in perpetuity.[12]

Implications of this kind gradually became explicit. By the end of the twelfth century specific endowment for the perpetual celebration of mass for the dead – the 'chantry' as it came to be called – is apparent in some religious houses. Other kinds of suffrage began to be specified too. Entry into the 'confraternity' of a religious house in return for benefaction had meant a vague expectation of commemoration within the general liturgical life of the house; but in the thirteenth century the content of these spiritual benefits came to be defined more precisely. Benefactors were increasingly inclined to indicate what they wished to be performed 'for their souls'. The cartularies of religious houses, certainly by the thirteenth century, begin to record smaller gifts in return for the setting up of altar lights, or 'obits' (anniversary services) or trental masses.[13] Such donations also allowed lower social groups, such as burgesses and free peasants, to gain association with a religious house. In part, these changes may well reflect a growing consciousness among lay people, from a widening social spectrum, of the concept of Purgatory and of a more precise need to tailor penitential good works to posthumous commemoration.

However important the penitential motive, monastic foundation and benefaction were also expressive of social power. The magnates who founded monasteries in the great period of monastic expansion in the twelfth century exhibited a strong desire for dynastic continuity and power over their feudal honour.[14] Lower down the social scale knightly benefactors emulated their social superiors in supporting monastic houses founded by their feudal lord, or in founding houses, such as Augustinian canonries or hospitals, which were more within their financial means. Despite the stricter separation of monastic life from the world demanded by Gregorian reformers, the expectations of lay patrons meant that separation could never be complete. To some Cistercians, even demands for specific religious services represented worldly intrusion into the cloistered life, and carried with them a suspicious whiff of simony.

Benefaction also brought worldly wealth – and its attendant troubles. The religious institutions which sought to capture and stabilize ideals of apostolic poverty found themselves judges against the very ideals they hoped to enshrine. The Cistercians took the spiritual high ground with the older Benedictine Order in their claim to be escaping from the world into the 'wilderness'. Yet their attraction of land from lay benefactors – not least because of their 'holiness' – left them open to the charge of hypocrisy. Walter Map, his pen dipped in the dark ink of sarcasm, marvelled at the lush pastures and thousands of pigs on the lands of an Order which claimed such proximity to holy poverty.[15] It was a pattern of complaint which continued long after the twelfth century. The popularity of the Franciscans, evident in the demand for their prayers and suffrages in return for gifts and bequests, quickly led critics inside and outside the Order to turn Franciscan ideals of poverty against the whole Order.[16] In towns built on lands owned by a local religious house, tensions with emergent civic governments dogged monastic relations with the laity for much of the period.[17]

In the later Middle Ages, the continuing (and often unavoidable) connections between religious houses and the world had other damaging consequences. Reliance on family patronage left monasteries vulnerable if the family died out or if patronage passed into hands which were not so disposed to generosity. The nuns at Lacock claimed in 1309 that the disappearance of aristocratic patronage necessitated their appropriation of the local parish church. The absence of direct aristocratic leadership in the region weakened ties with former feudal subordinates: local lordship in the region passed from the Bluet family to the Baynards who had themselves buried not in the priory, as the Bluets had done for the previous five generations, but in the local parish church.[18]

The patronage of Lacock in fact passed to the Crown. But the interest of kings in monastic property was double-edged. Some kings continued to found religious houses of a traditional kind, but others preferred newer orders, or (like many great aristocrats) established colleges of priests (like the Lancastrian hospital and collegiate church at Newarke) from whom they commanded specific religious observances.[19] More threateningly, the development of royal government and its growing demand for resources, particularly from the reign of Edward I (see Chapter 3: ii), led kings to cast predatory eyes on property given to religious houses which had effectively passed out of their financial reach and into the 'dead hand' of the Church. The 1279 Statute of Mortmain prohibited benefaction to religious houses, unless a fine were paid.[20] The Crown also began to draw out the implications of lay patronage over the religious. Monastic houses which did not fulfil the spiritual services demanded in benefactions were open to the charge of defrauding the souls of the dead. And those institutions which no longer seemed to fulfil their original functions were threatened with disendowment. 'Alien' priories, as cells of foreign monastic houses, and without native patrons, were increasingly susceptible to dissolution: royal demands for money to fight the French, particularly during the period of the Hundred Years War, made them easy targets.[21]

It is not surprising, then, to find a decline in benefaction to monastic houses. The flood of new religious foundations from the end of the eleventh century had already been reduced to a trickle by the middle of the thirteenth, and by then the flow of land into existing ones was drying up. Nevertheless, it would be misleading to represent late medieval monasteries as limping their way towards final Dissolution in the sixteenth century. Lay recognition of the value of the religious as intercessors did continue. Some families survived dynastic extinction to remain vital supporters of their local religious houses. The gentry (and particularly the aristocracy), more than other social groups, continued to remember monastic houses in their wills perhaps as a mark of their social status.[22] Religious houses were not solely dependent on aristocratic and knightly familial interests. The occasional late medieval list of benefactors – such as the *Liber Vitae* at Durham – show the inclusion of large numbers of people, from a broad range of social groups.[23] The wills of late medieval people below the rank of gentry also show a continuing need for the prayers of closed religious orders right up until their Dissolution in the 1530s. At least one in ten testators – one in six in some places – made some bequest to a closed religious house.

Not all religious houses were perhaps favoured in quite the same way. There are significant differences in the scale of bequest depending on local circumstances. Testators in fifteenth-century Reading left very few bequests to their local Benedictine abbey – perhaps because its overlord-ship of the town for long stifled the emergence of an autonomous town government. Salisbury citizens, untroubled by monastic domination, were more frequent benefactors, one in ten testators leaving bequests to religious houses outside the city.[24] The type of religious house also influenced testator choice. Many targeted the type which retained a reputation for austerity – Carthusian houses more than local Benedictine ones. Testator choice may have been influenced by gender. Nunneries seem to have netted relatively more bequests than monasteries. Female religious houses (with some notable exceptions) tended to be smaller and poorer foundations than their male counterparts, this enhancing their reputation for austerity and poverty which may itself have been perceived as gender specific.[25] On the other hand, late medieval testators placed a higher premium still on the kind of 'poverty' represented by (male) friars: bequests to Franciscan and Dominican houses outweigh bequests to closed religious houses, male or female.

In general, however, the religious of all orders continued to be valued for their intercessory functions; and if fewer gifts came in the form of land, the sums of money bequeathed by late medieval testators show a desire for the same kind of specific service – prayers, masses, altar lights – which had been required of religious houses since at least the thirteenth century. In any case, the drop in landed endowment was less the result of any perceived sense of monastic decline. Recent research suggests that even the most aged and wealthy of monastic institutions in the fifteenth century were centres of vibrant activity, spiritual, intellectual and even pastoral.[26] The relative decline in benefaction was more the result of competition. Even by 1300, the religious no longer had a monopoly on post-mortem commemoration. There were other ways for lay people to ensure suffrage for the soul.

(iii) Parishes and Guilds

Specific services for the dead were already being founded outside monastic houses in the late twelfth century.[27] 'Chantries' were being set up as free-standing chapels. Some of these may simply have been licences for divine service (for originally the term 'chantry' – 'cantaria' – referred to any service away from a parish or monastic church); but some were specifically for commemoration of the dead. Permission for a chapel to be set up in the cemetery of Melsonby for certain named souls was granted by the abbot of Durham in the early thirteenth century.[28] Many of these early chantry chapels betray similar monastic origins or show a wish for continued monastic patronage (though this may be only the impression produced by reliance on monastic sources). For instance, Sir Peter Mauley in 1238 founded a chapel by a bridge in a wood adjacent to Meaux abbey: in return for land the monks were to find two secular chaplains, one of whom was to sing masses for the dead.[29] By the end of the thirteenth century examples of free-standing chantry chapels with no apparent link with monasteries are more abundant.

By the thirteenth century too, endowments of masses for dead benefactors are evident in parish churches. Again early examples show links with religious institutions. A chantry chaplain for the parish of Langworth (Lincoln diocese) was provided by Barlings abbey in 1267.[30] But the shift of penitential benefaction from monastic to parish church is clear. By the early fourteenth century, it was much rarer for chantries to be founded within a monastic church or even as free-standing chapels. In 1322 John Alwyne might have endowed a separate chantry chapel in the parish of Broad Chalke (Wiltshire), yet he required that the endowment be used after his death to find a priest to celebrate at an altar within the parish church itself. By then only a quarter of perpetual chantries were being founded within monasteries.[31] Most were now set up within parish churches, usually as 'benefices', separate endowments under the general jurisdiction of a bishop.

Smaller gifts of altar lights, from peasants and burgesses, were already being made to local churches by the early thirteenth century. Endowments large and small were also being placed under the management of lay people. At Westbury (Wiltshire) in the early thirteenth century 'divine offices of the dead' were celebrated at St Thomas's altar, and it was at this altar that one local landlord gave land for a chaplain to say mass. In such cases, the chantry endowment may have been subsumed into the general fund which supported the parish priest. Yet it had already become possible to entrust endowments to a parish church – at first to the parish priest but increasingly to parishioners. The rector of Edington in 1235 left land to his nephew to provide distributions for the poor, to set up a light before two altars and to allow the parish priest to celebrate an anniversary mass for his soul: the reversion of the property to continue these arrangements for his soul was to pass to a 'trustworthy man or two' within the parish. Grants 'for souls' to the altar and mass of the Virgin Mary at St Helen's church, Abingdon, were being made by the 1240s to 'the parishioners or their proctors'.[32] By then the accumulation of funds of many kinds by parishioners for the souls of dead benefactors was common enough to attract legislatory attention from bishops. Early records of parish church visitations demonstrate the extent of the practice. Thorpe church, visited by St Paul's cathedral in 1251, had a stock of more than eighty sheep, hired out to forty-five people, sustaining five altar lights.[33]

The proliferation of religious guilds from the thirteenth century testifies in part to the increasing impact on the laity of the need for intercession and penance. The concern for decent burial and commemoration apparent in Anglo-Saxon guilds is even more acute in the abundant and varied guilds of later medieval England. Even though social activities continued to be an important dimension of many guild associations, these were invariably placed within the context of commemoration, and of penitential effort for the souls of their members, living and dead. Such was the approval in 1270 of the bishop of Worcester for the Holy Cross Guild at Stratford-upon-Avon, that he granted an indulgence so that all penitent benefactors of the guild might enjoy a shortening by forty days of the passage of their souls through Purgatory.[34]

Some of the Anglo-Saxon guilds had been attached to monasteries – and indeed relied on monastic suffrage to intercede for their brethren. In this early period, the guild could be one further way in which lay people profited from the intercession, even the devotional life, of monastic institutions which then still held a monopoly over *post-obit* commemoration. The association between guild and religious house continued throughout the later Middle Ages. In London and York, for instance, a significant number of guilds maintained altars in monastic and friary churches.[35] The prayers of monks and friars remained valuable commodities, and in a few isolated cases they may have been indispensable. In the impoverished parish of Middlesbrough (Yorkshire) in the late fifteenth century the 'prior' of a cell of Whitby abbey seems to have acted as priest of the parish, and of the guild of St Thomas within it.[36]

But the proliferation of guilds, as with the endowment of parishes, shows how far the monastic monopoly of commemoration had already been broken. Most late medieval guilds were not connected with religious houses; some founded their own chapels; many had chapels added to parish churches or adopted altars within them. Characteristic of them all was an emphasis on intercession, even if guilds often served a variety of other religious and social needs. All of them were placed under a patron saint or cult and offered some religious suffrage for their members, ranging from the lavish provision of chantry priests, through to the modest maintenance of an altar light or the simple payment of a parish priest to say a mass. The replies of over 500 guilds to the royal survey in 1389 sought to emphasize (for royal consumption) the centrality of penance and intercession to guild function: 80 per cent claimed to maintain altar lights; 60 per cent required the attendance of its membership at funerals or obits.[37]

(iv) Communities of the Living and the Dead

The corporate management by the laity of commemoration for the dead, already evident in the thirteenth century, is one of the most distinctive features of late medieval parish life. Churchwardens' accounts (at least in more urbanized parishes) which survive from the mid-fourteenth century demonstrate a continuing and systematic accumulation of endowments for souls of benefactors. Even in a small rural chapelry of Seend (Wiltshire) a list of its 'stocks' shows an accumulation by c.1500 of thirty-one endowments (of money and sheep or cows hired out for the profit of the church) for the celebration of anniversaries and the maintenance of altar lights for specific individuals. In larger urban churches, the number of souls to commemorate might be great: the fifteenth-century 'bede' roll (list of benefactors) at All Saints' Bristol runs to more than 150 folio pages.[38]

Parishioners had also developed a proprietorial interest over endowments for souls in Purgatory. Even chantries founded as separate 'benefices', under the direct supervision of the bishop, might include lay management.[39] The importance of the parish as a focus of endowment is also apparent in the manner in which chantries were increasingly founded. Instead of handing over land to an institution, and instead of setting up a separate 'benefice', by the fifteenth century chantry founders invariably gave the possession of their endowment to a group of 'feoffees' (trustees) who would use the profits of these lands to support a chantry priest. Such 'service' chantries escaped the fine payable under the Statute of Mortmain (because the endowment was not legally being given to the 'dead hand' of the church).[40] They were also a tacit recognition of the corporate strength of the late medieval parish, even though parishes were not yet regarded as 'corporations' in law. The trustees would often include the churchwardens whose continual reelection would ensure the kind of long-term supervision which had once been available only in monastic institutions.

Late medieval churchwardens had a heavy burden of duty for the souls of dead parishioners. They managed accounts which recorded a burgeoning list of benefactors; they supervised altar-light, obit and chantry foundations. Sometimes the continuation of these services was no mean feat. Churchwardens occasionally report defaulters on church rents to visitational officials; and in any case the original endowment might decline in value. Most of the 'perpetual' chantries which were recorded by commissioners in a royal survey of 1545 had been founded in the fifteenth century: far fewer from an earlier date seem to have survived. None the less, many a parish made considerable effort to keep these services going – not least by adding to the original endowment.[41]

Once again these efforts suggest the sense of duty that lay people had come to feel for the souls of their fellow parishioners in Purgatory. It was a sense stimulated by the benefit which services for the dead might bestow upon the living. The profits from endowments for altar lights, obits and service chantries invariably fed into communal coffers. The presence of chantry priests might considerably enrich the pastoral and liturgical life of the parish. Despite a reputation in late medieval satire for idle profiteering, they can be found contributing to education, musical instruction and preaching; and in a populous parish they might be invaluable in helping the parish priest to administer the Easter communion.[42] Such was the plea of a significant number of parishes to the commissioners in 1545 who heralded the eventual abolition of chantries during the Reformation. Perhaps by then parishioners were anxious to cling on to property which was threatened with royal confiscation. But at the very least it points to the significance of such property to many parishes.

It also points to another distinctive feature of late medieval parish life. The dead had become a constant and noisy presence. In some late medieval sermons and stories, souls apparently continued to return as ghosts;[43] but their demands on the living were much more regularly announced through the sounds created by the rituals and services set up to commemorate them. Outside the church bell-ringers and bedemen would parade publicly through town or village to announce the imminence of a funeral or anniversary service. Within the church sung masses for souls might capture the attention of the parishioner. The relationship between the living and the dead was thus a close and reciprocal one. The living interceded for souls in Purgatory, whose intercessory services they had founded; the dead, in turn, affected and benefited the 'divine service' of the living.[44] In the late medieval parish such reciprocity had assumed an institutional and corporate structure which lay people managed themselves.

The abundance of guilds must have added considerably to the visual and audible presence of the dead in late medieval society. At altars within parish churches, many guilds commemorated dead members in bede rolls, and at funerals, anniversaries and chantry services. The wealthier guilds supplied polyphonic music for the commemorative masses in parish churches. As providers of religious services, they attracted gifts and bequests; craft guilds too, maintaining religious services for their members, might attract bequests from people who belonged to a different craft. Many guilds received gifts from people who were already members of other guilds: multiple membership, for those who could afford it, was one way to generate a broadened range of good works for the soul. The penitential portfolio of a wealthy merchant like William Swayne of Salisbury in the late fifteenth century was impressive but not untypical: his good works, and his need for intercession, were announced visually in inscriptions inviting prayers for his soul on the roof beams of his parish church of St Thomas, and orally in the masses and anniversary services celebrated throughout the year by chantry priests in the parish and the cathedral, by the priests of the tailors' guild dedicated to St John the Baptist, and by the priest of the St George guild maintained by the town corporation.[45]

The growing importance of the late medieval parish as an institution, and the distinctive place occupied by the dead within it, found material expression in the fabric of the church itself. Investment in church building was a work of penance, and late medieval building projects were frequently the result of corporate effort, of parishioners and guild members, as the rebuilding of Bodmin church after 1469 shows (see Chapter 4: iii). Such projects could also be encouraged by parishioners acquiring an indulgence from their bishop, or even (with more trouble and expense) the pope himself. Significantly, whereas in the thirteenth century indulgences had generally been given to monastic institutions, by the fifteenth century bishops' registers record a far higher proportion being given to lay people, and in particular for building projects.[46]

Bodmin church (which may have acquired a papal indulgence) was almost completely rebuilt; but in the later Middle Ages, the rebuilding of parish churches was not always so comprehensive. The division of responsibility between lay parishioners and parish priests accounts for chronological differences in building work on nave and chancel. But the nave itself was not often rebuilt all of a piece: the intermittent addition of aisles and chapels was a result of liturgical need, above all the provision of altar space required for intercession, and it lent many late medieval parish churches their distinctively patchwork aspect. Lambourn church (Berkshire) had its twelfth-century cruciform structure altered by the addition of a south aisle in the fourteenth century, and from the late fourteenth to the early sixteenth centuries, by the addition of three tomb and chantry chapels belonging to the Estbury gentry family, clustered around the chancel end of the church.[47]

The dead were omnipresent in the late medieval parish church. Their names, invariably accompanied by a simple request for prayers, were glazed into the windows or carved into the rood screens which they paid for; they were stitched on to the back of priestly vestments or on to the parish hearse cloth and thus woven into the celebration of the liturgy; they were inscribed in the liturgical books or engraved on the brass candlesticks or silver chalices which they had bequeathed. Late medieval inventories of parish goods usually commemorate the benefactors who had provided them; and the length of some of these lists – which often reach far beyond what was required in each parish by synodal decree – is testimony to a need for commemoration which had become ingrained as part of a corporate enterprise. As an inscription at Steeple Ashton (Wiltshire) proudly declares, the church was completely rebuilt between 1480 and 1500 'by the whole parish'.

(v) Hierarchy and Community

However 'universal' the doctrines of penance and Purgatory, a great variety in their application was possible. There were significant differences between parishes and the financial regimes which churchwardens ran, and these affected the nature of parish life in particular areas. The dead were noisiest in populous or wealthier parishes, particularly in more urban churches. Such churches might have the personnel and endowments to allow more elaborate polyphonic masses to be sung. The importance of the dead to parish finances increased during the fifteenth century, even in more provincial market towns. Wimborne Minster in 1403 could expect some 20 per cent of its revenues to come from the 'dead' (rents of property from benefactors, charges for burials, or bequests). By the end of the century this figure had increased to 40 per cent. The change is still more noticeable in urbanized areas – many parishes in London or Bristol came to rely heavily on property gradually accumulated and managed by churchwardens. Their counterparts in rural parishes or smaller market towns depended more on regular collections from the living – church ales, plays and so on – even if the choices made by parishioners in these kinds of collections varied in scale and scope.[48]

Within individual parishes hierarchy could impose itself on 'community'. Death may have been the great leveller, and the need for corporate intercession powerful, but social status asserted itself beyond the grave. The inscription at Steeple Ashton singles out two cloth merchants, Robert Long and Walter Lucas (and their wives), for their contribution to the rebuilding of the northern and southern aisles: such benefactors were assured of suffrages commensurate with their munificence or social status. Even smaller gifts recorded on a parish bede roll – regularly read out to encourage collective prayers from the living – might be hierarchically arranged. Testators (as at St Albans in the late fifteenth century) could expect their names to remain longer on the bede roll, the larger their gift.[49] Parish bede rolls, in displaying hierarchy, indeed announced 'a social map of the community'.[50]

Church interiors were made to bear silent witness to rank. Graves of high-born lay people were sometimes marked out in non-monastic churches before the twelfth century; later recycling of stones may have obliterated evidence for a more general trend. The presence of lay effigies certainly became more common, and more three dimensional: by the early thirteenth century fully formed military effigies, assertive of social standing, are to be found. By the early fourteenth century, more churches were becoming populated by the sepulchral remains of gentry families: effigies intruded themselves upon aisles, and could even encroach on the chancel (especially in a parish where a gentry family retained the vestigial property right of advowson). Where the family was particularly dominant, the whole church (like an aristocratic secular college) could take on the aspect of a family mausoleum. None more so than at Etchingham, once the resident landlord family had shifted its penitential attentions, by the 1350s, from local priory to parish. The scheme of heraldic decoration on the windows of the rebuilt church which contained Sir William Etchingham's tomb, proudly displays the family's links with aristocracy and royalty.[51]

Lesser gentry might find other ways to ensure that their status – and that of their family – was made obvious in death. In 1460 Sir John Fetiplace left the lavish sum of £40 to pay for a 'closure' around the tomb of his parents in the church of East Shefford (Berkshire). There were cheaper options for self-advertisement: brasses were increasingly used, and as early as the thirteenth century they show signs of mass production. Gentry bequests to parish churches often had the effect of distinguishing their munificence from that of other parishioners. Their coats of arms were stitched to the vestments and engraved on the orna-ments they bequeathed. Their involvement in the more collective enter-prises of church-building tended to focus on gifts to particular aisles, chapels or towers. It is rare to find regular gentry involvement in the fund-raising activities of other parishioners or as donors to the altar lights which their social inferiors maintained.

The 'religion of the gentry' is not readily distinguishable from that of other aspirants of social status (see Chapter 4: ix). The parvenus of the later Middle Ages – merchants, yeomen, lawyers – could match or surpass many gentlemen with wealth and scale of benefaction. By the late fifteenth century the occasional wealthy peasant farmer might secure burial in the chancel. Wealthy merchants were often at the forefront of religious fashion in adoption of new feasts or even religious orders. William de la Pole, merchant of London, who had links with the royal court, was one of the first laymen to found a Carthusian house (in his native town of Hull).[52] They also contributed to the expanding market for brasses to cover their graves.[53] Cloth merchants in the West Country or in Suffolk ploughed their wealth into the more prestigious projects of their local parish churches.

Social aspiration and hierarchy in late medieval commemorative practice did not pass without comment. For some, it was a matter of great concern. Moralists voiced objections to competitive burial practice. Robert Mannyng in the early fourteenth century denounced the 'proud stones' of lords as instruments of damnation: rich men who bribed churchwardens to be buried within the chancel risked their corpses being ripped from their graves by devils.[54] Some laymen show an aware-ness of the sinful potential of 'proud stones'. Sir William Etchingham's tomb (d.1389) bears an inscription with a traditionally monastic message drawn from the Offices of the Dead: 'from earth you came and from earth you shall return'. Other contemporary gentry testators take this message further. A small minority deliberately rejected lavish funeral ceremony and material commemoration. For Sir Thomas Broke at Thornecombe (Devon) in 1415, burial under a flat paving stone in the cemetery was sufficient for his 'foul carrion'.[55]

Yet the pressure of social conformity was keenly felt. Sir Thomas's wife could not bring herself to follow her husband's direction, choosing to place his 'carrion' within the church itself, albeit under a brass of modest character.[56] The need to express the social status of the family overcame the pious wishes of the individual, and the absence of such expressions was worrisome. Margaret Paston in 1473 condemned her son's failure to commission a tomb for his father as 'a shame and a thing much spoke of in this county'.[57] There were competing attitudes at work even behind those graves and funerals which departed from social norms. The status of aristocrat or gentry was made all the more manifest in humble or gruesome grave markers by its apparently deliberate denial. Their distinctiveness drew attention. In the late medieval context of more frequent burial within churches, in which benefactors – now from a range of social 'classes' – clamoured for attention from their graves and from the fixtures and fabric of the church, distinctiveness was a desirable quality in post-mortem commemoration, as a social statement as well as a penitential necessity. Even double tombs with cadaver effigies, for all their eschatalogical message, did not entirely reject the things of this world: they were particularly fashionable in the first half of fifteenth-century England among high-ranking clerics and laymen who identified their connections with the Lancastrian royal court with stone badges on their tombs.[58] The stone corpse betrays an ambivalent attitude to death: it is a sharp reminder of mortality for even the most powerful, but a reminder too of social division even in death.

(vi) The Black Death: Attitudes to Plague

How were these attitudes and practices affected by the Black Death? So many were killed in the first visitation, let alone subsequent ones, that there seem to be *a priori* grounds for arguing that plague must have had a profound and long-term effect on attitudes to mortality. Reactions to plague could of course differ; and according to Boccaccio in *The Decameron* these ranged from a desire for withdrawal from society, or a careful moderation in behaviour, through to excessive hedonism in an effort to forget its menace. Whatever the reaction, the threat of death must have been ubiquitous. But the impact of plague on late medieval mentalities may have been more far reaching as a result of its indirect effects on socio-economic conditions. Changes in wealth and social conditions after 1348 also affected religious practice. Yet we have already seen over the whole period that there was significant continuity in attitudes to death and in penitential strategies adopted by lay people, especially from the thirteenth century onwards. In any assessment of the effects of plague on religion, such continuity may be of greater significance than any change after 1348.

Huizinga's characterization of late medieval attitudes to death as morbidly obsessive had the background and stimulus of the Black Death in mind. The notion that plague was a consequence of divine wrath at human sin certainly provoked some apocalyptic reactions, and to one London preacher in 1388 pestilence was a sign that the end of the world was nigh. It is true that representations of the Three Living and Three Dead and of the Dance of Death, even if they precede the advent of plague, seem to become more numerous thereafter. Some of the more gruesome portrayals of death may even have been prompted by the threat of plague. John Lydgate's poem (c.1440) inspired by the Dance of Death at St Paul's makes specific reference to death slaying me 'by the stroke of pestilence'.[59] The vision which so terrified Edmund Leversedge in 1465 was brought on by 'the plague of pestilence' which had turned his face as black as coal and his tongue as black as pitch.

However, too much can be made of post-plague morbidity. Gloomy representations of death are few; so too are direct allusions to plague as inspiration for spiritual thought. Cadaver tombs – which for Huizinga provided further evidence of morbid obsession – do not appear in England until half a century after plague first struck; nor do they direct attention solely towards bodily decay. As we have seen, the contemplation of 'death' (as of the Apocalypse) had enjoyed a much longer tradition, and within it, the attention of reader and spectator was steered not towards corporeal death but towards the ultimate fate of the soul on its journey to the Last Judgment and the promise of salvation.

There were other ways in which plague had a more profound effect on mentality. Its initial appearance heightened an awareness of sin among some. A few towns in continental Europe witnessed processions of flagellants who, in their effort to assuage the wrath of God made manifest through plague, whipped their naked torsos until the blood ran. Their presence was less welcome in England: a group of flagellants from the Low Countries who appeared in London in 1349 were treated with curiosity and faint disapproval. English bishops sought divine reprieve from plague by more measured encouragement of prayers, processions and masses, and by denunciation of sacrilegious behaviour.[60] The emphasis placed in the later fourteenth century by Archbishop Thoresby of York, among others, on catechetical and penitential instruction of clergy and laity might also be placed in the context of conditions brought

about by plague. Since death might indeed strike at any time, it was all
the more imperative to take precautionary measures. It is this thought
that lies behind *The Book of the Craft of Dying* which adds an introspective
depth to the traditionally monastic theme of instruction on how to
die well.

A mood of introspection is apparent in other contexts. Perhaps the
burgeoning of mystical literature in the later fourteenth century was
partly the result of plague. Julian of Norwich in 1373 celebrated the 'gift
of bodily sickness' which prompted her deathbed visions of Christ.[61]
Perhaps the more dour requests in some wills just after this period were
the product of a sharper sense of sin. Sir Thomas Broke, he of the 'foul
carrion', also declared himself a 'wretched sinner' whose soul was equally
'unclean'. But the connection between plague and either mysticism or
introspection is not made explicitly, while other impulses also stimulated
introspective devotion – which in any case may be observed directly only
among the literate few (see Chapters 2: iv; 6: iii).

As for the many, other conclusions might be drawn from the more
abundant evidence for penitential good works. Was the urge to go on
pilgrimage sharpened by plague? One chronicler in Ireland believed that
fear of pestilence prompted thousands to go on pilgrimage.[62] No such
chronicle references can be found for England, but other sources, like
the financial accounts at major shrines, are suggestive of this. Increased
offerings at St Thomas's shrine at Canterbury or St Etheldreda's at Ely,
have been interpreted as indicating an upsurge in pilgrimage after the
Black Death.[63] The numbers appearing at these shrines are unclear:
the sums collected do not tell us whether more people were attending
these shrines or were offering more when they arrived – or why they
went. So do these inflated sums reflect the collective response of people
threatened by imminent and arbitrary death? Or did survivors of plague
simply have more to spend? If the impulse to go on pilgrimage in these
decades was indeed prompted by plague, the response was not immediate. The survival of these accounts is patchy, and they might even suggest
that the real increase (for instance at St William's shrine at Norwich or
St Hugh's at Lincoln) occurred in the 1360s. Perhaps the second major
visitation of plague (1361) was more a trigger for this upsurge. Whatever
the case, the increased sums collected at these shrines were not sustained
after the 1370s. The long-term effect of plague seems to have left
unaltered the pattern of pilgrimage at least to these shrines.

What was the effect of plague on other kinds of penitential good
works? The fear of imminent death following in the wake of plague may

have sharpened a concern to ensure that post-mortem commemoration was in place. There was also the threat of inadequate provision for the soul – and body – after death. The major visitations of plague caused so many to die that mass burials had sometimes proved necessary: perhaps this also intensified an urge to ensure proper burial and individualized commemoration. Such a change has been identified in some North Italian towns.[64] The shift in testamentary practice – particularly after the shock of a second visitation of plague in 1363 – towards specifying the site of burial, demanding clear identification of the grave-site, towards more lavish funerals, towards narrower and targeted benefaction and away from 'scattered' bequests, might indeed point to a sharpened desire among testators to keep their memory after death more prominent in the minds of the living. Is post-Black-Death piety best described as a 'cult of remembrance'?

(vii) The 'Cult of Remembrance'

The desire for individualized commemoration might be discerned in England too. Testamentary evidence before the Black Death is not so abundant, but in some towns testators do seem to be more specific about the place of their burial from the mid-fourteenth century. In Salisbury, especially after 1361, not only did more citizens specify their place of burial but more asked for burial inside the church rather than in the cemetery. An increasing number of testators made detailed and lavish bequests by the 1400s.[65] The wills of gentry, in different parts of the country, seem to demand more lavish funerals – which may also explain the reactive request of some gentry (like Sir Thomas Broke) for more humble arrangements.[66] As for more long-term commemoration, some places do show greater provision of perpetual chantries. Such was the case at Gloucester, Reading or Norwich in the later fourteenth century.[67]

Membership of guilds had been one way to ensure a decent send off or commemoration, and in some areas the number of guilds do appear to have increased after the mid-fourteenth century. In London, the number of parish fraternities had risen dramatically by 1400. A similar trend seems true of towns like Bridport and Salisbury, and of the more rural regions of Cambridgeshire and Yorkshire. The frequency of reference to burial of dead members in the returns made to the Crown in the inquiry of 1389, might suggest a heightened concern for decent burial following the arrival of plague.

On the other hand, some of the evidence for a 'cult of remembrance' after the Black Death is more equivocal. Guild returns in 1389 only occasionally mention plague explicitly in the explanations for their foundation, and even then fear of anonymous burial is less important than concern at neglect of buildings or services. The Corpus Christi guild at Lynn claimed that the inspiration behind its foundation had been the sorry sight of the Host being carried through the town preceded by a solitary candle after the visitation of plague.[68] 'Extravagant' post-mortem commemoration of other kinds does not always seem to be timed with the appearance of plague. In Salisbury greater expenditure on funerals, anniversaries and temporary chantries occurs in the early 1400s rather than after major outbreaks of plague; so too, it seems, in Hull, Norwich and London. Evidence for perpetual chantry foundation is more ambivalent still. The number of licenses bought for chantries permitted under the Statute of Mortmain actually peaked in the 1330s.[69] Perhaps this means little: by the fifteenth century, many chantries were founded in a way which avoided the need for a license (making the number of mortmain licenses unrepresentative of the true level of foundation). But in some places where other evidence is also available, the effect of plague does not seem marked. There were no more perpetual chantries founded in Salisbury, Hull or Colchester after the Black Death than before; and fewer were founded in Bristol's churches in the late fourteenth century than previously.

There are other explanations besides attitudes produced by plague for these trends and differences. Endowments for chantries required property and wealth, but in the fourteenth century, rent from land in town and countryside was declining before, and more sharply after, the Black Death. Many a religious house struggled to maintain its incomes: the fear that a chantry endowment might become subsumed into the general and shrinking fund of the house may have been one reason why fewer were entrusted to the religious from the fourteenth century onwards. Fewer chantries were founded in certain rural areas: in Berkshire most of the perpetual chantries founded in parish churches before the Black Death occur in the rural parts of the county. Few were founded in these regions thereafter. Within larger towns, the endowments of chantries founded before the Black Death often needed shoring up during the fifteenth century.

On the other hand, economic conditions were improving in some places. In Berkshire it is not surprising to find a shift in perpetual chantry foundation after the Black Death from the rural regions to the flourishing towns of Reading and Newbury where more chantries were founded than ever before. The fortunes made by certain merchants were channelled into post-mortem commemoration. The city of Salisbury in particular profited from the wealth generated by the cloth trade in the early years of the fifteenth century: citizens continued to sow a respectable crop of perpetual chantries, and more striking are their efforts in rebuilding parish churches, and in founding a growing number of guilds. Membership of guilds depended upon the ability to pay the entrance fee and annual subscription, and in London increasing wages after the Black Death allowed more 'middling' Londoners (craftsmen and artisans) to found or join guilds. Surpluses of wealth accumulated by the upper strata of peasants might explain the apparent increase in guilds in rural Cambridgeshire from the 1370s.

Socio-economic conditions after the mid-fourteenth century, then, had their effect on *post-obit* commemoration. Plague may have been important in creating these conditions, even if these varied from region to region. But it may also have had an indirect effect on a further phenomenon. In many areas – whether flourishing or declining – religious associations run by the laity seem to become wealthier. Town governments, with their own religious fraternities, acquired more property. In late fourteenth-century towns across England – from Bath to Beverley, Wells to York, Salisbury to Colchester – gifts, bequests or acquisitions of rents by town corporations or councils were increasing. More vacant properties and the decreased profitability of rents may have allowed town corporations to step into holdings of individual townsmen who were heirless or who were reluctant to acquire more tenements. But many gifts of rents came with requests for anniversary services. Town governments (for instance at Bridport or Hartlepool) were also active in restructuring chantry and guild arrangements within town parishes. Some of this activity can be associated with efforts to increase the corporate power of town government – particularly in towns seeking to assert independence from a dominating landowner. But the more general accumulation of land by town governing bodies was also the result of a willingness to entrust property to institutions which could be relied upon to provide services for the dead.

Other kinds of guilds were becoming wealthier. If guilds were proliferating in the two decades before the 1389 inquiry, their endowments are likely to have been increasing too – an accumulation perhaps concealed by the reluctance of guilds to admit to the possession of property which might have seemed under threat of royal confiscation. A similar accumulation may also have occurred within parishes, at least those within more urbanized contexts. Here the accumulation of property is difficult to document, because so few churchwardens' accounts predate the outbreak of plague. But the annual rents belonging to the parish of St Michael's in Bath, at any rate, increased from less than half a pound in 1349 to over £4 by 1364, to over £6 by 1369 (increasing again in the early 1400s, before flattening out during the rest of the fifteenth century). If such a pattern is more general, it may be one further explanation why more parishes – at least in the more urbanized areas – were able to fund more elaborate ceremonies in the later Middle Ages (see Chapter 3: iv). The wealth of parish and town governments by the late fourteenth century is one explanation for the increasing expenditure on the 'ritual year'. More striking than any growth of individualized 'cult of remembrance' after the Black Death, is the growth of corporate regimes of *post-obit* commemoration, subject to the control of lay people and concentrated in guilds and parishes.

(viii) Ceremony, Social Change and the Poor

The accumulation of endowments may well indicate continuity rather than change: the collective desire to ensure intercession for souls had been stimulated by doctrines of penance and Purgatory which had long pre-dated plague. But it is also expressive of social anxieties.[70] The Black Death caused (or accentuated) changes with disturbing social implications. The foundation of guilds or the spending of surplus wealth may not be signs of confidence: social mobility in post-plague years, and immigration into some towns, may have reinforced a need to recreate a sense of family within a fraternity structure. Social disruption also threatened established hierarchy, breeding a widespread fear of social mobility even within towns which did not suffer economic decline. The royal inquiry into guilds from 1388 was part of a wider concern with collective lay activity, especially in the wake of the Peasants' Revolt (1381).

In both town and countryside guilds were identified, more often than not, with local ruling groups, and in ways which became more accentuated from the late fourteenth century. The growing landed wealth of guilds of urban patriciates was one facet of the increasing assertion of oligarchical control over many towns, and an expression too of the perceived threats to such control. Some (like the St George guild at Norwich) attempted to make their social composition more exclusive, and to assert greater control over craft guilds (see Introduction: iv).

The oligarchical character of guild life was accentuated in places (such as York) where craft guilds took over other devotional fraternities, or where a particular parish guild came to dominate all others. At Salisbury, in both the two main parishes in the late fifteenth century, a Jesus guild came to supplant all others and was run by a group whose ties with the civic elite were such that wardenship of the guild often led to wardenship of the parish, mastership of a craft guild and even mayoralty of the whole city. In many parishes, office-holding seems to have become more oligarchical.[71]

The elaboration of ceremony in parish and town was another consequence of the same social pressures. By the late fourteenth century, civic authorities (as at York and Coventry) had taken over processions of the Host, on Corpus Christi day, from ecclesiastical bodies within the town.[72] An idealized representation of civic society was constructed around the unifying presence of Christ's body: the processional order sanctified hierarchy by excluding the majority of city-dwellers, ranking craft guilds (some with their own pageants) in order, and placing the civic aldermen closest to the Host. But the civic procession did not always represent consensus: it reflected the forces of fragmentation as well as unity within the late medieval city. It enshrined the division of labour along craft guild lines, and these did not always submit to the prescribed civic order. Craft guilds could upset carefully calibrated hierarchies by challenging their place within them, while the pageants they put on could express their own group identity above that of the communal whole. Even powerful individuals might be able to use the procession as a forum to inscribe their social standing within the 'community'. In 1417 the York town council permitted plays put on by craft guilds during the Corpus Christi procession to be stationed before the houses of individuals who had paid for them – a contentious issue since some of them had already been suspected of profiteering.

Civic elites were also beset by divisions within their own social group. The closing of oligarchical ranks could be threatened by faction (see Introduction: iv). Even processions might reflect divisions within the body of aldermen. The Norwich merchant John Gladman apparently exploited the customary Shrovetide procession in 1443, riding through the town dressed as a 'king' to voice complaint in a dispute with the local priory which had caused factional tension among members of the dominant St George guild.[73] The rules of many top-ranking guilds in the fifteenth century evince a deep concern with unity and amity among their members. Social respectability might help to guarantee the civic order, and concern to uphold moral standards is evident both in guild rules and in more general civic regulation. Just as city governors sought to curb foul-mouthed behaviour or even adultery within their own religious guilds, so they legislated more frequently in the fifteenth century on behaviour in taverns, gambling and prostitution within the town.[74] In this process, the respectable urban 'household' was thought to have an increasingly important part to play.[75]

Socially restrictive legislation (as always) fell hardest on the dispossessed. Social upheaval in the later fourteenth century, whether as a direct result of plague or not, heightened sensitivities in the late fourteenth century to any activity which seemed to threaten the social order. Legislatory restriction on social mobility was reflected in suspicion of any movement by the lower orders, even as pilgrims.[76] Churchwardens appear as authoritarian figures, enforcing moral standards (in visitations) and social conformity. Attitudes to the poor may have hardened, although when precisely this happened is disputed. Some historians have argued that it was already present by the late fourteenth century: such was the perceived menace of the pauper by then that charitable giving assumed a more discriminatory guise; hospitals were founded with less frequency and admitted a more 'respectable' and local poor instead of vagrants; increasingly testators were less inclined to regard the poor as objects of charity in their own right than as liturgical appendages, tied into the 'cult of remembrance' of which more 'flamboyant' funerals were a part.[77] In fact evidence for this shift in attitude is not clear-cut, nor does it appear to have been immediate (or even entirely new). Foundation of smaller almshouses flourished in some places.[78] But it does seem that restrictions on the 'poor', and distinctions between 'deserving' and 'undeserving' poor, were sharper by the later fifteenth century. These restrictions formed part of a wider effort by the corporate regimes of towns, guilds and parishes to assert their authority – secular, religious and moral.[79]

(ix) Conclusion

The doctrines of penance and Purgatory developed within a universal Church had a profound impact on the laity. The proliferating strategies for the navigation of the soul through the afterlife greatly affected the character of religious life at a local level. By the later Middle Ages the reciprocal relationship between the living and the dead was stronger than ever, and in ways which encouraged corporate religious practices.

These practices were also accommodated into local society and under lay control: the relative shift away from benefaction of religious houses towards endowment of parishes and guilds, over which lay supervision was closest, had broken the monastic monopoly of *post-obit* intercession.

The strategies developed to deal with the afterlife were not fundamentally altered by the Black Death and subsequent plagues. In many ways they followed the patterns developed before the mid-fourteenth century and were inspired by the same penitential motives, though the threat of plague may have accentuated the desire to cultivate forms of remembrance which would ensure continued prayers and suffrage. Moreover, if (in some regions) more guilds or chantries were founded after plague struck, then such efforts seem to suggest confidence in an ability to make sound provision for the soul rather than the existence of a passive and morbid pessimism.

These long-term changes were partly the result of a concerted ecclesiastical effort, predating the Black Death, to Christianize lay society more thoroughly. But lay supervision of penitential strategies also meant that changes and tensions within society made their impact all the more forcibly on these religious practices. Social divisions projected themselves on to Purgatory itself; the strategies which helped reduce time spent in its cleansing flames were adapted to forms which allowed due expression of social status. Graves for the body or provision for the soul could become markers of social standing. Death was not the great leveller at all: it marked out the contours of social inequality – all the more so by the late fourteenth century when fears were sharpened (as an indirect consequence of continuing plague) that these contours were being eroded. The development of processions in towns, and perhaps too the expansion of festival at the parish level from the same period, were in part a response by civic and parish elites to the pressures of social upheaval.

It would be misleading to conclude that late medieval religion and strategies for the afterlife were merely tools wielded by those who held power. The civic order was readily contested, and within religious ceremony. In any case the requirement to perform penances was inherently corrosive of social pretension. It was a commonplace that the weight of sin bore down more heavily on the wealthy and powerful; and hostile reactions to flamboyant funerals or to 'proud stones' above graves were recognitions that lavish penance mattered little if inner contrition were absent. Ultimately, late medieval attitudes to death and the practices developed to deal with it were complex and not easily appropriated by the powerful. By the later Middle Ages, we can discern a confidence in the ability to navigate through the afterlife; a concern to ensure remembrance both for the soul in Purgatory and for earthly status; anxiety to stabilize social hierarchy in corporate penitential practices; but ambivalence too towards their proliferation and social implications.

Chapter 6:   Reforming the 'Inner' Life: Orthodoxy and Heresy

At the heart of reforming movements within the Church in the late eleventh and twelfth centuries had been a concern to deepen an understanding of the Christian faith within the 'community of the faithful' (see Chapter 2). The broader effort to encourage outward conformity to the requirements of corporate worship was an integral part of pastoral attention directed towards the cultivation of the inner life of the soul. Indeed, the one could complement the other. The implied distinction between 'outer' and 'inner', 'corporate' and 'personal' forms of devotion, can be misleading: attendance at mass or participation in a liturgical procession, for instance, would ideally create devotional experiences nourishing for the soul. But churchmen by the twelfth century had placed increasing stress on the need to examine conscience; while the search for fuller 'religious' life, in imitation of Christ and the apostles, made the performance of occasional devotional acts seem only the starting point for living a true Christian life. A fuller devotional life may once have been restricted to the cloistered, but from the thirteenth century in particular, there was an increasing number of ways in which lay people might also develop a more 'religious' or apostolic life, in imitation of the life of Christ. The growing number and variety of books acting as guides to develop inner devotion had meant that the contemplative life might be accessible to lay people. The life of 'Mary' (contemplation) was potentially open to the laity; the life of 'Martha' (action) was potentially valuable for its spiritual possibilities: the 'mixed life', advocated in a wide variety of devotional texts from the late fourteenth century onwards, allowed the laity to combine contemplation with an active life in the world.

Such were the ideals; their translation into practice is the subject of this chapter. As we shall see, the process raised more problems than it solved. The idea of allowing the laity access to a more contemplative life troubled and divided some churchmen. Moreover, the interpretation of 'apostolic' or contemplative ideals in society could not be entirely controlled: lay people constituted neither a passive nor a uniform audience, and their responses to ideals were altered by variables such as social status and gender. In any case ideals were inherently unstable. Calls for inner spiritual renewal, in imitation of Christ or the life of the apostles, invited comparison with 'outer' contemporary practice, and perhaps criticism of the Church itself. At what point did criticism become heresy? From the later fourteenth century these problems became more pressing. A demanding and literate laity is increasingly in evidence; under the inspiration of John Wyclif, a new heresy, Lollardy, was reckoned to have appeared in England. The response was persecution.

The connections between literacy, heresy and persecution need careful exploration. For one thing, 'heresy' is not easily defined, nor is it easily distinguished from 'orthodoxy'. In some senses, heresy needs persecution to exist at all. 'Heretics' do not usually regard themselves as 'heretics': they are more accurately defined as dissidents or nonconformists who acquire the pejorative label of 'heretics' from persecutors. Whether they acquire the label or not might also depend on circumstance. So the appearance of a new 'heresy' in England needs to be placed in a wider context, both of trends within 'orthodoxy' and of concerns which generated a heightened need to identify and label a new sect of 'heretics'.

This need is more evident in the fifteenth century than before, and some recent historians commenting on the period have emphasized the persecutory nature of English society: the lines between 'heresy' and 'orthodoxy' were more sharply drawn; men and women attempting to live out contemplative or devotionally more intense lives were liable to find themselves whisked smartly into courtrooms. But these views can be questioned. As one fifteenth-century text, *The Book of Margery Kempe*, demonstrates, experimentation and reinterpretation of the ideal spiritual life lived in the world, was still possible – even if attitudes towards it were ambivalent and contentious.

(i) The 'Inner' Life and the Laity c.1100–1400

In many ways the increasing quantity and variety of instructional literature was the product of clerical initiative and pastoral reform. But they were also the product of lay demand, fuelled by rising levels of lay literacy. The term 'literacy' covers a wide range of meanings (as we shall see), but it is evident that devotional texts were acquiring a wider audience. Psalters and books of hours, first owned by the higher nobility, began to appear in the hands of the gentry, and by the end of the fourteenth century in those of the wealthier townspeople. Such an audience, moreover, was not a passive one. Patrons influenced the content of devotional texts. Collections of particular saints' Lives, like those of the Campsey manuscript, produced for Isabella, countess of Arundel, in the late thirteenth century, reflected the devotional interests of their patrons. Psalters and books of hours could be personalized by the addition of prayers, saints and images which reflected their own tastes and concerns. The Luttrell psalter, written and illuminated in the 1330s, was not thrust on to a grudging layman by a confessor: 'The Lord Geoffrey Luttrell caused me to be made' proclaims an inscription accompanying the image of a fully armoured mounted knight. The countess of Derby in the late fourteenth century introduced select prayers into her father's psalter which show the influence of Richard Rolle.[1]

By the later Middle Ages, the literature which encouraged inner reflection was not all 'officially' promoted. Walter Hilton's *Epistle* and Nicholas Love's *Myrrour* received the seal of episcopal approval, yet much of this kind of literature, unlike the catechetical and penitential instruction of the twelfth and thirteenth century, was not turned out by reforming churchmen anxious to impose a certain kind of religious behaviour on the laity. Instead much of it was produced for lay people on their command, and by a wide variety of clerics – confessors, canons, friars and hermits.[2] The diffuse provenance of these texts made for diffuse interpretation of contemplative ideals.

By the fourteenth century some lay people were also writing texts for themselves. Henry of Grosmont, earl of Derby, composed his own examination of conscience. The threat of the seven deadly sins in his *Livre de Seyntz Medicines* (*c*.1354) is made vividly appropriate to his military and aristocratic background: sins attack the soul as deadly foes a fortress; they lurk as foxes in their holes on a lord's estate. Sir John Clanvowe, a knight in Richard II's chamber (d.1391), wrote a more introspective tract *Of the Two Ways*, contrasting the narrow way of inner truth with the broad way of the world and its 'foul stinking muck' of transient riches.[3]

Such works might indeed suggest that the pastoral efforts of the Church had come to fruition: laymen internalizing the spiritual emphases of the cloistered. Clanvowe's introspection followed a monastic line of thought and a wider clerical concern to carve the Christian message more deeply upon the individual soul. As one of Clanvowe's clerical contemporaries, Walter Hilton, put it: 'the more I sleep from outward things, the more wakeful I am in knowing Jesus and of inward things'.[4] Yet there were inherent tensions contained within the pastoral concern to promote self-help for the soul. What was the balance between interior meditation and the exterior requirement of priestly mediation? The monastic withdrawal from the world of 'outer things' had always implied a sense of the world as corrupt. Confessional literature – sermons, manuals for priests or penitents – encouraged examination of conscience with a rhetoric which also emphasized the dangers and falseness of outer things.

The world of outer things might also include the Church and clergy: the same confessional literature warned the priest against clerical abuses. Richard Rolle and Walter Hilton did not rail against the clergy; but their emphasis on the inner life implicitly increased their readers' responsibility for their own souls and reduced lay dependence on ecclesiastical structures. The author of the *Book to a Mother* (written in the 1370s) extended his condemnation of society to include the outer Church, and went further by implying that the true Church comprised all those who would be saved.[5] Clanvowe's *Of the Two Ways* has little to say about the visible Church's role in the process of salvation. Emphasis on the inner life, however monastic and clerical in origin, might lead to a denial for any need of priestly mediation. *Of the Two Ways* does not go so far, but it begins almost as a preacher would a sermon, and its lay author was rumoured, as we shall see, to be a heretic. The cultivation of the inner life could take some disturbing directions.

(ii) Social Status and Gender c.1100–1400

The emphasis on inner devotion was one part of a more spiritually intense life. Lay people (unless they became hermits) could not be expected to partake fully of the 'monastic' life of self-denial or of the 'apostolic' life of preaching and 'poverty', stressed in reforming currents of the twelfth and thirteenth centuries. Yet there were ways in which they might share in these ideals, by meditating on the life of Christ or outwardly expressing their adoption of a more 'religious' life – for instance in dress, regime of devotion, or perhaps by a vow of chastity. But such ideals were not uniformly laid down, and there might be great variety in their interpretation.

To begin with, constructions of the ideal life for women were different from those of men. 'Estates' theory, after all, tended to make gendered distinctions (see Introduction: iii); and while the threefold hierarchy of the flesh was not gender-specific, the faithful wife figured prominently in manuals of conduct, and in the exemplary literature of female saints' lives, virginity was the ideal most emphasized for women – even married women. Virgin martyrs loom large in the late thirteenth-century collection assembled for Isabella, countess of Arundel.[6]

Such theories and ideals were no doubt constraining on women. They smack of patriarchal containment and scrutiny. Just as rules on the enclosure of religious women became more tightly defined during the twelfth century, ideals of female piety prescribed for lay women were more limited than they were for men (see Chapter 2: vi). Ideal types of lay women lived lives framed by their households, and were closely connected with religious houses: Beatrice de Say, sister of Earl Geoffrey de Mandeville, described as a 'model among women', was a frequent visitor of the monks at Walden whom she called her sons, and from her house at Rickling (Essex), five miles from the abbey, she fed the hungry and visited the sick.[7] Others had suitable instructional works conveyed from monastic house to their households. Such (apparent) constraint arose in part from misogyny: the frequent association of women with the 'body' and its fleshly fluidity – in contrast to the more male 'spirit' – made containment of women all the more necessary.

On the other hand, to follow the influential arguments of Caroline Bynum, the association of women with the 'body' was not necessarily negative: it might even allow them a closer identification with the body of Christ than was possible for men, especially because Christ's humanity came from his mother and because his body did 'womanly' things, bleeding on the cross and nourishing the faithful through the Eucharist.[8] The affective spirituality focused on the humanity of Christ was not restricted to women, and its language had been developed particularly by the Cistercians in the twelfth century. But certain practices of female mystics were peculiar to women: some of them (like Mary of Oignies d.1213 at Liège) experienced divine visions through frequent consumption of the body of Christ while penitentially starving their own bodies of other food.

Such practices could not be expected of lay women, and in England they are absent even amongst the religious. English women apparently missed out on the so-called 'golden age' of female mysticism experienced on the continent (particularly in 'beguinages', collective houses of semi-religious women) in the thirteenth and early fourteenth centuries.

On the other hand, 'golden-age' practices which allowed the bodies of Eucharist-consuming women to dissolve and disappear served other agenda: Jacques de Vitry who applauded the disintegration of Mary of Oignies' flesh in the Life he wrote of her, could confirm thereby the integrity and power of the body of Christ, consecrated by the priesthood, which she had consumed.[9] Texts which seem to bring us closer to the 'experience' of female spirituality, often bring us closer instead to the anxieties of clergymen who wrote them. In any case, the differences between England and the Continent can be overdrawn. There was certainly an interest, judging from the countess of Arundel's collection, in the lives of contemporary continental 'saints' and an interest too in visions. There were no 'beguinages' founded in England, yet types of religious life were available – evident in the connections and exchanges, personal and textual, between lay households, anchorages and nunneries – that allowed aristocratic women to share in devotional concerns similar to those on the Continent.[10] The *Ancrene Wisse* in the early thirteenth century speaks of a 'community' of solitary anchoresses who had spread throughout England, and the spiritual guidance it offered was adaptable for women (and men) in the household.[11]

The narrower range of spiritual practices prescribed for women was less constraining than at first might appear. Enclosure contains, but it also creates space and autonomy; prescribed ideals confine, but they might not be interpreted along authorized lines. The ideal of virginity could be read in various ways. Virgin martyrs were evidently troublesome role models for clerical commentators: some felt the need to comment that St Katherine's outspoken behaviour against authority was not to be taken literally.[12] Lives of penitent women or mothers, accorded honorary virginity, were models which might well have appealed to the mother or widow who commissioned them: perhaps Countess Isabella found in the Life she owned of Mary Magdalen an ideal which valorized her single status against potentially enforced remarriage. There were other more positive and accessible models for laywomen: Bozon's life of Martha in the late thirteenth century suggested an ideal of active holiness, asceticism and chastity outside enclosure, and one which did not have to end in martyrdom.[13]

Whether enclosed in religious houses or monitored within secular households, women did not have to live solitary lives. The spaces they occupied could be communal; and the household of an aristocratic lady was one in which a 'female subculture', nourished by exterior contact with anchoresses and religious houses, could be allowed to thrive.[14] Yet if such a subculture existed, it was one permeated by concerns other than those generated by gender, and concerns that overrode gender distinctions. Lives of redoubtable virgin martyrs who resisted pagan demands on their person or property suited an ecclesiastical agenda of resistance to secular interference, as much as they might a widow resisting remarriage. Moreover, gender could be constructed differently depending on social position. Saints' Lives owned by high-ranking women reflected aristocratic concerns, resonating with their social status rather than gender. As an aristocrat Countess Isabella would have found parts of her Life of St Modwenna disturbingly instructive. In one episode certain rebellious villeins are punished and killed. But after death the rebels are seen carrying their own coffins and changing shape into animals; their bodies have to be disinterred, their hearts cut out and burned until dusk. Even then the seigneurial nightmare continues: a black crow flies up from the ashes.[15]

Fearful attitudes towards the lower orders are a reminder that devotional contemplation might acquire connotations of social exclusiveness. Moreover, the categories of gender could also be employed to construct barriers of social exclusion, thus complicating certain stereotypes of gender identity. The association of women with 'the body' was frequent but not entirely exclusive. Some theologians and authorities in the thirteenth and early fourteenth centuries could associate male beggars with female prostitutes: both deceived the respectable by distorting the appearance of their bodies (in the beggars' case to avoid work) and by putting their bodies on the 'market'.[16]

These views tended towards the support of the social order. Yet ideals to which elites aspired did not always do so. Just as the devotional concerns of aristocratic women could undermine misogyny, so those of men and women might subvert other hierarchies. Ideals which encompassed austerity and even 'poverty' based on the life of Christ, pointed to attitudes which directly undercut the trappings of aristocratic living. Perhaps a Grosmont or Clanvowe felt these inherent contradictions. Instructional literature had indeed encouraged clergy and laity to seek them out. How far these contradictions were even more evident to those outside an aristocratic elite is hard to say, but perhaps even 'illiterate' rustics by the fourteenth century were familiar with ideals of reform and renewal. The peasants who rebelled in 1381 seem to use the language of homily, psalter and liturgy. One of them, a Jack Trewman, is reported to have made moral criticisms of English society: 'falseness and guile have reigned too long…falseness reigns in every flock'.[17] These were terms long emphasized in confessional instruction, as well as in more contemporary literature.

There were then uncomfortable social implications in such ideals – even in some which seemed to support social hierarchy and patriarchy. But the social dimension of these ideals, contained in texts, raises another question: how far was their influence restricted by levels of literacy?

(iii) Literacy and the Vernacular c.1100–1409

Undoubtedly, levels of literacy were increasing during the period, especially by the fourteenth century with the appearance of schools in which a wider group of lay people could receive a basic education.[18] The broadening social base of literacy no doubt helped drive a demand for devotional instruction – a demand also suggested by the gradual reappearance of works in the vernacular, first in French or Anglo-Norman, the language of the elite after the Conquest. This elite had other reading material – like *chansons de geste* – of a more secular nature, and some devotional or instructional texts (like the Beaulieu sermon – see Chapter 2: iv) adopted their forms, perhaps to make their message more accessible. Accessibility appealed to a reformer like Bishop Grosseteste (d.1253): the faithful needed to learn their prayers in the vernacular, while instructional texts needed to be understood to be widely disseminated. From the thirteenth century, especially from c.1300, religious works appear in Middle English, the language of the lower (and increasingly the upper ranks) of society. By the mid-fourteenth century a Richard Rolle or a Walter Hilton could still compose works in Latin, but their vernacular writings suggest an awareness of a wider audience.

Relatively few lay people, even by the later Middle Ages, were literate enough to read devotional works for themselves. Yet this deficiency need not have excluded the illiterate from the spirituality encouraged within these works. 'Literacy' is a term which can encompass a wider range of abilities, and literacy of a 'pragmatic' or more passive kind can be found among a broader spectrum of lay people, including the peasantry.[19] The impact of literacy, increasingly important for instance in government even at local levels, meant that those still illiterate were involved and influenced by literate culture. In any case the distinction between literate and oral or visual cultures can be overdrawn. Books were written explicitly to be read out loud; sermons were read as well as preached. Devotional works might urge the visualization of images or include them alongside texts. The fluidity between image and word, written and spoken, tended to break down any sharp distinction between a 'literate' elite and 'illiterate masses'. It is no surprise therefore to find 'peasants' in 1381 familiar with the language of homily and psalter.

Nevertheless, literacy – variously defined – could be used in the construction of difference. If, during the fourteenth century, a more complete literacy was within the reach of people below the rank of aristocrat or gentleman, a sense of literacy remained a mark of social exclusiveness and a tool for social exclusion. An aristocrat might occasionally decry the possession of books by socially inferior merchants – whose acquisition of psalters or lives of saints (such as the socially elevated St Katherine) confirmed their own participation in 'aristocratic' culture.[20] Literacy marked them out too from the peasantry who wished to subvert the social order. The 'peasants' who rebelled in 1381, although 'pragmatically' literate and evidently versed in homiletic language, were constructed by those in authority as being hostile to all literate culture. According to Walsingham, monk of St Albans, an ink-well was enough to invite murderous violence on its owner by rebels who were more animal in their behaviour than human.[21]

Literacy also informed gender distinctions in several different contexts. Devotional reading was considered more appropriate for women than for men: by the fourteenth century images of the Virgin Mary or St Anne with book in hand begin to appear, without a corresponding male equivalent. Yet reading by women, defined innately as the more impressionable sex, was also deemed to require more careful scrutiny. The existence of a female readership might be put forward as a pretext for translation into the vernacular in the interests of pastoral welfare; the vernacular itself acquired gendered associations (positive and negative) when described as the 'mother tongue'.[22]

Here we encounter the concerns of the Church hierarchy about literacy and the vernacular. Literacy also marked out potential differences between clergy and laity. Traditionally, the 'literate lay person' was a contradiction in terms, for the Church had enjoyed a monopoly of literacy which was in any case equated with a knowledge of Latin. The thrust of pastoral reform from the later twelfth century, however, was towards the greater dissemination and deepening of the Christian message: rising lay literacy in the vernacular was an opportunity for churchmen wishing to lay down catechetical syllabuses or devotional instruction, and the flourishing of devotional texts in Middle English in the late fourteenth century suggests a Church hierarchy prepared to accommodate the

growing demands of the laity. Yet the use of the vernacular raised troubling questions: how appropriate was it for the moralizing on clerical
abuses in Latin instructional texts to appear in the vernacular before a
wider lay audience? And how much religious knowledge was a literate lay
person required to know? Archbishop Pecham had laid down a catechetical syllabus in 1281; and although his minimum was not necessarily
a maximum, there remained a clerical perception that the vernacular lay
reader was too naive to understand more. Even if it did not correspond
to social reality, the perception persisted that the layman's 'book' was the
image not the written word. Texts like the Northern Homily which seem
to encourage reading in the vernacular did not advocate lay people reading for themselves. What indeed was the use of casting religious pearls
before lay swine? Those lay people, on the other hand, who did presume
to know more, might be labelled simply as lustful for knowledge. By the
later fourteenth century, such lay presumption was thought by some clerics to be increasing. John Mirk wished to equip the parish priest against
awkward questions from 'lewed men which be of many words and proud
of their wit'.[23]

Concern about how much religious knowledge the laity should know,
and in what form, crystallized around a more central question: what
access should lay people have to the Bible? Debate on the matter at
Oxford around 1401–07 showed that some conservative theologians were
fearful of the social consequences of biblical translation.[24] Dissemination
of scripture in the vernacular, unmediated and unglossed, would
inevitably lead to error, where normal social structures would be turned
on their head. Lay people – women and rustics no less – would presume
to teach what they were ill-equipped even to learn. Here again we meet
gender and social distinctions used to buttress clerical fears of lay learning; and a little later, Hoccleve was to equate heresy with the habits of
female readers whose mental deficiencies led them to quibble with the
wording of Holy Writ.[25] The laity need not know more than the basic
catechism: deeper biblical truth had to be kept from them. Yet there
remained an alternative viewpoint. In the same Oxford debate, Richard
Ullerston followed an evangelical line of argument to defend translation
of the Bible. The laity were willing to learn, able to understand, as well as
able to teach within proper contexts – husbands informing wives and
children, women instructing other women. In many ways Ullerston
encapsulates the dream of pastoral reformers: the vision of an educated
and ordered Christian community which the spread of biblical truth
would foster rather than undermine.

Ullerston's arguments did not prevail – and were unlikely to in the religious climate of the early fifteenth century. Shortly after the debate (1407–09) Archbishop Arundel formally prohibited all vernacular translation of the Bible. But he also voiced a more general suspicion with vernacular theology: even possession of a devotional text in the vernacular was open to suspicion. His reactionary Constitutions were the result of concerns that had been mounting since the late fourteenth century, above all because of the threat, as we shall see, of a new heresy. Lollardy, as it had come to be called, seemed to embody the worst of clerical fears about the consequences of lay literacy and vernacular religious writing.

(iv) Heresy in England before 1380

The implications of a more literate laity and of the varied interpretations of leading a more 'holy' life could lead to troubling questions, even to criticism of society and Church. It might seem a short step from criticism to heresy. In parts of continental Europe, critical dissent and heresy seem to have increased from the mid-twelfth century onwards. Not so, apparently, in England: why, before the appearance of Lollardy, was there so little heresy in England?

The question seems valid if we treat heresy as an ideology or a sect independent of the Church. In Catharism, the Church may indeed have been faced by a sect separate from Catholic traditions. Its dualist theology had begun to spread from the Balkans in the twelfth century, finding adherents in the alpine and urban regions of southern Europe. Some English Cathars were also picked up by inquisitors in these areas; shortly before 1166 a group of German heretics, apparently Cathars, attempted to spread their 'sickness'; an isolated individual was found in London in 1207.[26] But there is nothing to suggest that this heresy ever took root in England.

The question also seems valid if other comparisons with the continent are made. Apparently absent in England are other kinds of 'heretic', dissenters who did not necessarily believe in alternative theologies, but whose criticisms of the Church eventually led to their denunciation as heretics. Charismatic individuals like Arnold of Brescia or Peter Valdes, preaching the gospel, contrasting the poverty of the Christ and the Apostles with the wealth of the contemporary Church, attracting followings, and who then drew condemnation as heretics from Church authorities: such figures abound on the continent but were, as far as we know, completely absent from England.

One simple explanation might be that secular and ecclesiastical authorities in England were powerful enough to suppress heretical sects. Given the traditional strength of the English episcopacy, this argument has some force. Another theory lends a more benign gloss to episcopal power: such was its strength and success in creating a parish system, meeting the pastoral needs of local people, that dissent found no place to fester. Another answer might be that the social conditions which created heretical dissent were not so intense in England as in other parts of the Continent. Radical preachers found their most responsive audiences in more urbanized regions such as the Low Countries, the Rhineland, Southern France or Northern Italy, where sharper extremes of wealth and poverty were more likely to agitate volatile crowds.[27] England was more rural. On the other hand, London was of a size comparable to the larger continental towns, and its crowds were not unresponsive to demagogues: William FitzOsbern, the bearded rabble-rouser against the rich, gathered a following in 1196. Moreover, religious enthusiasm could be whipped up in other areas of England, as Abbot Eustace of Flay found on his revivalist preaching tour of England in 1200 (to the outrage of English churchmen).[28] A relative absence of large towns did not prevent Lollardy appearing later – although perhaps by the later fourteenth century social disruption in the wake of plague made dissent of all kinds more likely.

However, identifying reasons for the presence or absence of heresy presupposes that 'heresy' is easily defined. The radical idealism of a Peter Valdes, of course, was not in itself 'heretical': it needed labelling as such by the Church. In that sense, 'heresy' was the creation of orthodoxy. Even 'Catharism' was not necessarily a clearly identifiable sect. Not all those prosecuted for 'Catharism' were Cathars; in any case, in their ascetic practices they shared traits similar to those of Valdes or St Francis. The identity of Catharism in Christendom was also shaped by similar processes of labelling by orthodox authorities. Indeed the enforcement of orthodoxy perhaps required the existence of an anti-society, or a sect whose strength and coherence could be exaggerated. Heresy requires the existence of a persecuting society. Even so, not all demagogues or dissenters were branded as heretics: William FitzOsbern, despite proclaiming himself in apocalyptic terms as 'the saviour of the poor', seems to be a case in point. In England, the interesting question is not why there were so few preachers like William FitzOsbern, but why none of them were apparently labelled as heretics. A more appropriate question to ask, then, is why Church authorities in England did not choose to identify (or 'create') more heretics than they did.

The answer is not obvious. Many of the processes which created 'heresy' were the same in England as elsewhere. At the root of these processes was the reforming impulse to return to primitive ideals and the Church of the apostles. These ideals had been embraced by the papacy, but neither wholly contained nor sustained by it (see Chapter 2: ii, vi). Those seeking a more perfect 'religious' life tended to look back to the Church of the apostles and contrast it with its contemporary successor. Their sense of contrast may have been sharpened by a growing shift from an oral to a more literate culture: critics often shared a sense of disparity between a degenerate present and an apostolic past which could be read about or preached from the gospels.[29] 'Literacy' perhaps helped the creation of a persecuting society.[30] By the later twelfth century, the process of creating a more universal Church, where definitions of orthodoxy were tightened and enforced by a new professional class of literate clerks, had made variety of religious opinion less tolerable.

Twelfth-century England seemed ripe for the appearance of 'heresy'. It was certainly affected by an enthusiastic atmosphere of reform, new orders being founded, new hermits appearing. Conditions for a 'persecuting society' were also present, perhaps earlier in England than elsewhere (which suggests that 'literacy' may be a necessary cause of heresy, but not always a sufficient one). Expanding bureaucracies of ecclesiastical and secular government, and the beginnings of academic schools, imply the growth in England both of a 'literate' culture and of a class of clerks capable of acting as agents of conformity and repression. The treatment of the Jews (before their final expulsion from England in 1290) indicates a willingness to persecute a minority group to reinforce a sense of Christian solidarity.[31] There was certainly a will among authorities to repress what was identified as heresy. The German heretics rounded up in 1166 were treated with summary harshness: William of Newburgh gratefully reported how even the houses in which they found refuge were taken out of the village or town and burned. Chapter 21 of the Assize of Clarendon in 1166 which condemned these heretics was the first secular legislation against heresy anywhere in Western Europe.

Was there quite the same will in England to 'create' heresy, to identify and brand apparent nonconformity as heretical? The power to repress might explain an absence of heresy, but the same power is important in its presence: repressive authorities often need, and can manufacture, scapegoats to legitimate their power or enforce conformity. In periods where this need is not so great, 'heresy' does not appear so rampantly. The later eleventh century saw less repression of new religious enthusiasms: popes and bishops seem more prepared to 'take risks' both in allowing new experiments in religious life and in licensing preachers who took up their reforming zeal.[32] After 1150, however, a greater unease at experiment might be associated with a growing number of prosecutions for heresy. In England that unease was less apparent.

The support of Church authorities for reforming preachers and hermits had been 'remarkable' in the late eleventh century. Perhaps this kind of support continued in England into the later twelfth century and beyond. It suited Norman and then Angevin rulers to tolerate potentially disruptive hermits.[33] They were a useful safety-valve for potential friction between themselves and the native population even in the later twelfth century. The rapid advance of a predatory Angevin government left subjects more alienated and rulers less sure of their own sacrality. Henry II was quite prepared to crush 'heretics' and also, more inadvertently, to murder recalcitrant archbishops; but he was apparently ready to listen meekly to the reproofs against his regime of a hermit like Hugh of Lincoln (d.1200), whose asceticism was proof of a link with the divine (see Chapter 3: ii, iii).

Of course, Hugh of Lincoln was a hermit of a safer type. He was a Carthusian who later became a bishop. Churchmen in authority certainly preferred 'holy men' not to wander, and to remain in a solitary cell, or better still within an enclosed order. But in England they also seemed relatively confident that the call for reform, even if it came from more mobile ascetics, could be harnessed to wider pastoral aims. Gilbert of Sempringham turned from his hermitage to reforming the local parish – and enforcing the payment of tithes. The enthusiasm he encouraged could be contained in the creation of a new religious order. The English anchorite Wulfric of Haselbury (d.1155) made potentially inflammatory denunciations of those who departed from primitive ideals; but he did not apparently attract episcopal suspicion, perhaps because his relationship with the local village priest was close, and a benefit rather than a threat to parochial finances. His ascetic lifestyle could be accommodated within the parish structure (see Chapter 2: iii).

In the thirteenth and early fourteenth centuries there was a continuing confidence in an ability to contain potential sources of religious disruption. Whereas spiritual enthusiasm of the beguines in the Low Countries attracted accusations of heresy, in England potentially similar enthusiasm did not induce the same ecclesiastical panic. Perhaps this was also one reason why England apparently missed out on the 'golden age' of female mysticism: to the extent that Eucharist-consuming women were the creation of clerics concerned to defend the reality and power of Corpus Christi (see Chapter 6: ii), their presence was perhaps less needed by Church authorities in England. There were occasional warnings, in late twelfth- and early thirteenth-century synods, to be alert for heresy; but when Bishop Bingham of Salisbury (*c.*1240) ordered the razing of old 'reclusaria' in churchyards and prohibited the building of new ones, he did not imply that these were breeding grounds of heresy.[34] Most bishops were content to exercise control over anchorites by licensing; some even offered indulgences for their support. Other churchmen promoted direction for their lifestyle, for instance in the early thirteenth-century text, *Ancrene Wisse* (possibly written by a friar or canon).[35] Moreover, royal approval of hermit or anchorite continued, and was echoed by aristocrats, and gradually by gentry and townsmen who occasionally acquired the right to appoint individuals to an anchorhold. Concern that such individuals were agents of disorder was infrequent. A hermit at Fisherton in 1352 brought episcopal condemnation upon himself only because he seems (unlike Wulfric of Haselbury) to have attracted people (and funds) away from the parish church. Rare indeed was the kind of accusation made by the bishop of Lincoln of a recluse at Huntingdon in 1346 that he had 'introduced doctrines contrary to the Catholic faith'.[36]

So England had become a persecuting society, but one in which authorities did not feel the same need as elsewhere to 'create' heretics to legitimate their authority or enforce conformity. Perhaps their authority was more assured than on those parts of the continent where social tensions were likely to produce dissent and where agents of secular and ecclesiastical government were less powerful. Perhaps their confidence rested simply on an ability to persecute. But it also rested on an ability to contain and harness enthusiasms which might otherwise have caused persecutory panic. Conversely, it was a loss of confidence at the end of the fourteenth century that in a sense created Lollardy.

(v) Wyclif and Lollardy

'Lollardy' was a term of abuse applied to a collection of beliefs that owed their origin and coherence to John Wyclif (d.1384).[37] Wyclif was hardly the kind of reformer who had worried Church authorities in the past: as an Oxford academic, and one who had entertained hopes of advancement within the Church hierarchy, he was not the typical ascetic or charismatic preacher who stirred up crowds. But he did preach; and he also wrote works which (although mainly in Latin) reached a much wider audience and which shared the concerns of previous reformers. Like earlier 'heretics', he advocated a return to the 'poverty' of Christ and a more literal interpretation of scripture. Like earlier churchmen, he was anxious to promote pastoral reform. In Bishop Grosseteste's writings, Wyclif found a concern for the education of the laity in the vernacular, a fundamentalist approach to scripture, and a strong sense that the visible Church had become corrupt.[38]

Wyclif's criticisms of the Church in the 1370s also drew on other more contemporary concerns, most of which did not lead to the charge of 'heresy'. In 1376 he was employed as a spokesman by the English government to defend the royal right to tax the clergy. His views on dominion which emerged from this were potentially radical, since they questioned the right of churchmen to acquire wealth and exercise authority; but they were ideas also borrowed from the respectable 'Poverty of Christ' written in the 1350s by no less an authority than Archbishop FitzRalph. In fact, Wyclif was the kind of reformer who was not untypical in the later fourteenth century. His reforming voice, especially after the Papal Schism, joined a chorus of complaint: other educated clerics, all over Europe, became increasingly alarmed at the state of a Church of which they too were inextricably a part. The Schism had raised new questions about the nature of the Church, sharpening as never before a sense of disjuncture between the contemporary and the apostolic Church, and between the visible outer Church and the true inner Church of the saved. Wyclif's Church of the 'predestined' elect did not necessarily include the clergy as its members.

Wyclif's disgust at the hypocrisy of outer things drew also from his academic background (his neo-Platonic philosophy), and perhaps more importantly from other contemporary spiritual concerns. He shared with Walter Hilton a desire to develop the inner life and to meditate on the life of Christ. His criticism of 'outer religion', as practised by the laity, only made explicit what mystics and some high-ranking churchmen had tended to leave implicit. His dislike of images of saints and the 'magical' use made of their cults was part of his distrust of corporate devotion which took the individual away from the study of scripture and scrutiny of conscience. It is no accident that Wyclif's distrust was nurtured at a time when corporate devotion was being reasserted in the wake of profound social disruption after the Black Death. Episcopal emphasis on communal ceremony and the efforts of lay people in founding guilds, bolstering parochial regimes, perhaps in funding more elaborate funeral and *post-obit* services (see Chapter 5: vii), may have provoked a wider reaction of which Wyclif's attitudes were part.

What Wyclif's views amounted to was a radical programme of reform: detaching the Church from its endowments, restricting the automatic right of the clergy to exercise authority through the sacraments, and providing the laity with wider access to the scriptures, stripped of clerical gloss. But for none of these views, however potentially subversive, was Wyclif initially condemned for heresy. Not until 1382 was Wyclif finally prosecuted – and only on one issue, concerning the Eucharist. His denial of transubstantiation derived once again from his platonic philosophy, from his literal attention to scripture, as well as from his disgust with the uses to which the Eucharist had been put. Corpus Christi processions, part of the reassertion of corporate devotion, allowed the Host to be paraded in a manner which Wyclif had come to regard as idolatrous.[39]

In the years that followed, his other views were gradually condemned. Yet the support that Wyclif's ideas gained suggests that in the later fourteenth century there was still scope for toleration of more radical beliefs, even within the higher echelons of society. Wyclif had himself been patronized by John of Gaunt, the king's uncle, who supported (if only as a matter of political expediency) the disendowment of the Church; and although Gaunt was urged to drop his client after the Eucharist controversy, he shared other links with Wyclif's reforming spirituality.[40] Gaunt was also the patron (like other aristocrats) of hermits and recluses, one of whom, William Swinderby, was condemned in 1389 for preaching views very similar to Wyclif's (except, ironically, on the Eucharist). His iconoclastic views (apparently dating back to 1382) went further than even Wyclif's dislike of the cult of saints. Swinderby was one of several recluses who attracted the alarmed attention of bishops in the 1380s in a way that previous recluses had not. Alarming for bishops too was the activity of other preachers who began to disseminate Wyclif's ideas. Philip Repingdon was one of several clerics who had known Wyclif in Oxford (and had hoped to secure John of Gaunt's support); by his preaching he intended to bring reformist ideals to a much wider public.

Gaunt's support was not forthcoming, but there were others within courtly circles who were prepared to flirt with ideas increasingly seen as subversive. Clerical chroniclers like Henry Knighton were convinced that a group of 'Lollard' knights lurked close to the royal chambers.[41] One of these, Sir Thomas Latimer, was indeed accused later of sponsoring a scriptorium for Wyclifite texts at his manor of Braybrooke (Northants.). Others included Sir John Clanvowe, author of *Of the Two Ways*, and

Sir Lewis Clifford. Such men were perhaps receptive to reforming ideas which emphasized attention to the inner life of the soul and to scripture in the vernacular. Sir Thomas Latimer's penitential concerns had predated Wyclif's radicalism, although in an orthodox fashion: in 1366 he had petitioned the pope for his own confessor and portable altar.[42] Sir John Clanvowe's own meditative tract expressed disgust at outer things. Sir Lewis Clifford's will combined an ascetic contempt for his 'stinking carrion' (like other knights in this period – see Chapter 5: v, vi) with a rejection of elaborate funeral ceremony.

The accusation of heresy levelled at such men is instructive in several ways. It shows that part of the attraction of Wyclifite ideas lay in their similarity to much wider patterns of piety. The boundary between heresy and orthodoxy was blurred on many issues, so blurred that the 'heresy' of 'Lollard knights' is notoriously hard to pin down. Sir Lewis Clifford's testamentary contempt for the flesh (itself of monastic origin) is reflected in a clutch of similar contemporary wills from testators of unimpeachable orthodoxy, including the most formidable persecutor of Lollardy, Archbishop Arundel. As we have seen, a concern for devotional texts in the vernacular, and the cultivation of inner piety was of much broader concern by the late fourteenth century. A wider wish, even in ecclesiastical circles for scripture in the vernacular (as seen in the Oxford debate 1401–07) sometimes makes it difficult to determine whether certain biblical texts of this period are 'Lollard' or not. Moreover, just as Wyclif had drawn on ideas of unquestioned orthodoxy, later Wyclifite writings made use of texts (like the *Lay Folk's Catechism* and the works of Richard Rolle) which had received ecclesiastical approval.

The boundary between heresy and orthodoxy was permeable as well as blurred. Individuals in the later fourteenth century who drifted in too radical a direction could move back to greater conformity with relative ease. Philip Repingdon returned to the ecclesiastical fold, eventually becoming bishop of Lincoln (1404–19). In any case there were respectable forms of piety which could accommodate aspects of his radicalism. His earlier zeal for preaching found later expression in his scheme to unleash educated preachers on to his diocese. Nicholas Hereford, another evangelical cleric close to Wyclif, ended his days in a Carthusian house at Coventry. Carthusian houses, as communal hermitages, had long represented the kind of ordered asceticism preferred by the ecclesiastical hierarchy: within them, individual meditation and even Bible reading and dislike of corporate devotion – attitudes close to Wyclifite views – were acceptable by being made institutionally safe.

Many Wyclifite ideas, then, were not necessarily 'heretical'; and their apparent adherents were drawn to them not because they were new, but because they were so close to familiar and 'orthodox' currents of piety. Yet a heresy was made out of these ideas. Indeed the accusation of Lollardy directed at 'Lollard' knights is instructive in another way. It represents a rising panic within the Church hierarchy at the implications of radicalism. Chroniclers like Knighton were quick to identify a sect centered on Wyclif and his evangelizing acolytes. They appear, as early as 1382, if not before, 'as if educated in a single school and nurtured in the classroom of a single master'. They spread their sedition as though administering 'phials of poison'.[43] There were certainly grounds for concern. The activities of Wyclif's associates, the early production of Lollard books and even bibles in the 1380s, the patronage of preachers by certain gentry suggests a wider network of radicalism. However the hysterical tone adopted by Knighton and others exaggerates, in much the same way as did previous persecutors of heresy, the strength and coherence of a heretical sect. Lollardy began to be used as a label to define this sect; and the definition of what constituted Lollardy was increasingly tightened within restrictive legislation which culminated in Arundel's Constitutions.[44]

Why the panic? Alarm at heresy was part of a wider concern over sedition. The spectacle of rebellious peasantry in 1381 horrified most in the upper echelons in society; and since heretics were 'rebels' it is not surprising to find some churchmen quick to blame Wyclif himself for fomenting peasant dissent. The use that the peasants made of the vernacular (and their apparent quotation of homily) served as another reason to link vernacular writing with potential dissent.[45] But there was also a concern that sedition of all kinds resulted from a lack of vigilance and disunity among the elite. The crown's financial trouble in the late 1370s was the context for John of Gaunt's early and, according to Knighton, gullible patronage of Wyclif's call for disendowment. The last two decades of the fourteenth century saw churchmen increasingly anxious to engage the power of king, lords and commons in the persecution of Wyclif's subversive 'sect', not least because secular authorities did not appear to share the same anxiety. The commons might have agreed to set up a new commission of laymen and ecclesiastics to deal with Lollardy in 1388, yet they were apparently willing to entertain a Lollard petition for disendowment of the Church in 1395. Even Richard II, for all his high-flown ideals of kingship, did not choose to establish himself as a clear and vigorous champion of orthodoxy.[46]

A more decisive change came after his deposition and the change of dynasty in 1399.[47] The Lancastrian usurpation provoked political rebellion against the new king Henry IV who was quick to link opposition to his rule with the charge of heresy. Preachers were suspected of treason. The fusion of state and ecclesiastical power is first manifest in the royal statute of 1401 (*de Heretico Comburendo*) which gave sheriffs the power to burn relapsed heretics. Even before the statute was officially promulgated, the first burning had been carried out. The hapless victim, John Sawtry, seemed to confirm the imagined link between heresy and rebellion: he died apparently prophesying doom for the Lancastrian regime. By the time Thomas Hoccleve (a clerk in the office of the Privy Seal) came to address his *Regiment of Princes* (1410–11) to the future Henry V, orthodoxy had been firmly yoked to Lancastrian legitimacy. Henry V's reburial of the bones of Richard II in Westminster abbey (1413) was an event intended to heal the scars of usurpation: in Hoccleve's poem of the event it is transfigured into a healing act that might also prevent heretical dissent.[48]

Hoccleve's hopes were misplaced. A year later Sir John Oldcastle rebelled against the king, clearly following a Wyclifite programme of reform.[49] A captured king was to be forced to disendow the Church. How popular Oldcastle's rebellion was is unclear. Chroniclers like Walsingham are unduly (or deliberately) dismissive of the rebels' pious intentions but careful to inflate their number. The tally of rebels finally captured was not large, but many came from areas where Wyclifite preachers had been active, while the organization of Oldcastle's rebellion suggests networks of communication between them. Yet the rebels barely reached their destination; Oldcastle was captured and escaped from the Tower, spending the next two years in hiding. The first and last serious Lollard rebellion was a dismal failure. Its only achievement was to consolidate the equation of heresy and treason in the minds of the ruling elite. It confirmed the existence of a Lollard 'sect' that needed ecclesiastical and secular persecution to administer its eradication: Hoccleve's diatribe against Oldcastle applauded Henry V as the enforcer and champion of orthodoxy. It confirmed too that political society in England had become a more persecutory one with a will to seek out its imagined ideological enemies.

(vi) Lollardy after 1414

There is little dispute that it became more dangerous after 1414 to express publicly views which could be connected with Wyclif. Heresy trials became more frequent, forcing heretics underground. Some of those accused appear to have lost touch with the more coherent creed of earlier Wyclifite reformers. It would be difficult to blame Wyclif for the cosmological assertion, attributed to a 'Lollard' butcher at Standen in 1452, that there was no God but the sun and the moon.[50] Yet the statements of those accused of Lollardy, recorded at trials, do not give a full or fair account of later Lollard belief. Anne Hudson has argued that the surprisingly large amount of Lollard literature that was produced, even after 1414, shows the survival of a coherent set of beliefs which lay behind even the more outlandish statements recorded at trials. In any case, trials as late as the 1420s reveal the existence of itinerant preachers still visiting households who studied vernacular scripture and other texts with their neighbours.[51] These groups continued to operate throughout the fifteenth century and beyond. Best known is the outspoken Margery Baxter, tried before the bishop of Norwich in 1428, whose husband read to her and others at home from a book given by the preacher William White, active in East Anglia. Her observation on the consecrated Host – its passage, after digestion, into base stinking privies – perhaps lacked the academic elegance of Wyclif's metaphysical analysis of the Eucharist. Yet there is a coherence to her crudely expressed views that shows the continuing currency of Wyclifite ideas.[52] Reginald Pecock writing against the Lollards in the 1440s and 1450s certainly thought that he was dealing with a sect of 'bible men' who needed skillful persuasion if they were to abjure their beliefs.[53]

The dissemination of Wyclifite ideas by preachers and books partly explains the relative coherence of later Lollardy. But Lollard ideas did not exist in a vacuum, and their adherents also maintained a sense of coherence by reflecting on the religion practised within their neighbourhood. Some to their cost reflected a little too audibly. Alice Tailor of Bisham in 1502 could not contain her displeasure at what she took to be the idolatrous behaviour of a neighbour during a procession of the cross: 'Stand up old foole! Whereto knelist thou?'[54] Others openly scorned pilgrims on their way to shrines, offerings to saints or church-building projects. Wyclif's venom towards 'outer' religion had flowed partly from a disgust at the morass of ceremonies that had come to entangle the Eucharist. Later Lollardy was also shaped by reaction to the ceremonies and corporate practices of other parishioners. It is no accident that many of the places that were uncovered as 'hot-spots' of Lollard activity were within regions (such as the cloth-producing areas of the west country or East Anglia) where investment in penitential good works in church-building, parish and guild was at its heaviest.[55]

The case for the popularity and even coherence of Lollardy, however, can be pressed too far. What was certainly missing from Lollardy after 1414 was the presence of any significant aristocratic or gentry support. Perhaps patronage of Lollard scriptoria continued: books did continue to be produced. Perhaps the powerful could simply evade prosecution so that evidence for their heresy is lacking. But the sharpening definitions of orthodoxy and the now proven link between heresy and sedition, made it much more difficult to maintain, as the so-called Lollard knights had done, an ambiguous sympathy for Wyclifite attitudes. Moreover, after about 1440 there seems to have been a rapid drop in Lollard book production, and perhaps therefore a corresponding decline in intellectual coherence. Even Hudson detects a variety of opinion amongst Lollards on a wide range of practices and beliefs. Wyclif had disliked the cult of saints; Swinderby had encouraged iconoclasm; but Margery Baxter revered the preacher William White as a saint and prayed to him daily. Such variety may not mean incoherence, and to Hudson it suggests 'vibrancy'; but it also points to a certain fragmentation of the original core of beliefs.[56]

It also seems evident that those who met and discussed radical beliefs, like Margery Baxter, were few in number. Arguably the number actually prosecuted for heresy may only represent the tip of the iceberg; and the rising number of prosecutions in the latter half of the fifteenth century (after a lull) suggests that Lollard groups were still active. But even this increase may tell us more about the worries of prosecutors than Lollard numbers. Signs of heightened concern with disorder and rebellion at a national level surface in 1467: fears that robbers 'as irreverently as Lollards and heretics' were daily taking ornaments from churches – including vessels containing the Host – provoked a commons petition demanding that the king should see the crime as an 'offence to God' and 'the most damnable and cursed example that may be suffered in any Christian realm'.[57] The commons were in no doubt about the strong connections between royal and spiritual authority within the kingdom: they also demanded that the crime be regarded as high treason. Concern about Lollardy in the later fifteenth century was part of the wider concern with social order within the realm.

Moreover, those prosecuted for Lollardy in this later period sometimes indicated that their opinions were very much in the minority. Some had escaped detection only by dint of outward conformity. Several report at their trial that they would not have come to church as often 'but for the rumour of the people'. Despite his belief that Christ was not present in the consecrated Host, Thomas Boughton of Hungerford (Berkshire) in 1499 said that he received it every year, and 'feigned with his hands to honour it as cristen men use to do', so that 'he should not be noted and knowen of the people'. Others were unearthed, like Alice Tailor, precisely because they publicly denounced popular practices.[58]

Despite the worries of some churchmen, Lollardy was never a threat to the beliefs of the majority. It is not always easy to regard it as a minority 'sect', even though prosecuting bishops attempted (sometimes with difficulty) to fit it into a preconceived mould. There were certainly studious groups who continued to meet in households in a sectarian fashion. But the diversity of opinion amongst those accused of 'Lollardy' is a reminder that it was a term which covered a wide range of nonconformity and did not always indicate an attachment to a specific Wyclifite creed. Moreover, even sectarian groups were not necessarily detached from the religion practised by the majority of parishioners; nor did they take part in it merely to avoid detection. Thomas Boughton claimed to be attentive to orthodox preachers, and so long as they spoke 'the veray wordys of the gospel' he took 'great delight' in hearing them. There were aspects of orthodox practice which radicals could still find acceptable. There is even evidence, as we shall see, for a certain acceptance by the majority for the views of the radical minority.

(vii) Orthodox Devotion c.1409–1500

Catholic England in the fifteenth century has come to assume, for some historians, an authoritarian and narrow-minded aspect. Arundel's Constitutions of 1409 seem to mark 'an end' to vernacular theology.[59] Translation of the Bible was forbidden; the possession of any religious work in the vernacular became suspect, even works previously considered orthodox. Consequently, in contrast to the wealth of speculative theology to be found in vernacular writing of the late fourteenth century, the decades after 1410 are marked by a corresponding paucity in such material. Arundel recommended restricting lay theological knowledge to the basic catechism first outlined by Archbishop Pecham. Hoccleve, in his denunciation of Oldcastle, blamed the errors of the rebels on the private reading of Holy Writ. Reginald Pecock was made to regret his attempt at a more expansive explanation of theology: despite his efforts to win back heretics, by 1457 his use of the vernacular had brought the charge of 'Lollardy' down on his own head.

Moreover, the kind of texts officially encouraged were ones that discouraged theological speculation. Arundel endorsed the *Myrrour of the blessed lyf of Jesu Christ* by Nicholas Love: it unashamedly offered its readership the 'milk of light doctrine' in preference to the 'sad meat of high contemplation', affective devotion rather than intellectual inquiry, heavily glossed scripture rather than the naked text. Most of the homiletic texts in circulation in the fifteenth century (like the widely read *Book of the Craft of Dying* or the personalized 'Instructions' for laymen) are catechetical, emphasizing morality above knowledge of doctrine.

The kind of affective piety encouraged through reading of the *Myrrour* also found royal support. It could be harnessed to the wider interests of public worship and social conformity which Oldcastle's rebellion had apparently shown to be dangerously fragile. The 'mixed' life allowed lay people to participate in the sort of contemplative devotion once found exclusively in monastic circles, but it could also be promoted to allow a comfortable marriage of personal introspection with a public life of social conformity.[60] Love's *Myrrour* identified obedience to Jesus with obedience to the clergy. The churchmen who surrounded Henry V were anxious to promote common public worship of all kinds, and channel devotional energies, however introspective, towards public expression in ceremony or new feasts and cults. Henry V's own foundation of a Carthusian house at Sheen and a house of Brigittine nuns at Syon harnessed introspective piety to the needs of public worship by engaging the spirituality of two orders, renowned for their austerity, in a permanent round of prayer for a dynasty whose legitimacy could still be questioned.

It is as well to be reminded that Catholicism in the fifteenth century was at least in part a religion which the powerful sought to control and impose on others. Such a view is a useful corrective to Eamon Duffy's more holistic vision which tends to play down the formative role of political and social agency in the creation of late medieval piety. But it is also a view which comes close to characterizing the religion of the period, in distinctly twentieth-century terms, as a repressive adjunct to state power, enforced by a clerical army of thought-police. Yet the gap between principle and practice in medieval legislation was often wide: what effect could Arundel's Constitutions have had?[61] It is obvious that its terms were applied sporadically and were open to evasion, not least by the upper classes, whose possession of English books, even of parts of the Bible, are not infrequently mentioned in their wills. Late fourteenth-century texts (*Piers Plowman* or 'The Fire of Love') through which literate lay people could still have access to speculative theology continued to circulate. The biblical content of sermon literature does seem to have become more limited, but by the end of the fifteenth century there was a reemergence of sermon collections and homiletic literature with a weightier diet of scriptural quotation.

The relative absence of intellectual speculation, especially on scripture, may also be an issue of exaggerated significance. Wyclifite (and later Protestant) criticism turns the scarcity of complete vernacular Bibles into the glaring weakness of pre-Reformation piety and the fault of a restrictive Church hierarchy, unwilling to bend to new lay demands. But the need to study the Bible as a whole text had not been a priority within the monastic tradition: parts of it had always been favoured, the gospels and psalms above all.[62] It was these parts too that had been strongly represented in the psalters which had begun to form the basis of literate lay devotion in the twelfth century. If, by the late fourteenth century, some lay people were demanding wider access to the Bible, it is not at all clear that the majority wished for such access in a wholly unmediated way. Arundel's promotion of Nicholas Love's text may have been intended to promote social conformity, but it was also a response to demand. Its harmonizing of gospel narrative with explanation was an extension of the need met by earlier psalters, while its affective dimension responded to the new emphasis on mystical introspection which had gathered pace in the late fourteenth century.

The paucity of theology in the homiletic literature produced for lay people in the fifteenth century was similarly demand-led as well as clerically driven. Guides to achieve salvation, tracts to nourish religious sensibilities, texts like books of hours with little scriptural content, were what the literate faithful wanted most. The growing number of primers and instructional texts produced for the laity in the fifteenth century represents the continued extension of the catechetical programme which had antedated Lollardy. Some of them were addressed to individual lay readers and tailor-made to their devotional needs. The spiritual demands of certain aristocratic ladies like Cecily Neville, duchess of York, or even of townsmen were met in personalized regimes worked out for them by their confessors. The anonymous town-dweller, with his own programme for moral self-improvement, was not alone in wishing to bring spiritual concerns, once restricted to the cloister, into his own household (see Chapter 2).

Arundel's endorsement of Love's treatment of scripture was also a response to the challenge of Lollardy. The repressive prosecution of heretics needs to be balanced against the more positive efforts of fifteenth-century bishops to continue pastoral reform. Repingdon's efforts to educate the priesthood of his diocese, were matched by the efforts of other bishops who had never been associated with Wyclifite ideas. Bishop Fleming founded Lincoln College in Oxford as a seminary for anti-Lollard preachers. Preaching seems to have become more regular in parish churches.[63] In any case, the treatment of those accused of Lollardy was relatively lenient, and prosecutors preferred abjuration to burning.

Fifteenth-century England was still a place where toleration of religious experimentation was possible. Although some heretics expressed fear of discovery, others claimed that they had been able to keep their beliefs from prosecutory inquiry for a long time, a few for decades. Some had expressed their doubts more openly and with impunity: one Philip Broune of Hinton Waldrist (Berkshire), put on trial in 1486, had been persuaded, temporarily, by a parish priest and an abbot to believe in the sacrament of the altar.[64] Moreover, those who withdrew into the privacy of their houses to discuss scripture and Wyclifite texts were not necessarily isolated from local society or indeed the communal life of the parish. Lollards uncovered from the late fifteenth century onwards were not social misfits. Some were men of substance in their local communities – not gentry, perhaps, but husbandmen, yeomen or millers who had profited from economic change and who were active in the affairs of their own parish churches. A few even became churchwardens. Others perhaps were selective in the cults or ceremonies they supported. The Castelyn family at Tenterden (Kent) were seemingly able to accommodate their heretical leanings with patronage of the new cult of the Holy Name of Jesus: perhaps they found its Christocentric emphasis (despite the indulgences and ceremony that surrounded it) compatible with their more radical tastes.[65]

Conversely, certain radical attitudes could be contained within orthodoxy. The evangelical fervour which had inspired early Wyclifite preachers, but which had also been a part of pre-Wyclifite preaching, continued into the fifteenth century, in the sermon of the friar, for instance, who condemned the festive motives of those who attended Corpus Christi dramas in York.[66] The taste for austerity, found in the wills of the 'Lollard' knights, continued with the occasional testator who preferred to do without 'sumptuous funerals' or in the relative popularity of the Carthusians as beneficiaries of bequests. Hermits and anchorites continued to be patronized and revered by gentry and, perhaps even more so in the fifteenth century, by townsmen.[67] Books – including parts of the Bible – appear in orthodox wills more frequently in the fifteenth century than before; and religious houses, especially Carthusian, continued to disseminate texts and encourage private reading amongst its patrons. In some ways, these trends were a response to the challenge of Lollardy, the orthodox accommodation of certain Wyclifite ideas. But it is a reminder too that ideas that came to be labelled as 'Lollard' were part of a broader trend of evangelical and 'puritanical' piety which continued to be accommodated within 'orthodoxy'.[68] Orthodox and heretical beliefs, and those who held to them, were not always at opposite poles.

(viii) Social Status and Gender c.1400–1500

This variety of religious attitudes becomes more complex when considering the social context. Gender, and perceptions of gender, could affect religious choices, though not always in straightforward ways. It may be the case, as is sometimes claimed, that women were more attracted to heresy than men. There are certainly cases of women opposed to orthodox religious practices. So opposed had one Alice Hignell become, according to her own testimony in 1491, that she had been driven to violent thoughts. Parishioners who offered candles to the image of St Erasmus in her parish church at Newbury (Berkshire) had apparently risked finding her hatchet embedded in the back of their heads.[69] There are, on the face of it, logical reasons why women might seek alternatives to orthodox religious practice: denied access to the priesthood, and to its sacramental and pastoral powers, women might have gravitated towards Wyclifite teaching which weakened the authority of priests and elevated the role of the laity as preachers and interpreters of scripture. 'Every man and every women being in good life out of sin', Lollards in Norfolk were accused of saying, 'has as much power of God in all things as any priest ordained'. Moreover, although female illiteracy was greater than male, women were not necessarily excluded from activities which were central to Lollard concerns: Alice Collins of Ginge (Hertfordshire) had such a good memory that she was often sent for to recite scriptures and other good books.[70]

Heresy trials, however, do not seem to confirm any innate appeal of Lollardy to women.[71] More men were brought to trial than women, and of those women who were, few occupied a dominant position in the Lollard groups in which they were found. Margery Baxter in 1429, active in drawing others to her home and explaining the errors of orthodox religion, deferred to her husband as 'the best teacher of Christianity'. The patriarchal structure of the household within these Lollard groups was generally upheld: in any case, Wyclif himself had tended to follow the traditional Pauline teaching on the subordination of wife to husband. It is not surprising to find that those heretical women who were more influential were either widows or wives of more socially elevated husbands. It was not gender alone which explains heretical activity of these women, but the social position – as women – that they occupied. Different women from different social backgrounds may have had different reasons for being attracted to heresy.

The relative lack of women brought to trial for Lollardy may suggest another explanation: that women were more attracted to orthodox practices. There were roles that women were able to play within the parish, particularly in the cults surrounding saints (see Chapter 4: x); there were also types of Eucharistic devotion (to be found among mystics and visionaries) which were more adaptable to women – the select few – than men. The attacks of Lollards on saints' cults and the Eucharist were assaults on practices which particularly involved women. But such an argument seems to reduce 'femaleness' to a single gender identity which affected all female attitudes to religion, and to ignore the different ways in which women, from different social backgrounds, were involved in orthodox religious practices, just as they were in 'heresy'. Aristocratic women appear overwhelmingly orthodox compared to their social inferiors. Perhaps their greater access to English books (even scripture) satisfied a need for religious experimentation which, for their social inferiors, was more liable to attract persecutory attention.

The attempt to find connections between gender and heresy is further complicated by the nature of heresy itself. Issues of experimentation and persecution raise once more the question of boundaries between orthodoxy and heresy. To ask whether women were attracted to or 'better served' by Lollardy assumes that Lollardy itself was a coherent sect. Even in Hudson's characterization of Lollardy as a sect there were shades of Lollard opinion. Not all those accused of Lollardy attacked the cult of saints in quite the same way. Perhaps some women (from different social groups) were attracted to certain aspects of Lollard opinion.

We have also seen that 'Lollardy', as well as being the pejorative term for minority groups of like-minded individuals, was also an ideological construct, and in the minds of persecutors various shades of 'nonconformist' practice might, sometimes arbitrarily, be labelled as 'Lollard'. In the construction of this label, gender also played its part. Persecutors were just as inclined as those persecuted (like Michael Gamare – see Chapter 4: x) to denigrate the religious practices they opposed with misogynistic rhetoric. It is no accident that Margery Kempe (see later) could be accused by the Mayor of Leicester of being 'a false Lollard' and 'a false strumpet' in almost the same breath: perceived heresy and prostitution were linked as weaknesses deemed to be typically female. The most explicit connections between women and Lollardy are to be found at a rhetorical level, when 'gender' and 'heresy', for ideological purposes, are assumed to have single origins: at this level the attraction of women to heresy was purely a result of gender. But the complexities of gender identity and the nature of Lollardy make the connections between the two far from straightforward.

Similar issues are apparent in more 'orthodox' religious behaviour. The 'mixed life' was intended for women as well as men, perhaps especially so: its advocates often addressed their texts specifically to women, and some of its most dedicated exponents, it seems, were women. Cecily Neville, duchess of York, combined her status as lay person (and widow) with an almost monastic discipline of daily observances. In the fifteenth century there is stronger evidence than before for networks of female readers among aristocratic and gentry ladies who sponsored and exchanged texts from local religious communities – and who seem closer to nuns, than laymen were to monks, in their religious interests. The Augustinian canon Osbern Bokenham between 1443 and 1447 wrote lives of several female saints for individual ladies in the vicinity of his East Anglian house.[72]

None of this need suggest the flourishing of a 'female' piety. The 'mixed life' for women was subject to patriarchal circumscription. The closeness of religious interests between gentlewoman and nun partly reflects the ecclesiastical construction of female reading as a habit to be monastically contained. The virgin martyrs presented as role models (for men and women) tend to be shorn of disruptive potential: Bokenham's female saints are courteous housewives in life and passive sufferers in death; John Lydgate's St Margaret (1414–26) is an introspective martyr rather than a stubborn teacher of rulers.[73] Such saints' lives were incorporated into household manuscripts, in aristocratic, gentry and in merchant circles; and in these contexts they served social functions, whatever the pious intentions of their patrons.[74] In the 'Book of the Knight of La Tour Landry', St Katherine is a role model for the trainee housewife: demure, practical, charitable and chaste.[75]

Yet once again, there is no need to assume that female readers of these texts internalized their patriarchal values. Perhaps Bokenham's readership constituted a female 'subculture', encompassing wives, vowesses, recluses and nuns, capable of interpreting authorized texts in 'unauthorized' ways.[76] The meaning of saints' Lives could vary with the audience; and their authors could not always control interpretation. However glossed, the behaviour of a St Katherine or a St Margaret towards pagan (male) authority remained an unstable model for patriarchy. For the late medieval widow, the image of St Katherine, before her martyrdom, maintaining her household with 'full right governance', might have valorized her own independence. In *The Book of Margery Kempe*, St Katherine's chastizement of Roman Emperors seems to have justified Margery's outspokenness before the mayor of Leicester.[77]

Some modern critics are able to hear, within the written lives of virgin martyrs, alternative 'voices' fighting the suppression of 'censorship' – rebellious voices behind the passively presented martyr.[78] Whether these voices were audible to Margery Kempe is less clear; at any rate her hearing was also tuned into voices of disturbing and celestial provenance, to which her more socially well-adjusted contemporaries were deaf. The great lady in her household may have been less inclined to reject the model of quiescent behaviour so strongly advocated in these saints' lives. Social context as well as gender varied the responses of women to models of religious life. The privacy apparently enjoyed by a Cecily Neville was an image of aristocratic exclusivity, while ownership of expensive books was a mark of social prestige.

The 'mixed life' itself could be fashioned as a statement of social respectability. Household manuscripts or courtesy texts which incorporate saintly models served social purposes. The Knight of La Tour Landry was anxious that his daughters understand 'how they ought to governe themself', 'to have the love of God' but also 'the love and grace of their neyghbours and of the world'. These concerns appear in an urban context too. Texts like 'What the goodwife taught her daughter' seem intended for an urban household keen to maintain respectability by schooling daughters and female servants in manners and morals.[79] Perhaps they reflect an anxiety, especially in the changing economic environment from the later fourteenth century, that such values were being threatened by social mobility – not least by the increase of migrant female workers into towns. By the later fifteenth century, further change and economic contraction in some towns, made urban governments more sensitive still to social order at civic and household level. In Coventry in the 1490s this was a concern in which 'Lollards' among the civic elite could also share.[80] Thus, the deportment in public of women, even more than of men, reflected back on to the household: the construction of religious life for women was part of a wider attempt to construct the moral values, in a climate of social change, of the 'bourgeois' male, his household and his urban community.

(ix) The Book of Margery Kempe

The variety in fifteenth-century religious attitudes, and issues of gender and society may also be identified in *The Book of Margery Kempe* (1436–38). But there are problems. It used to be possible to mine the text for nuggets of evidence about actual contemporary religious life. Not that all conclusions reached were the same: Margery has appeared as proof of the profound orthodoxy of her contemporaries on the one hand, and as proof, in her exceptional life, of the spiritual shallowness of fifteenth-century Englishmen, on the other.[81] Recent commentary about the text's authorship and purpose, however, has made it a more complicated text to handle. At least four approaches to it might be adopted. First, we might still see Margery and the events described as in some sense 'real'. It is, on the face of it, an autobiography of the spiritual experiences of a well-to-do but unusually pious laywomen from King's Lynn. Perhaps we do hear the authentic voice of an unusual fifteenth-century woman, for the text seems to preserve the imprint of oral dictation. But another approach, to some extent compatible with the first, is to emphasize its exemplary function, as a text which (since Margery was apparently illiterate) has passed through the medium of at least three scribes, one a priest, who have constructed Margery's life in a certain way. In the process, the text may have accumulated other ideological deposits from a literate clerical culture.[82] A third approach is to treat the scribes as fictional, part of a strategy deployed by Margery herself, to authorize actions and utterances which would otherwise have been condemned by men as subversive.[83] But a fourth approach is to treat both scribes and subject as entirely fictional: 'Margery' and scribes are ciphers, used by a highly skilled and literate author to validate spiritual experiences or mask other agenda.[84] Debates about authorship may be unresolvable; and they may lead to very different conclusions about the context in which it was written. Yet they can point to similar conclusions about fifteenth-century religious attitudes.

Let us take a traditional approach and read the Margery in the text, and the events she describes, as in some sense 'real'. What unfolds is the search by a married woman for a perfect religious life. Margery leaves her husband, takes a vow of chastity, and undertakes many pilgrimages in search of religious advice. The search, however, is a difficult one. She encounters gendered criticism. Her mobility, even if on pilgrimage, raises the patriarchal eyebrows of urban authorities. Her effusive tears in church raise 'bourgeois' and clerical shackles. Her quotation of scripture provokes the charge of heresy, despite her deep devotion to the Eucharist: here the label of 'Lollardy' was applied to force conformity on the unconventional.[85] Her troubles reveal a persecutory society.

Yet there is toleration of her lifestyle too. Alongside the suspicions of authorities and the 'grutchings' of parishioners Margery has her 'maintainers'. Hermits, anchorites, doctors of divinity, friars, nuns, the prior who lets her sit in a chapel of his church: all seek her out for her revelations. Widows, burgesses, high-ranking ladies, even the parishioners who sometimes scorn her, ask for her prayers.[86] Intensive persecution of her as a 'Lollard' is relatively short-lived, mostly contained within the period between September and November 1417, when, just prior to Oldcastle's final capture, heresy trials and sensitivity to any kind of nonconformity were at a peak.[87] As for her own wish to hear scripture, there are clearly clerics who were ready to provide greater access.[88]

Opinion about her is divided. But one group is constant in its support for Margery: the episcopacy.[89] Bishops in the text do not appear as persecutors. They are active preachers: the bishop of Norwich's own sermon in the parish church of King's Lynn reduces Margery to tears (admittedly an unexceptional feat). They are listeners, open to discussion on approaches to the ideal life which might be construed by some as subversive. Perhaps (to go beyond the text) these bishops saw different things in her. She appealed to the once Wyclifite bishop of Lincoln, Philip Repingdon, who urged her to have her thoughts written down – unfearful it seems of vernacular writings prompted by the inspiration of the Holy Ghost. Perhaps she also appealed to others, through her life of contemplation lived in the world, as a living example of the 'mixed life'. Perhaps it was his continuing pastoral search for the ideal life for the laity that Archbishop Arundel, the persecutor of Lollards, the censor of scripture, and the patron too of the *Myrrour of the blessed lyf of Jesu Christ*, sat listening to Margery 'till the stars appeared in the firmament'.[90]

Read as an account of actual events, the text seems to demonstrate contradictory impulses within fifteenth-century society – at times persecutory and closed, yet at others tolerant and still open to alternatives. But the text is also an exemplary one: Margery's life is constructed in a particular way. Let us now read the text as more exemplary than

'real'. Clerical scribes and other voices in the text are to be found deliberately suggesting precedents and role models which 'validate' Margery's
experiences and visions.[91] Some of these precedents were inherently
problematic.[92] The female visionaries who voraciously consumed the
body of Christ, and whose own bodies dissolved into tears (or into nothing) were admired by some clerics, yet they seem by the same token to
transgress taboos associated with the integrity of the body – especially the
female body. The construction and validation of the female 'mixed life'
was more difficult than it was for its male counterpart. In Margery's case
it was evidently more difficult still. In the end, her life as a whole seems
to fit none of the models found for her. Her dedication to chastity is that
of a widowed vowess, yet she remains married (with fourteen children).
Her affective tears are validated with reference to Mary of Oignies, but
not her bellowings. Her frequent consumption of the body of Christ
and occasional vegetarianism seem to place her in the mould of other
continental mystics; yet unlike Mary of Oignies who wastes away amid
the odour of sanctity, Margery ends the account alive, redoubtable and
carnivorous. Her visions mirror those of previous female mystics; but
unlike Julian of Norwich whom she visits, Margery has her visions outside
the safe confines of cell or nunnery.

The construction of Margery as an exemplary life is evidently difficult.
The text narrates how troublesome a process it is for the scribes. Perhaps
they intended to promote a particular view of the perfect religious life. If
so, it was contentious. Or perhaps they had other agenda. Eucharist-
devouring, body-dissolving women on the Continent had served clerical
purposes: upholding the power of Corpus Christi against heretical threat.
In England the need for such women in the thirteenth century was not
as great: the threat to the symbol of Christian unity and clerical authority
was felt more keenly after the appearance of Wyclif. Margery's emotional
visions at the site of Christ's Passion in the Holy Land, and in front of
the consecrated Host or Corpus Christi processions,[93] are validations
of Christ's real presence in the Eucharist which English churchmen
hotly defended against a perceived army of Wyclifite disciples. Even so,
Margery does not entirely fit the conventional vehicle for this agenda:
her scribes might have done better.

Are the scribes 'real'? Are they fictional devices behind which the
Margery of the text can validate her account with the seal of male and
clerical approval? If so, it points once again to the greater difficulty experienced by women in attempting to live out a more perfect life. If the
scribes are invented authors, what if the subject is invented too? Let us

read the text as a work of fiction. Perhaps the scribal convention was used to mask criticisms of contemporary Church and society, as an attempt to avoid persecution. What is described in the text is a dystopia of commercialism, hypocrisy and persecution, painfully exposed by a member of the 'weaker sex'. The 'Margery' in the text who breaks away from the conventional life, who is attacked by its agents, and who seeks solace in utopian encounter with like-minded individuals (such as the 'Pentecostal' meal enjoyed with the foreign confessor who, ironically, confounds the English pilgrims gathered there by understanding her every word[94]), is a vehicle for social criticism.[95]

Such a view of the text, where scribes, author and subject are fictional will not command universal assent: some prefer their Margery Kempe to be 'real'. However the text is read, and even though it is a text unlikely to have been read by many contemporaries, what it suggests is a social context of uncertainty and tension. Even as pure fiction the text points in different and contradictory directions. On the one hand, the elaborate scribal conventions adopted reveal a context in which discussions of unconventional behaviour (particularly by women) were liable to invite persecutory attention. On the other hand, the criticisms of complacent clergy and laity follow well-trodden paths. As a 'mirror' in which contemporaries might see and repent of their own inadequacies, 'Margery' functions as a tool of spiritual renewal within a long tradition of pastoral reform. Contemporary ideals about the inner life of the soul, and how it might be cultivated by men and women in society were still matters of deep and tense concern.

(x) Conclusion

The search for a more perfect religious life had taken many paths from the twelfth century onwards. By the later Middle Ages, regimes of religious observance, self-denial and meditation were possible for lay people. The spiritual ideals of the cloister, one might say, had been taken out and aired in a wider world; currents of spiritual renewal based on the 'apostolic' life were adaptable in secular contexts. Pastoral reform in part had made this possible. Yet the passage of ideals from cloister to world was a fraught one. From an ecclesiastical point of view, there were inherent difficulties in defining and limiting how far the laity might develop their own 'inner' lives. Among those labelled as Lollards in the fifteenth century were lay people who saw themselves as 'true Christians' against the Church. Moreover, the attempt to define and limit had other consequences. There was just a short step between careful prescription and proscription – and therefore persecution. Although in England active persecution of 'heretics' is not apparent before the late fourteenth century, English society was already persecutory.

In many ways the idea that spiritual ideals passed from 'cloister' to 'world' is too simplistic. The application of ideals in lay society involved reinterpretation, and by lay people themselves. Social change, not least the rise of a more literate culture, profoundly altered perceptions of how ideals might be realized and by whom. Social context altered the meaning of monastic spiritual language. In some ways, devotional ideals could be reconstructed to support social hierarchy, and possession of devotional texts could become a mark of social status for male and female aristocrats. Yet the same ideals, reinterpreted, might subvert constructions of social hierarchy or gender. Examination of inner conscience questioned the possession of outer wealth and authority; ideals of virginity could empower rather than contain the women who upheld them.

By the early fifteenth century, models of holy living were becoming more closely defined. The 'mixed life' was being carefully constructed as a safe form of devotional behaviour for the laity; indeed, under the direction of Henry V's churchmen, it had become a tool of social and political conformity. 'Heresy' served the same function. Tightening definitions of 'orthodox' behaviour meant specifying what was unacceptable: Lollardy and the 'mixed life' became reverse sides of the same coin. Debate on how the inner life of lay people should be conducted was more likely to be a troubled one in the fifteenth century.

Although constraint and persecution are more evident, there were limits to the control that authorities, ecclesiastical or secular, could exercise over interpretations of devotional ideals. Definition and persecution of Lollardy had been responses to social disorder and a loss of confidence in the ability to contain the radical implications of lay literacy and of pastoral reform itself. Those in authority continued to be fearful of disorder and radicalism in a climate of social change and mobility. Household manuscripts which contain saints' lives or instructive texts reflect such anxiety at a local level. Prescriptive models of religious and social behaviour (particularly for women) were the product not just of pious impulses, but also of concerns that social boundaries were under threat.

Moreover, control over the definition of ideals, even of the 'mixed life', could not be total. Reinterpretation of their meaning continued, and the boundaries between heresy and orthodoxy were not (or could not be) so sharply drawn as to preclude variation and experiment in living out a more perfect religious life. *The Book of Margery Kempe*, in its construction and content, is illustrative of the forces of constraint and persecution. But it is also illustrative of the ways in which a 'mixed life', using a variety of precedents and models, could be reconstituted, and along lines which exposed the perceived failings of contemporary Church and society. Such exposure in itself followed a pastoral tradition of self-examination and criticism: the desire to reform and reevaluate the inner life for the laity remained strong even in fifteenth-century English society.

Conclusion

Between 1000 and 1500 the pastoral efforts of the Church made a considerable impact on English society. Even by the late Anglo-Saxon period, they had already affected decisively the religious practices of lay people, and in subsequent centuries this impact was to harden. It makes sense to speak of medieval society or culture in this period, at a general level, as 'Christianized', if by the term we accept a broad definition which would not always have pleased the theologically refined, and if we accept that pre-Christian beliefs had generally been absorbed and accommodated within a broad Christian framework, by the end of the period even more than at the beginning. A firm distinction between pagan or folkloric beliefs and Christian beliefs cannot be sustained; and the same may be said (though with certain qualifications) of the distinction between 'popular' and 'elite' religion, not least because elements deemed to be the distinctive features of the one (such as a 'cultic' approach to religion) or of the other (a 'literate' mentality, for instance) can usually be found in both.

One of the features of religious mentality which became increasingly common in society, even though it underwent change in the process, was a spirituality which had once been confined to the cloister. The influence of monastic ideals is already observable in Anglo-Saxon England, at least among an aristocratic elite of men and women; but by the later Middle Ages, the opportunity for reflection on the life of Christ, on sin or on death, formerly the exclusive province of the cloistered, was open to many more, through the greater availability of devotional literature and of spiritual regimes which could accommodate contemplative devotion with a life lived in the world. Such an influence had been made possible both by pastoral effort and increasing levels of literacy, but it was not an influence restricted to the literate alone – if only because it could be absorbed in oral and visual forms. In particular, the emphasis on penance had perhaps the most profound impact of all, especially because refinements of doctrine and the construction of Purgatory offered lay people means of salvation which were more easily within their grasp.

By the later Middle Ages, observances and practices which had been concentrated within monastic houses were also in much wider circulation – though in altered forms. In the eleventh century, the monopoly of monasteries (or minsters) over religious life, as prime centres of pastoral care or post-mortem commemoration, was already disintegrating. By the thirteenth century, parish churches or guild associations fulfilled most of the pastoral and commemorative requirements of most lay people; and by the fifteenth century, the larger and wealthier parishes, and even humbler ones, could expect a level of liturgical observance which rivalled that of any religious house. The daily round of masses provided by chantries or guilds, the unfolding vision of the Christian year painted on nave and chancel walls, the rood screens and retables which divided and defined spaces within the church, were all features borrowed from a monastic environment, and had become the common experience of lay parishioners from almost all social ranks.

The increasing homogeneity of Christian culture had been promoted by the effort to create a more universal Church. The encouragement of greater uniformity in doctrine, cult and administration, especially from the twelfth century onwards, had tended to iron out the rucks and creases of regional difference within Christendom as a whole. By the later Middle Ages, for instance, there was a greater uniformity in the cults of saints, even though local saints retained devotees, and even though unapproved 'saints' continued to appear. The ubiquity in the fifteenth century of church dedications to 'universal' saints such as the Virgin Mary or St Katherine, or of guild foundations dedicated to Corpus Christi or the Holy Name of Jesus, suggests a 'community of the faithful' sharing a common culture as never before.

Yet in so many ways, this culture was more diverse and fragmented than it was unified. Visions of universality and ideals of a 'community of the faithful' were rhetorical, in part designed to set up boundaries of exclusion, and in part emphasized to obscure difference and tension. The process of defining faith and doctrine meant that 'paganism', 'superstition' and 'heresy' became useful labels in strengthening a sense of community. An emphasis on Christian society as united within the 'body of Christ' tended to hide the divisions between social groups, however much individuals genuinely aspired to Christian charity and communal peace. Literacy may not have been the exclusive preserve of the elite, but it could be used as a rhetorical tool to separate clergy from laity, or great landowner from peasant. Liturgical practices and religious observances may have been the common currency of all levels of society, but they could be deployed to mark out the contours of social division and hierarchies of status and gender.

Religion in this period, however, cannot be seen merely as the projection of dominant social groups. In its many forms – as institutionalized worship, as religious practice, devotional observance, ideals, doctrine and belief – religion was too diverse in nature and meaning to be harnessed easily by those in authority. From the clerical point of view, the creation of a universal Church – which emphasized the subordination of laity to clergy, and prioritized an inner spirituality above outer and localized devotion – was never fully practicable. Moreover, the ideals and doctrines of churchmen were not always malleable to clerical control or supportive of the Church as an institution. The ideal of 'imitating' Christ or the emphasis on sin and its dangers (not least in the light of the impending day of Judgment), could lead to unfavourable reflection on the state of the contemporary Church. The pastoral desire to reform society led in problematic directions, such as the possibility of lay people taking control over their own inner lives. In any case, Church and religion were shaped by the laity too. If a more monastic kind of spirituality became increasingly influential, it had become so as a result of lay demand rather than of pastoral effort; and in the process it was appropriated, reinterpreted and transformed under the influence of wider social pressures. The 'mixed life' pursued by Margery Kempe did not meet with general clerical approval.

Lay influence shaped Church and religion in more direct ways. In the late Anglo-Saxon period, lay people had exercised considerable control over churches and their priests, over religious forms of association like guilds, and perhaps too over cults of saints. Although Gregorian reform theoretically was to limit such control, it nevertheless continued, albeit in modified ways, allowing lay people to tailor religious practices to suit local needs. Devotion to a particular saint at a parish level or management of parochial finances, for instance, were matters over which parishioners enjoyed both choice and control.

From a papal point of view, the ideal of a universal Church was also undermined by the hold that kings (and even bishops) developed over the Church in England. The strength of royal government is a feature already apparent at the beginning of the period, and the extent to which Anglo-Saxon kings attempted to exercise authority over saints and relics, or legislate on local religious observance, is striking. Despite Gregorian reform, it was a feature of English religious life, in contrast to many places in continental Europe, which continued throughout the period. Ecclesiastical government in England was also comparatively strong, its control perhaps made easier by the relative absence of large towns which on the continent were often the seedbeds of volatile religious enthusiasms. The strength of episcopal government and of the parish framework meant a firmer control over the appearance of new cults, and it also acted to mute the influence of the friars who (from the thirteenth century) could sometimes inspire more radical religious behaviour. The persistence of local traditions in England, notably the survival of Anglo-Saxon saints within a more universal Church, was partly a consequence of a tradition of strong government.

By the later Middle Ages, certainly under Henry V, it is possible to speak of a 'national' church under the close control of the king. The papal Schism in 1377 had seen secular powers all over Europe encroach upon the papal authority within their own territories. Secular government in England had advanced to such an extent that it was already able to tax clerical wealth at will, seize the property of monastic institutions, promote royal saints, and turn the public and private devotion of its subjects into expressions of loyalty to the realm.

Yet it is important to stress the limitations of any authoritarian control over religion. Royal control even in England was qualified. Royal saints might be ignored by a wider population, or appropriated to serve local needs; the charisma of unofficial saints was capable of contesting royal authority; royal attempts to monitor parish and guild life could not override the priorities of lay people who controlled them. The 'mixed life' as explored by *The Book of Margery Kempe* was scarcely a model to suit the royal requirement of social conformity.

Other dominant social groups were similarly restricted in attempts to exploit religious practices. Undoubtedly, thegns in Anglo-Saxon England who built churches and owned their priests, or gentry in the later Middle Ages who erected elaborate tombs and hired their own chantry priests, were making public statements in a religious context about their authority. The Lives of saints promoted by Aelfric, or the courtesy texts within late medieval households, undoubtedly promoted social mores which supported patriarchal ends. But it would be misleading to dismiss the piety of the powerful as an instrument of their social dominance.

Lavish benefaction was framed within a penitential context; and late medieval gentry had only to glance at their psalters and confessional instructions to be made uncomfortably aware that their family tombs were no more than 'proud stones', and that their wealth would avail them little in the afterlife. Patriarchal models of female behaviour were also open to ambiguous interpretation. The Lives of virgin martyrs may even have served to stimulate a female religious 'subculture' undercutting misogynistic assertion.

The religious identities of social groups, however, are not easily characterized. To stress the 'performative' nature of gender is to emphasize that even 'women' or 'men' cannot be treated as separate groups within society with distinct religious attitudes. Also, categories of gender were to some extent fluid: how they were deployed might depend on social context. The Lives of female saints served not only to represent ideal role models for women, but also to express other purposes – clerical agenda or even 'bourgeois' constructions of male and civic identity. Gender mattered in forming patterns of religious behaviour, but different gender identities were possible within different social contexts. The religious behaviour of an aristocratic woman might be distinct from that of her social inferiors, male and female.

The definition of other social groups, and where the divisions between them lay, are also a matter of debate, and even contemporaries had different means of categorizing them. But hierarchy mattered, and although a common religious culture may be identified, religious behaviour or action could be interpreted differently depending on context. Wandering pilgrims, or the owners of a vernacular religious text, might be perceived as pious or dangerous depending on their status or gender – and depending on the period.

From the second half of the fourteenth century, an even more homogeneous religious culture is apparent. The elaboration of the 'ritual year' and of communal celebration within the parish context was partly the continuation of pre-existing developments, following their own internal logic. It undoubtedly contributed to a growing depth of religious experience. But set against the background of social tensions between landlord and 'peasant', or within 'peasant communities' and towns, and in the context of social mobility, commercial opportunity and greater 'literacy', such elaboration is best explained as a reaction to perceived threats to the social order. With it came a more persecutory society. In this context too, religious attitudes which have been viewed by some historians (suspicious of the spiritual depth of the average Englishman), as 'complacent' or 'comfortable', might also be reinterpreted. Elaborate chantries and benefaction, or socially normative religious texts, were partly the product of social disquiet. But once again, spiritual anxieties may also lie beneath seemingly serene surfaces. There was a diversity of religious practices in fifteenth-century England, and a concern (certainly within *The Book of Margery Kempe*) about how a holy life might be lived in the world, which suggests that fifteenth-century England was still a place where religious experimentation and reevaluations of 'society' were present.

Greater upheaval, of course, came in the following century. Why the Reformation happened is a question which lies well beyond the scope of this book, for part of the answer must lie in events peculiar to the six-teenth century. The Protestant tradition of explaining the Reformation by the long-term failings of the Catholic Church used to determine per-ceptions of medieval religion – as moribund in its spirituality, and run by a corrupt Church which was already being undermined by the heroic spadework of the proto-Protestant Lollards. In the light of much revisionist research, none of these views can be decently sustained.

It is worth attempting to understand late medieval religion, Church and society in their own terms, without recourse to teleologically driven historiography – or to the dubious benefit of hindsight. But any book which claimed complete success in such a feat would require of its author an amnesia clinical in form. Moreover, attempts to look for long-term causes of the Reformation do not need to be dismissed as subservient to a Protestant tradition. One revisionist line of argument is that the Reformation happened because it was imposed by royal policy, despite the overwhelming popularity of the old faith amongst the majority: if so, it makes better sense within the context of a kingdom which, from at least the Anglo-Saxon period, was accustomed to the heavy hand of royal government, and whose kings had been able to exercise considerable control over the religious lives of their subjects. On the other hand, as we have seen, there were limitations to this royal control: from a medieval perspective, it would seem surprising indeed if a sweeping religious change in the sixteenth century could be entirely imposed from above. The earlier transition from paganism to Christianity had been a slow process, and perhaps one which was never completed to the satisfac-tion of churchmen. The transition from Catholicism to Protestantism in England, although a different kind of transition in many ways, was sim-ilar in that it was neither swift nor total. An alternative (post)-revisionist view is that the Reformation was not about the sudden imposition of

Protestantism but a more gradual process which was never to reach completion; and that despite 'the stripping of the altars' decreed by royal authority, there was a good deal that survived from Catholic practice, from the liturgy to habits of behaviour and lay control at a parish level.[1] From a medieval perspective, this explanation too makes better sense: royal or ecclesiastical accommodation or compromise with local practices had always been necessary.

None of this need imply that the Reformation was in any way inevitable. Even habits of lay control or of powerful kingship did not lead inexorably to a layman becoming head of the Church. But from the medieval perspective once more, the Reformation does not need to be seen as a surprising event. Although it involved serious theological matters (and it would not do to underplay the passions that these stirred), it was also about the moral reform of society and the Church itself; while a central concern to reformers was how best to live life, at a spiritual level, in an inherently sinful world. These questions were being asked, in a variety of ways, throughout our period: the Reformation, at a certain level, was one further manifestation of deep-rooted concerns.

At the very least, emphasis on the survival of late medieval religion into the Reformation period, whether in terms of the habits it encouraged or the questions it raised, helps to redress the historiographical balance. The Protestant Reformation used to cast a long shadow over the medieval Church and religion; now, perhaps, the shadow is cast the other way.

Notes

Introduction

1. For excellent studies of 'Church and Society' with the institutional Church as the main (though not exclusive) focus, see, of course, R.W. Southern, *Western Society and the Church in the Middle Ages* (Harmondsworth, 1970); and for England, R.N. Swanson, *Church and Society in Late Medieval England* (Oxford, 1989).
2. For an enjoyable overview see R.G. Davies, 'Religious Sensibility', in *An Illustrated History of Late Medieval England*, ed. C. Given-Wilson (Manchester, 1996), pp. 103–26; and see P. Heath, 'Between Reform and Reformation: the English Church in the Fourteenth and Fifteenth Centuries', *Journal of Ecclesiastical History* xli (1990), pp. 647–78.
3. For medieval definitions, and for a historiography of 'popular' religion, see P. Biller, 'Popular Religion in the Central and Later Middle Ages', in *Companion to Historiography*, ed. M. Bentley (London, 1997), pp. 221–46. For modern definitions see G.I. Langmuir, *History, Religion and Antisemitism* (Oxford, 1990).
4. On these issues see in particular: S.J. Tambiah, *Magic, Science, Religion, and the Scope of Rationality* (Cambridge, 1990).
5. For examples of such contemporary criticisms of Catholic practices, see K.V. Thomas, *Religion and the Decline of Magic* (1971; Harmondsworth, 1978), pp. 30, 33–4. Thomas certainly does not take Protestant diatribe at face value (cf. pp. 52–3); but for the criticism that he preserves distinctions between 'religion', 'magic' and 'superstition', and treats the Church as complicit in its perceived status as magical agency, see for instance, Tambiah, *Magic, Science, Religion*, chaps 1 and 2.

6. R. Kieckhefer, 'The Specific Rationality of Medieval Magic', *American Historical Review* xcix (1994), pp. 813–37.

7. G.W. Bernard, 'Vitality and Vulnerability in the Late Medieval Church: Pilgrimage on the Eve of the Break with Rome', in *The End of the Middle Ages in the Fifteenth and Sixteenth Centuries*, ed. J.L. Watts (Stroud, 1995), pp. 199–233.

8. For further references, see Chapter 3.

9. R. Manselli, *La Religion Populaire au Moyen Age* (Paris, 1975). Or for the 'Annales' view of 'superstition' as the authentic non-Christian religion of the people which a clerical and bookish culture wished to suppress, see J. Le Goff, *Time, Work and Culture in the Middle Ages* (1977; Chicago, 1986), pp. 159–88, or J-C. Schmitt, *The Holy Greyhound: Guinefort, Healer of Children since the Thirteenth Century* (1979; Cambridge, 1983), esp. pp. 40–8. For the view that medieval folk were only superficially Christianized even by the sixteenth century see (among others): J. Delumeau, *Le Catholicisme entre Luther et Voltaire* (Paris, 1971), esp. pp. 234–5.

10. For the view that the religion of the people, at least in the early Middle Ages, was 'religion danced', where action was more important than belief, see P. Geary, *Living with the Dead in the Middle Ages* (Ithaca, 1994), p. 178. Although for criticism of the tendency to view 'ritual' as practice or action rather than as thought, see C. Bell, *Ritual Theory, Ritual Practice* (Oxford, 1992), pp. 19–32.

11. For one of many critiques of distinctions between 'popular' and 'elite' since at least the 1970s, see: N.Z. Davis, 'Some Tasks and Themes in the Study of Popular Religion', in *The Pursuit of Holiness in Late Medieval and Renaissance Religion*, ed. C. Trinkaus and H. Oberman (Leiden, 1974), pp. 307–36.

12. E. Duffy, *The Stripping of the Altars: Traditional Religion in England 1400–1700* (New Haven, Conn., 1992), pp. 2–3.

13. J. van Engen, 'The Christian Middle Ages as an Historiographical Problem', *American Historical Review* xci (1986), pp. 519–52 (and for further discussion of the historiography). For a riposte which defends a more permeable distinction between 'folkloric' and 'learned' culture, and also emphasizes the fractures behind the visions of Christian unity, see: J-C. Schmitt, 'Religion, Folklore, and Society in the Medieval West', in *Debating the Middle Ages*, ed. L.K. Little and B.H. Rosenwein (Oxford, 1998), esp. pp. 379–87.

14. R.G. Davies, 'The Church and the Wars of the Roses', in *The Wars of the Roses*, ed. A.J. Pollard (London, 1995), pp. 134–61; C. Richmond,

'Religion', in *Fifteenth-Century Attitudes. Perceptions of Society in Late Medieval England*, ed. R. Horrox (Cambridge, 1994), pp. 191, 196; P. Heath, 'Urban Piety in the Late Middle Ages: the Evidence of Hull Wills', in *Church, Politics and Patronage in the Fifteenth Century*, ed. R.B. Dobson (Gloucester, 1984), p. 229.

15. G. Macy, 'The Dogma of Transubstantiation in the Middle Ages', *Journal of Ecclesiastical History*, xlv (1994), pp. 11–41.

16. See for instance, K. Ashley and P. Sheingorn (eds), *Interpreting Cultural Symbols. Saint Anne in Late Medieval Society* (London, 1990), pp. 4–5; J. Eale and M.J. Sallnow (eds), *Contesting the Sacred. The Anthropology of Christian Pilgrimage* (London, 1991).

17. This is the essence of D. Aers's critique of Duffy (D. Aers, 'Altars of Power: Reflections on Eamon Duffy's Stripping of the Altars', *Literature and History* third series, iii (1994), pp. 90–105).

18. E. Durkheim, *The Elementary Forms of the Religious Life* (1915; London, 1964), esp. pp. 225–6. For recent sociological overviews of various ways in which 'religion' and society' have been interrelated, see M.B. McGuire, *Religion. The Social Context* (4th edn; London, 1997) and M.B. Hamilton, *The Sociology of Religion. Theoretical and Comparative Perspectives* (London, 1995).

19. For a brief survey of the ways that 'religion' and 'society' have gradually come together in historical writing, see S. Farmer and B.H. Rosenwein (eds), *Monks and Nuns, Saints and Outcasts. Religion in Medieval Society in Honour of Lester K. Little* (Ithaca, 2000), pp. 1–15.

20. P. Brown, *The Cult of Saints. Its Rise and Function in Latin Christianity* (Chicago, 1981), pp. 62–3; M. James, 'Ritual, Drama and Social Body in the Late Medieval English Town', in his *Society, Politics and Culture* (Cambridge, 1986), pp. 16–47; or see J. Bossy, *Christianity in the West 1400–1700* (Oxford, 1985), p. 13.

21. Duffy, *Stripping of the Altars*, p. 7.

22. M. Weber, *The Sociology of Religion*, trans. E. Fischoff, ed. T. Parsons (London, 1965); and see B.S. Turner, *Religion and Society. A Materialist Perspective* (London, 1983), esp. pp. 78–80.

23. For overviews see Bell, *Ritual Theory*; C. Bell, *Ritual. Perspectives and Dimensions* (Oxford, 1997); for an emphasis on uncertainty as an essential element in the ritual process, see D. Handleman, *Models and Mirrors: Towards an Anthropology of Public Events* (Cambridge, 1990), e.g. p. 66; for emphasis on the potential of a ritual event, depending on circumstance, either to uphold or to subvert social order, see: Handelman, *Models*, pp. 52–3, 59–60; J.C. Scott,

Domination and the Arts of Resistance: Hidden Transcripts (London, 1990), pp. xii, 30, 54–5; P. Stallybrass and A. White, *The Politics and Poetics of Transgression* (London, 1986), pp. 11–14.

24. For instance, S. Beckwith, *Christ's Body. Identity, Culture and Society in Late Medieval Writings* (London, 1993), esp. chap. 2.

25. G. Constable, *Three Studies in Medieval Religious and Social Thought* (Cambridge, 1995), pp. 251–341. See also useful essays in: J. Denton (ed.), *Orders and Hierarchies in Late Medieval and Renaissance Europe* (Houndmills, 1999).

26. See C. Dyer, *Standards of Living in the Later Middle Ages. Social Change in England c.1200–1520* (Cambridge, 1989), pp. 10–26.

27. Etienne de Fougères, *Le livre des manières*, ed. R.A. Lodge (Geneva, 1979), esp. 94–100.

28. John Gower, *Mirrour de L'homme* and *Vox Clamantis* (texts in R.B. Dobson (ed.), *The Peasants' Revolt* (2nd edn; London, 1983), pp. 97, 388).

29. Particularly useful on 'estates of the flesh', from a gendered perspective are: J. Wogan-Browne, *Saints' Lives and Women's Literary Culture c.1150–1300. Virginity and its Authorizations* (Oxford, 2000), chap. 1; and for the later Middle Ages: C. Beattie, 'Meanings of Singleness: The Single Woman in Late Medieval England' (Unpublished doctoral dissertation, University of York, 2001), esp. part. 1.

30. For women (and their relative absence) in penitential literature, see M.F. Braswell, 'Sin, the Lady, and the Law: the English Noblewomen in the Late Middle Ages', *Medievalia et Humanistica* new series, xiv (1986), pp. 81–101.

31. For overviews see Dyer, *Standards of Living*, pp. 10–26; M. Keen, *English Society in the Later Middle Ages 1348–1500* (London, 1990), pp. 1–24.

32. For general overviews, see J.L. Bolton, *The Medieval English Economy 1150–1500* (London, 1980); R.H. Britnell, *The Commercialisation of English Society 1000–1500* (2nd edn; Manchester, 1996).

33. M.T. Clanchy, *From Memory to Written Record. England 1066–1307* (2nd edn; Oxford, 1993).

34. For the following (and for the advocation of 'closure theory' in the description of medieval society, which has its roots in both Marxist and Weberian thought and emphasizes antagonisms between social groups, or rather 'systacts') see S.H. Rigby, *English Society in the Later Middle Ages. Class, Status and Gender* (London, 1995).

35. See again, Rigby, *English Society*, chap. 7.
36. For a useful overview of historiography of medieval women and gender, see: J.M. Bennett, *Medieval Women in Modern Perspective* (Washington, 2000). For gender as 'performance', see J. Butler, *Gender Trouble: Feminism and the Subversion of Identity* (rev. edn; London, 1999); but for a critique on the history of distinctions made between 'sex' and 'gender', see T. Moi, *What is a Woman? And Other Essays* (Oxford, 1999), pp. 3–121.
37. For overviews, see J. Bolton, ' "The World Upside Down". Plague as an Agent of Economic and Social Change', in *The Black Death in England*, ed. W.M. Ormrod and P. Lindley (Stamford, 1996), pp. 17–78; M. Bailey, 'Population and Economic Resources', in *Illustrated History of Late Medieval England*, ed. Given-Wilson, pp. 41–57.
38. Perhaps in a fundamental sense, the Black Death was itself an endogenous product of social problems – a Malthusian check on population or part of a 'crisis of feudalism' resulting from structural imbalances in society. On the other hand, the weight of scholarly opinion is tipped towards viewing plague as an exogenous event which struck without warning. (See T.H. Aston and C.H.E. Philpin (eds), *The Brenner Debate* (Cambridge, 1985).)
39. But whether social change fundamentally altered the position and status of women in society is much more questionable. For introductions to these debates see M.E. Mate, *Women in Medieval English Society* (Cambridge, 1999), pp. 27–61, and J.M. Bennett, 'Medieval Women, Modern Women: Across the Great Divide', in *Culture and History, 1350–1600: Essays on English Communities, Identities and Writing*, ed. D. Aers (London,1992), pp. 147–75. See too: P.J.P. Goldberg, *Women, Work and the Life Cycle in a Medieval Economy: Women in York and Yorkshire 1300–1520*, (Oxford, 1992); and P.J.P. Goldberg (ed.), *Woman is a Worthy Wight. Women in English Society c.1200–1500* (Stroud, 1992). For perceptions of female work identities see C. Beattie, 'The Problem of Women's Work Identities in Post Black Death England', in *The Problem of Labour in Fourteenth-Century England*, ed. J. Bothwell, P.J.P. Goldberg and W.M. Ormrod (Woodbridge, 2000), pp. 1–19.
40. See R.H. Hilton and T.H. Aston (eds), *The English Rising of 1381* (Cambridge, 1984).
41. I.M.W. Harvey, 'Was there Popular Politics in Fifteenth-Century England?', in *The McFarlane Legacy. Studies in Late Medieval Politics and Society*, ed. R.H. Britnell and A.J. Pollard (Stroud, 1995), pp. 159–74

(esp. pp. 167–8). For possible pre-plague traditions of dissent see for instance R.H. Hilton, 'Peasant Movements in England Before 1381', in his *Class Conflict and the Crisis of Feudalism* (2nd edn; London, 1996), pp. 49–65.

42. R.M. Smith, ' "Modernization" and the Corporate Medieval Village Community in England: Some Sceptical Reflections', in *Explorations in Historical Geography. Interpretative Essays*, ed. A.R.H. Baker and D. Gregory (Cambridge, 1984), pp. 140–79; C. Dyer, 'The English Medieval Village Community and its Decline', *Journal of British Studies* xxxiii (1994), pp. 407–29.

43. C. Liddy, 'Urban Conflict in Late Fourteenth-Century England', *English Historical Review* (2003). I am grateful to Dr Liddy for allowing me to cite his article in advance of publication.

44. H. Swanson, 'The Illusion of Economic Structure: Craft Gilds in Late Medieval English Towns', *Past and Present* cxi (1988), pp. 29–48; D.J.F. Crouch, *Piety, Fraternity and Power. Religious Gilds in Late Medieval Yorkshire 1389–1547* (York, 2000), chap. 4.

45. See for instance: M.K. McIntosh, 'Finding Language for Misconduct. Jurors in Fifteenth-Century Local Courts', in *Bodies and Disciplines. Intersections and History in Fifteenth-Century England*, ed. B. Hanawalt and D. Wallace (Minneapolis, 1996), pp. 87–122; M.K. McIntosh, *Controlling Misbehaviour in England 1370–1600* (Cambridge, 1998), e.g. pp. 11–14; or S. McSheffrey, 'Men and Masculinity in Late Medieval London Civic Culture. Governance, Patriarchy and Reputation', in *Conflicted Identities and Multiple Masculinities. Men in the Medieval West*, ed. J. Murray (New York, 1999), pp. 243–78; and for the intensification of repressive legislation in the early Tudor period see: J.A. Sharpe, *Judicial Punishment in England* (London, 1990), pp. 27–9.

46. See in particular R.H. Hilton, 'Ideology and Social Order in Late Medieval England' in his *Class Conflict*, pp. 246–52; J. Hatcher, 'England in the Aftermath of the Black Death', *Past and Present* cxliv (1994), pp. 3–35.

47. See chaps 4 ix and 5 v. For the application of 'structuration' theory to elucidate the function of spaces within parish churches, see C.P. Graves, 'Social Space in the English Medieval Parish Church', *Economy and Society* xviii (1989), pp. 297–322. The distinction here between 'religious' and 'secular' discourses is perhaps a little overdrawn.

48. *Rotuli Parliamentorum*, (6 vols, Record Commission; n.p., n.d), iii, 273.

49. D. Aers ('Altars of Power') rather exaggerates the extent to which Duffy ignores problems of social conflict and dominance (see for instance, Duffy, *Stripping of the Altars*, pp. 12 or 33). It is more the case that when Duffy addresses these issues, the emphasis of the argument does slide away from these problems towards a discussion of religion as internalized and communally shared (see *ibid.*, esp. p. 15, first sentence). And on this issue Duffy's book is splendid.

50. Beckwith, *Christ's Body*, chaps 1 and 2.

51. Aers comes close to this view, though stresses resistance to 'dominant groups' (D. Aers, *Community, Gender and Individual Identity* (London, 1988), pp. 1–19).

Chapter 1: Anglo-Saxon Church and Society c.1000

1. W.D. Macray (ed.), *Chronicon Abbatiae Ramesiensis* (Rolls Series; London, 1886), lix–lxxiv (for Miracula S. Iovinis), esp. lxxi–lxiii.

2. A. Thacker, 'Saint Making and Relic Collecting by Oswald and His Communities', in *St Oswald of Worcester. Life and Influence*, ed. N. Brooks and C. Cubitt (London, 1996), p. 258; P.A. Hayward, 'Translation-Narratives in Post-Conquest Hagiography and English Resistance to the Norman Conquest', in *Anglo-Norman Studies* xxi, ed. C. Harper-Bill (Woodbridge, 1999), pp. 84–5.

3. H. Mayr-Harting, *The Coming of Christianity to Anglo-Saxon England* (London, 2nd edn, 1991); C. Cubitt, *Anglo-Saxon Church Councils c.650–c.850* (Leicester, 1995), esp. pp. 99–122; N. Brooks, *The Early History of the Church of Canterbury: Christ Church from 597 to 1066* (Leicester, 1994); J. Blair, 'Secular Minsters in Domesday Book', in *Domesday Book; A Reassessment*, ed. P. Sawyer (London, 1985), pp. 104–42; J. Blair, 'Local Churches in Domesday Book and Before', in *Domesday Studies*, ed. J.C. Holt (Bury St. Edmunds, 1987), pp. 265–78.

4. S. Foot, 'Anglo-Saxon Minsters: A Review of Terminology', in *Pastoral Care Before the Parish*, ed. J. Blair and R. Sharpe (Leicester, 1992), pp. 212–25; E. Cambridge and D. Rollason, 'Debate: The Pastoral Organization of the Anglo-Saxon Church: a Review of the 'Minster Hypothesis', *Early Medieval Europe* iv (1) (1994), pp. 87–104; J. Blair, 'Debate: Ecclesiastical Organization and Pastoral Care in Anglo-Saxon England', *Early Medieval Europe* iv (2) (1995), pp. 193–212.

5. P.H. Hase, 'The Church in the Wessex Heartlands', in *The Medieval Landscape of Wessex*, ed. M. Aston and C. Lewis (Oxford, 1994),

pp. 47–81; J. Blair, *Early Medieval Surrey. Landholding, Church and Settlement before 1300* (Stroud, 1991), p. 105.

6. N. Orme, *English Church Dedications with a Survey of Cornwall and Devon* (Exeter, 1996), pp. 21–4; N. Orme, *The Saints of Cornwall* (Oxford, 2000).

7. D. Whitelock (ed.), *English Historical Documents, Volume 1, c.500–1042* (London, 1955), pp. 411–2.

8. See generally H.R. Loyn, *The English Church 940–1154* (Harlow, 2000), chap. 2; J. Hill, 'Monastic Reform and the Secular Church', in *England in the Eleventh Century*, ed. C. Hicks (Stamford, 1992), pp. 103–16.

9. Loyn, *English Church*, pp. 150, 155; *English Historical Documents*, i, pp. 411–2; A.S. Napier (ed.), 'Visio Leofrici,' in *Transactions of the Philiological Society* (1900), pp. 182–5.

10. Cf. the vision of Dryhthelm in Bede, *The Ecclesiastical History of the English People*, ed. J. McClure and R. Collins (Oxford, 1999), pp. 253–8 (Bk. V.12).

11. *English Historical Documents*, i, pp. 650–1; J. Frantzen, *The Literature of Penance in Anglo-Saxon England* (New Brunswick, 1983), esp. chap. 6.

12. D. Whitelock (ed.), *Anglo-Saxon Wills* (Cambridge, 1930), *passim.*

13. M. McC. Gatch, *Preaching and Theology in Anglo-Saxon England: Aelfric and Wulfstan* (Toronto, 1997); *Chronicon Abbatiae Ramesiensis*, pp. 90–101, 447–8; M. Lapidge, 'Byrhtferth and Oswald', in *St Oswald of Worcester. Life and Influence*, ed. N. Brooks and C. Cubitt (London, 1996), pp. 64–83.

14. D. Rollason, *Saints and Relics in Anglo-Saxon England* (Oxford, 1989), pp. 174ff; S.J. Ridyard, *The Royal Saints of Anglo-Saxon England: A Study of West Saxon and East Anglian Cults* (Cambridge, 1988), pp. 107–21; A. Thacker, 'Cults at Canterbury: Relics and Reform under Dunstan and his Successors', in *St Dunstan. His Life. Times and Cult*, ed. N. Ramsay, M. Sparks and T. Tatton-Brown (Woodbridge, 1992), pp. 221–45; Aelfric, *Lives of Saints*, ed. W.W. Skeat (Early English Text Society, 2 vols; London, 1881–1900), i, pp. 441–71 (esp. 469).

15. D. Rollason, *The Mildrith Legend. A Study in Early Medieval Hagiography in England* (Leicester, 1992), pp. 64, 66–7.

16. P.J. Geary, *Furta Sacra: Theft of Relics in the Central Middle Ages* (Princeton, 1978), pp. 59–63; M. Winterbottom, *Three Lives of English Saints* (Toronto, 1972), pp. 67–87 (for Abbo's *Passio Sancti Eadmundi*); T. Arnold (ed.), *Annals and Memorials of St Edmund's*

Abbey, vol. i (Rolls Series; London, 1890), pp. 42–6; Rollason, *Saints and Relics*, pp. 155–8; Brooks, *The Early History of the Church of Canterbury*, pp. 291–2.

17. Mayr-Harting, *Coming of Christianity*, pp. 245–9; Cubitt, *Anglo-Saxon Church Councils*; Brooks, *The Early History of the Church of Canterbury*, p. 315; C. Cubitt, 'The Making of Angelcynn: English Identity Before the Norman Conquest', *Transactions of the Royal Historical Society* sixth series, vi (1996), pp. 25–49.

18. Loyn, *English Church*, chaps 1 and 2; M. Lapidge and M. Winterbottom (eds), *Wulfstan of Winchester, The Life of St Aethelwold* (Oxford, 1991), xlv; J. Nelson, 'Royal Saints and Early Medieval Kingship', in *Sanctity and Secularity: the Church and the World*, ed. D. Baker (Studies in Church History x; Oxford, 1973), pp. 39–44; *English Historical Documents*, i, pp. 846–9

19. G. Klaniczay, *Holy Rulers and Blessed Princesses. Dynastic Cults in Medieval Central Europe* (Cambridge, 2000), pp. 89–96.

20. *English Historical Documents*, i, pp. 411, 471–6; Brooks, *The Early History of the Church of Canterbury*, pp. 87–96.

21. M. Clayton, *The Cult of the Virgin Mary in Anglo-Saxon England* (Cambridge, 1990); M. Clayton, 'Centralism and Uniformity Versus Localism and Diversity: the Virgin and the Native Saints in the Monastic Reform', *Peritia* viii (1994), pp. 95–106.

22. For the following see: Rollason, *Saints and Relics*, chap. 6; D. Rollason, 'Relic-Cults as an Instrument of Royal Policy *c.*900–*c.*1050 in Anglo-Saxon England', in *Anglo-Saxon England*, xv, ed. P. Clemoes (Cambridge, 1986), pp. 91–103; Ridyard, *Royal Saints, passim*; Brooks, *Canterbury*, p. 227; Thacker, 'Cults at Canterbury'; B. Yorke, *Wessex in the Early Middle Ages* (London, 1995), p. 209; P. Stafford, *The East Midlands in the Early Middle Ages* (Leicester, 1985), pp. 175–6. But for an attempt to see these royal cults as the product of more 'popular' origins see C. Cubitt, 'Site and Sanctity: Revisiting the Cult of the Murdered and Martyred Anglo-Saxon Royal Saints', *Early Medieval Europe* ix (2000), pp. 53–83.

23. Aelfric, *Lives of Saints*, ii, pp. 332–5.

24. J. Gerchow, 'Prayers for King Cnut: The Liturgical Commemoration of a Conqueror', in *England in the Eleventh Century*, ed. C. Hicks (Stamford, 1992), pp. 219–38.

25. Ridyard, *Royal Saints*, pp. 160–8; D.J.V. Fisher, 'The Anglo-Monastic Reaction in the Reign of Edward the Martyr', *Cambridge Historical Journal* x (1952), pp. 254–78.

26. Clayton, 'Centralism and Uniformity', pp. 95–106; and cf. A. Thacker, 'Kings, Saints and Monasteries in Pre-Viking Mercia', *Midland History* x (1985), pp. 1–25.

27. Constable, *Three Studies*, pp. 279–86; *English Historical Documents*, i, pp. 853–4; Loyn, *English Church*, pp. 5–7.

28. For the following see: C. Cubitt, 'Virginity and Misogyny in Tenth- and Eleventh-Century England', *Gender and History* xii (2000), pp. 1–32; P. Stafford, 'Women and the Norman Conquest', *Transactions of the Royal Historical Society* sixth series, iv (1994), pp. 221–49.

29. S. Foot, *Veiled Women 1: The Disappearance of Nuns from Anglo-Saxon England* (esp. chaps 6–7); *Veiled Women II: Female Religious Communities in England, 871–1066* (Aldershot, 2000).

30. P. Stafford, *Queen Emma and Queen Edith: Queenship and Women's Power in Eleventh-Century England* (Oxford, 1997); M. Otter, 'Closed Doors: An Epithalamium for Queen Edith, Widow and Virgin', in *Constructions of Widowhood and Virginity in the Middle Ages*, ed. C.L. Carson and A.J. Weisl (Basingstoke, 1999), pp. 63–92.

31. *English Historical Documents*, i, pp. 855–9.

32. V. Ortenburg, *The English Church and the Continent in the Tenth and Eleventh Centuries* (Oxford, 1992), pp. 133–94.

33. Cubitt, *Anglo-Saxon Church Councils*, pp. 99ff; Bede, *Ecclesiastical History*, pp. 350–2 (Letter to Egbert).

34. Blair, 'Local Churches', pp. 265–78.

35. R. Faith, *The English Peasantry and the Growth of Lordship* (London, 1997), chap. 6.

36. F. Hill, *Medieval Lincoln* (Cambridge, 1948), pp. 136–8.

37. J. Stevenson (ed.), *Chronicon Monasterii de Abingdon* (2 vols; Rolls Series: London, 1858), ii, pp. 18–19.

38. For the following see: J. Campbell, 'The Church in Anglo-Saxon Towns', in *The Church in Town and Countryside*, ed. D. Baker (Studies in Church History, xvi; Oxford, 1979), pp. 119–35; C.N.L. Brooke and G. Keir, *London 800–1216: The Shaping of a City* (London, 1975); C.N.L. Brooke, 'The Medieval Town as Ecclesiastical Centre: General Survey' in *European Towns. Their Archaeology and Early History*, ed. M.W. Barley (London, 1977), pp. 459–74; C.N.L. Brooke, 'The Churches of Medieval Cambridge', in *History, Society and the Churches: Essays in Honour of Owen Chadwick*, ed. D. Beales and G. Best (Cambridge, 1985), pp. 49–76; G. Rosser, 'The Cure of Souls in English Towns before 1000', in *Pastoral Care Before the Parish*, ed. J. Blair and R. Sharpe (Leicester, 1992), pp. 267–84; R. Morris,

Churches in the Landscape (London, 1989), chap. 8; R. Fleming, 'Rural Elites and Urban Communities in Late-Saxon England', *Past and Present* cxli (1993), pp. 3–37.

39. R.R. Darlington (ed.), *The Vita Wulfstani of William of Malmesbury* (Camden Society, second series, l; 1928), p. 45.

40. For the following see *English Historical Documents*, i, pp. 603–7; G. Rosser, 'Anglo-Saxon Gilds', in *Minsters and Parish Churches: the Local Church in Transition 950–1200*, ed. J. Blair (Oxford University Committee for Archaeology, Monograph xvii; Oxford, 1988), pp. 31–5.

41. Stafford, *The East Midlands*, pp. 173–5.

42. Whitelock (ed.), *Anglo-Saxon Wills*, p. 18.

43. *English Historical Documents*, i, pp. 472, 475.

44. Bede, *Ecclesiastical History*, 57 (Bk i, p. 30).

45. K.L. Jolly, *Popular Religion in Late Saxon England. Elf Charms in Context* (University of North Carolina Press, 1996), pp. 5–23, 71–95; Arnold, *Memorials*, 90–1; A. Gurevich, *Medieval Popular Culture. Problems of Belief and Perception*, trans. J.M. Bak and P.A. Hollingsworth (Cambridge, 1988), pp. 78–103; Morris, *Churches*, pp. 58–63.

46. *Vita Wulfstani*, p. 27.

47. William of Malmesbury, *Gesta Regum Anglorum. The History of the English Kings*, ed. R.A.B. Mynors, R.M. Thomson and M. Winterbottom (Oxford, 1998), 196. For other examples see *infra*, chap. 5 i.

48. T.P. Hudson, 'The Origins of Steyning and Bramber, Sussex', *Southern History* ii (1980), pp. 12–29. Cubitt goes further ('Sites and Sanctity'), arguing that royal martyred saints may also have had 'popular' and 'pagan' roots and sprung up spontaneously. Whether the elements identified as 'pagan' (such as a sense of injustice provoked by violent death) were in fact 'popular' or 'pagan' when these cults appeared, may be a contentious issue. Even so, the presence of so many royal martyrs in England compared with continent again points to the relative strength of Anglo-Saxon kingship.

49. Clayton, 'Centralism and Uniformity', pp. 95–106.

50. J.M.H. Smith, 'Oral and Written: Saints, Miracles, and Relics in Brittany, *c*.850–1250', *Speculum* lxv (1990), pp. 309–43.

51. J. Rattue, *The Living Stream: Holy Wells in Historical Context* (Woodbridge, 1995), pp. 52, 68–71.

52. Orme, *Saints of Cornwall*.

53. Rollason, *Mildrith*, pp. 66–7; Winterbottom, *Three Lives*, pp. 67–87.

54. P. Wormald, 'Bede, Beowulf and the Conversion of the Anglo-Saxon Aristocracy', in *Bede and Anglo-Saxon England*, ed. R.T. Farrell (Oxford, 1978), pp. 32–95.

Chapter 2: The Universal Church and the Laity *c.*1050–1500

1. W.A. Pantin, 'Instructions for a Devout and Literate Layman', in *Medieval Learning and Literature: Essays Presented to Richard Wilson Hunt*, ed. J.J.G. Alexander and M.T. Gibson (Oxford, 1976), pp. 398–422.
2. For the following see especially: C. Morris, *The Papal Monarchy. The Western Church from 1050 to 1250* (Oxford, 1989); G. Constable, *The Reformation of the Twelfth Century* (Cambridge, 1996); Southern, *Western Society and the Church*; J.A.F. Thomson, *The Western Church in the Middle Ages* (London, 1998), part ii.
3. A. Vauchez, *Sainthood in the Later Middle Ages* (1988; Cambridge, 1997), pp. 22–57.
4. For the following see: P.J. Geary, *Furta Sacra: Theft of Relics in the Central Middle Ages* (Princeton, 1978), esp. pp. 25–8; B. Abou-el-Haj, *The Medieval Cult of Saints. Formations and Transformations* (Cambridge, 1994), esp. pp. 16, 31; T. Head (ed.), *Medieval Hagiography. An Anthology* (New York, 2000), Introduction; A.M. Kleinberg, *Prophets in their own Country. Living Saints and the Making of Sainthood in the Late Middle Ages* (Chicago, 1992), pp. 21–39; K. Ashley and P. Sheingorn, *Writing Faith. Text, Sign and History in the Miracles of Saints* (Chicago, 1999), esp. chap. 2; R.C. Finucane, *Miracles and Pilgrims: Popular Beliefs in Medieval England* (London, 1977), chap. 11; M. Bull, *The Miracles of Our Lady of Rocamadour* (Woodbridge, 1999), esp. p. 29.
5. Quoted in J. Sumption, *Pilgrimage. An Image of Medieval Religion* (London, 1975), p. 44.
6. For a recent general survey: J. Burton, *Monastic and Religious Orders in Britain 1000–1300* (Cambridge, 1994), chaps 2–6.
7. H. Leyser, *Hermits and the New Monasticism. A Study of Religious Communities in Western Europe 1000–1150* (London, 1984), pp. 1–4 and *passim*.
8. R. Foreville and G. Keir (eds), *The Book of St Gilbert* (Oxford, 1987), pp. 16–18; B. Golding, *Gilbert of Sempringham and the Gilbertine Order c.1130–c.1300* (Oxford, 1995), esp. chap. 1; and for numbers of Gilbertine houses, *ibid.*, pp. 448–9.

9. Constable, *Reformation*, esp. chap 7.
10. For a general survey, see C.H. Lawrence, *The Friars. The Impact of the Early Mendicant Movement on Western Society* (London, 1994).
11. For the following see: A. Murray, *Reason and Society in the Middle Ages* (Oxford, 1978), pp. 337–42; Vauchez, *Sainthood*, esp., chaps 11, 12, 13.
12. But for continuities with earlier penitential practices, see S. Hamilton, *The Practice of Penance 900–1050* (Woodbridge, 2001), esp. pp. 202, 209.
13. M. Chibnall (ed.), *The Ecclesiastical History of Orderic Vitalis* (6 vols; Oxford, 1969–80), iv, 102–9; D. Greenway (ed.), *Henry, Archdeacon of Huntingdon, Historia Anglorum* (Oxford, 1996), 702 (x, 2).
14. D. Crouch, 'The Culture of Death in the Anglo-Norman World', in *Anglo-Norman Political Culture and the Twelfth-Century Renaissance*, ed. C. Warren-Hollister (Woodbridge, 1997), pp. 157–80.
15. Quoted in R. Bartlett, *England Under the Norman and Angevin Kings* (Oxford, 2000), p. 592.
16. Greenway, *Henry of Huntingdon*, pp. 598–9.
17. Constable, *Three Studies*, p. 324.
18. Constable, *Reformation*, pp. 291–3.
19. J. Le Goff, *La naissance du purgatoire* (Paris, 1981); R.W. Southern, 'Between Heaven and Hell: A Review of J. Le Goff La Naissance du Purgatoire', *Times Literary Supplement* (18 June 1982), pp. 651–2.
20. C. Burgess, ' "A Fond Thing Vainly Invented": An Essay on Purgatory and Pious Motive in Late Medieval England', in *Parish Church and People: Local Studies in Lay Religion, 1350–1750*, ed. S.J. Wright (London, 1988), pp. 56–84.
21. *Ibid.*, p. 61; H. Leyser, 'Hugh the Carthusian', in *St Hugh of Lincoln*, ed. H. Mayr-Harting (Oxford, 1987), p. 13.
22. J-C. Schmitt, *Les revenants: les vivants et les morts dans la société médiévale* (Paris, 1994), esp. pp. 79–83, 110.
23. For Walter Map, William of Newburgh, and the following, see Bartlett, *England*, pp. 603–12.
24. R.W. Southern, *St Anselm. A Portrait in a Landscape* (Cambridge, 1990), pp. 95, 181–6, 344–5.
25. H.W. Saunders (ed.), *The First Register of Norwich Cathedral Priory* (Norfolk Record Society, xi; London,1939), pp. 30–3.
26. *Book of St Gilbert*, 18–20; Golding, *Gilbert of Sempringham*, p. 14.
27. For the following see C.R. Cheney, *From Becket to Langton: English Church Government 1170–1213* (Manchester, 1956); M. Brett, *The English Church under Henry I* (London, 1975).

28. For the council at Windsor in 1070, see D. Whitelock, M. Brett and C.N.L. Brooke (eds), *Councils and Synods with Other Documents Relevant to the English Church* (1981), ii, pp. 577–80.

29. Saunders, *Register of Norwich Cathedral,* pp. 30–3.

30. F. Barlow (ed.), *English Episcopal Acta XI, Exeter 1041–1184* (Oxford, 1996), ii, No. 188.

31. J.E. Burton (ed.), *English Episcopal Acta V, York 1070–1154* (Oxford, 1988), No. 22.

32. *Book of St Gilbert,* 18–20; Golding, *Gilbert of Sempringham,* p. 14.

33. L.E. Boyle, 'The Fourth Lateran Council and Manuals of Popular Theology', in T. Heffernan (ed.), *The Popular Literature of Medieval England* (Knoxville, 1985), pp. 30–43.

34. J.T. McNeill and H.M. Gamer (eds), *Medieval Handbooks of Penance* (New York, 1928; repr. 1963), p. 354.

35. M. Haren, *Sin and Society in Fourteenth-Century England. A Study of the Memoriale Presbitorum* (Oxford, 2000), esp. chap. 12.

36. F.M. Powicke and C.R. Cheney (eds), *Councils and Synods with Other Documents Relating to the English Church (1205–1313)* (2 vols; Oxford, 1964), i, pp. 72.

37. *Ibid.,* ii, pp. 1003, 1005–8.

38. Southern, *Grosseteste,* pp. 257–60; Powicke and Cheney, *Councils and Synods,* i, pp. 261–5.

39. M.D. Legge, *Anglo-Norman Literature and its Background* (Oxford, 1963), pp. 134–8, and *passim*; C. Cannon, 'Monastic Productions', J.V. Fleming, 'Friars and Literature', M. Curry Woods and R. Copeland, 'Classroom and Confession', in *The Cambridge History of Medieval English Literature,* ed. D. Wallace (Cambridge, 1999), chaps 12–14.

40. M. Camille, *Mirror in Parchment. the Luttrell Psalter and the Making of Medieval England* (London, 1998), esp. p. 177. Although the text is in Latin, Camille argues that we need to recognize the importance of French and English in the way that Geoffrey would have understood the visual clues (*ibid.,* pp. 160–72).

41. Quoted in T. Hahn, 'Early Middle English', in *Medieval English Literature,* ed. Wallace, p. 85.

42. E.W. Tristram, *English Wall Painting of the Fourteenth Century* (London, 1955), p. 265.

43. Southern, *Grosseteste,* pp. 272–91. For late medieval English bishops: R.G. Davies, 'The Episcopate', in *Profession, Vocation and Culture in Later Medieval England: Essays Dedicated to the Memory of A.R. Myers,* ed. C.H. Clough (Liverpool, 1982), pp. 51–89.

44. R.W. Pfaff, *New Liturgical Feasts in Late Medieval England* (Oxford, 1970).

45. M.G. Dickson, 'Patterns of European Sanctity: the Cult of Saints in the Later Middle Ages' (Unpublished PhD thesis; Edinburgh, 1975), esp. chap. 1.

46. Vauchez, *Sainthood*, esp. pp. 444–53.

47. A.E. Malden (ed.), *The Canonization of St Osmund* (Wiltshire Record Society; Salisbury, 1901), pp. 35–45, 55–83.

48. Vauchez, *Sainthood*, esp. chap. 17.

49. For the following two paragraphs see: Sumption, *Pilgrimage*, esp. chaps 6, 7, 15; D. Dyas, *Pilgrimage in Medieval English Literature 700–1500* (Cambridge, 2001), esp. pp. 2–6, 247–9; D. Webb, *Pilgrims and Pilgrimage in the Medieval West* (London, 1999), chaps 1–3; D. Webb, *Pilgrimage in Medieval England* (London, 2000), chap. 5.

50. G. Dickson, 'The Crowd at the Feet of Pope Boniface VIII: Pilgrimage, Crusade and the First Roman Jubilee', *Journal of Medieval History* xxv (1999), pp. 279–307.

51. See W.A. Pantin, *The English Church in the Fourteenth Century* (Cambridge, 1955), pp. 189–262; J. Hughes, *Pastors and Visionaries: Religion and Secular Life in Late Medieval Yorkshire* (Woodbridge, 1988), chap. 3; C. Harper-Bill, 'English Religion after the Black Death', in *The Black Death in England*, ed. W.M. Ormrod and P. Lindley (Stamford, 1996), pp. 79–123; W.J. Dohar, *The Black Death and Pastoral Leadership. The Diocese of Hereford in the Fourteenth Century* (Penn Press State, 1995).

52. See R.N. Swanson, *Religion and Devotion in Europe c.1215–c.1515* (Cambridge, 1995), pp. 59–71.

53. P.H. Barnum (ed.), *Dives and Pauper* (Early English Text Society, cclxxv; London, 1976), p. 189.

54. F.M.M. Cowper (ed.), *The Book of the Craft of Dying and Other Early English Tracts Concerning Death* (London, 1917); A.C. Cawley (ed.) and A. Rooney, *Everyman and Medieval Miracles Plays* (London, 1993).

55. R.N. Swanson, *Catholic England. Faith, Religion and Observance Before the Reformation* (Manchester, 1993), pp. 14–18.

56. See text in *ibid.*, pp. 96–104.

57. Constable, *Three Studies*, pp. 3–141 (esp. pp. 89–92).

58. H.G. Hewlett (ed.), *Chronica Rogeri de Wendover qui dicitur Flores Historiarum* (3 vols; Rolls Series; London, 1886–9), ii, pp. 16–35 (esp. p. 19).

59. J.A. Brundage, 'Enclosure of Nuns: the Decretal Periculoso and its Commentaries', *Journal of Medieval History* xx (1994), 143–58; S.K. Elkins, *Holy Women of Twelfth-Century England* (London, 1988), pp. 105, 117–20, 144, 161–2; though for more positive assessments of the religious life for women, see D.M. Kerr, *Religious Life for Women c.1100–c.1350* (Oxford, 1999), pp. 238–9.

60. Macy, 'The Dogma of Transubstantiation', pp. 11–41.

61. *Dives and Pauper*, p. 189.

62. Haren, *Sin and Society*, chaps 1, 6, 7.

63. R. Brentano, *Two Churches. England and Italy in the Thirteenth Century* (Princeton, 1968), pp. 207, 221–2, 226, 288.

64. Le Goff, *Naissance*, pp. 305, 409.

65. A. Vauchez, 'Female Prophets, Visionaries, and Mystics in Medieval Europe', in *The Laity in the Middle Ages: Religious Belief and Devotional Practices*, ed. D.E. Bornstein, trans. M.J. Schneider (Notre Dame, Ind., 1993), pp. 219–29.

66. M. Rubin, 'Europe Remade: Purity and Danger in Late Medieval Europe', *Transactions of the Royal Historical Society* sixth series, xi (2001), pp. 101–24.

67. D. Hay, 'The Church of England in the Later Middle Ages', *History* liii (1968), pp. 35–50.

Chapter 3: Saints, Cults and the Holy

1. *Calendar of Entries in the Papal Registers Relating to Great Britain and Ireland: Papal Letters*, iv, p. 101; and see D.M. Owen, *Church and Society in Medieval Lincolnshire* (Lincoln, 1971), pp. 126–7.

2. Ridyard, *Royal Saints*, pp. 196–210.

3. T. Arnold (ed.), *Historia Dunelmensis Ecclesiae* in *Symeonis Monachi Opera Omnia* (2 vols; Rolls Series, 1882–5), pp. 99–100; *Ecclesiastical History of Orderic Vitalis*, ii, 346–50; A. Williams, *The English and the Norman Conquest* (Woodbridge, 1995), chap. 6.

4. Ridyard, *Royal Saints*; Rollason, *Saints and Relics*, chap. 9.

5. *Ecclesiastical History of Orderic Vitalis*, ii, 344; Hayward, 'Translation-Narratives', pp. 67–93 (p. 93 n.122).

6. A peasant attempting to cheat the patron saint of land had his head severed off with his own scythe: 'Vita Sancti Ecgwini', in J.A. Giles (ed.), *Vita Quorundum Anglo-Saxonum* (London, 1854), pp. 387–93.

7. J. Campbell, 'Some Twelfth-Century Views of the Anglo-Saxon Past', in his *Essays in Anglo-Saxon History* (London, 1986), pp. 209–28.

8. P.A. Hayward, 'The *Miracula Inventionis Beatae Mylburge Virginis* attributed to the Lord Cardinal of Ostia', *English Historical Review* cxiv (1999), pp. 543–73.

9. J.F. Benton and C.C. Swinton (eds), *Self and Society in Medieval France, The Memoirs of Abbot Guibert of Nogent* (New York, 1978), pp. 191–7.

10. Abou-el-Haj, *The Medieval Cult of Saints*, esp. pp. 1–3, 13–15, 17–19.

11. Cf. Webb, *Pilgrimage in Medieval England*, p. 11.

12. T. Arnold (ed.), *Symeonis Monachi Opera Omnia*, i, pp. 255.

13. Southern, *St Anselm*, esp. p. 294. For Becket's devotion to St Aelfeah (Alphege) see F. Barlow, *Thomas Becket* (London, 1986), pp. 233, 247.

14. Orme, *Saints of Cornwall*, p. 31.

15. V. Tudor, 'The Cult of St Cuthbert in the Twelfth Century: the Evidence of Reginald of Durham', in *St Cuthbert, His Cult and His Community to AD1200*, ed. G. Bonner, D. Rollason and C. Stancliffe (Woodbridge, 1989), pp. 447–62.

16. N. Vincent, *Peter des Roches: An Alien in English Politics 1205–1238* (Cambridge, 1996), pp. 243–7.

17. Malden, *Canonization of St Osmund*, pp. 35–45, 55–83.

18. R. Bartlett, 'The Hagiography of Angevin England', in *Thirteenth-Century England V*, ed. P.R. Coss and S.D. Lloyd (Woodbridge, 1995), pp. 37–52.

19. Golding, *Gilbert of Sempringham*, p. 10.

20. See Vauchez, *Sainthood*, chap. 10.

21. G. Dickson, 'Encounters in Medieval Revivalism: Monks, Friars, and Popular Enthusiasts', *Church History. Studies in Christianity and Culture* lxviii (1999), pp. 265–93 (esp. pp. 292–3).

22. Quoted in P. Heath, *Church and Realm 1272–1461* (London, 1988), p. 29.

23. *Ibid.*, pp. 34–54, 312–16.

24. See Clanchy, *From Memory to Written Record*, p. 67 for the Weberian 'routinization of charisma'.

25. K.L. Leyser, 'The Angevin Kings and the Holy Man', in *St Hugh of Lincoln*, ed. H. Mayr-Harting (Oxford, 1987), pp. 49–73.

26. For late medieval examples see A.K. Warren, *Anchorites and their Patrons in Medieval England* (London, 1985), chap. 5.

27. M. Bloch, *The Royal Touch. Sacred Monarchy and Scrofula in England and France*, trans. J.E. Anderson (London, 1973); F. Barlow, 'The King's Evil', *English Historical Review* xcv (1980), pp. 3–27; G. Koziol,

'England, France, and the Problem of Sacrality in Twelfth-Century Ritual', in *Cultures of Power: Lordship, Status and Process in Twelfth-Century Europe*, ed. T.N. Bisson (Philadelphia, 1995), pp. 124–48; M. Prestwich, 'The Piety of Edward I', in *The Proceedings of the 1984 Harlaxton Symposium*, ed. W.M. Ormrod (Stamford, 1985), pp. 120–8.

28. N. Saul, 'Richard II and Wesminster Abbey', in *The Cloister and the World. Essays in Medieval History in Honour of Barbara Harvey*, ed. J. Blair and B. Golding (Oxford, 1996), pp. 196–218.

29. D. Webb, *Pilgrimage in Medieval England* (London, 2000), chap. 5. For the European-wide development of ideas of dynastic or hereditary sanctity by the fourteenth century, see Klaniczay, *Holy Rulers*, chap. 6. In England these ideas seem to have been latent before then.

30. G. Williams (ed.), *Memorials of the Reign of Henry VI. Official Correspondence of Thomas Bekynton* (Rolls Series; London, 1872), i, pp. 118–19. The brief effort to achieve King Alfred's canonization (1441) was linked in with the ongoing efforts in the papal curia to secure Osmund's canonization.

31. Webb, *Pilgrimage in Medieval England*, p. 125.

32. W.M. Ormrod, 'The Personal Religion of Edward III', *Speculum* lxiv (1989), p. 862.

33. William of Newburgh, 'Historia Rerum Anglicarum', in *Chronicles of the Reign of Stephen, Henry II, Richard I*, ed. R. Howlett (Rolls Series; London, 1884–9), i, pp. 187–9.

34. Matthew Paris, *Chronica majora*, ed. H.R. Luard (7 vols; Rolls Series; London, 1872–83), iv, pp. 642–3; vi, pp. 138–44; and see now N. Vincent, *The Holy Blood. King Henry III and the Westminster Blood Relic* (Cambridge, 2001).

35. J. Bengtson, 'St George and the Formation of English Nationalism', *Journal of Medieval and Early Modern Studies* xxvii (1997), pp. 317–35.

36. A. Goodman, 'Introduction', in *Richard II. The Art of Kingship*, ed. A. Goodman and J.L. Gillespie (Oxford, 1999), pp. 10–11.

37. See for instance N. Saul, 'The Kingship of Richard II', in *Richard II*, ed. Goodman and Gillespie, pp. 37–41. And for earlier developments in this process M. Vale, *The Princely Court. Medieval Courts and Culture 1270–1380* (Oxford, 2001), pp. 200–46.

38. G. Kipling, *Enter the King: Theatre, Liturgy and Ritual in the Medieval Civic Triumph* (Oxford, 1998); F. Taylor and J.S. Roskell (eds), *Gesta Henrici Quinti*, (Oxford, 1975), pp. 106, 108.

39. J. I. Catto, 'Religious Change under Henry V', in *Henry V: the Practice of Kingship*, ed. G.L. Harriss (Oxford, 1985), pp. 97–115.

40. C.M.D. Crowder, *Unity, Heresy and Reform 1378–1460: the Conciliar Response to the Great Schism* (London, 1977), pp. 111–26 (esp. pp. 118–9). And see Hay, 'The Church of England in the Later Middle Ages'.

41. R.B. Dobson, *Durham Priory 1400–1450* (Cambridge, 1973), p. 30; D.H. Farmer, 'Some Saints of East Anglia', *Reading Medieval Studies* xi (1985), pp. 31–49; Orme, *English Church Dedications* and Orme, *Saints of Cornwall.*

42. Kleinberg, *Prophets in their own Country*, p. 31.

43. H. Mayr-Harting, 'Functions of a Twelfth-Century Recluse', *History* lx (1975), pp. 337–52.

44. M. Bell (ed.), *Wulfric of Haselbury by John of Ford* (Somerset Record Society, xlvii; 1933), pp. 28–9, 65.

45. See M.G. Dickson, 'Patterns of European Sanctity', chaps 2 and 3.

46. William of Newburgh, *Chronicles*, i, pp. 310–11; ii, pp. 466–73.

47. Quoted in J.C. Cox, *The Sanctuaries and Sanctuary Seekers of Medieval England* (London, 1911), pp. 244–6.

48. Quoted in J.A.F. Thomson, *The Later Lollards 1414–1520* (Oxford, 1965), pp. 148–50.

49. F.C. Hingeston-Randolph (ed.), *The Register of John de Grandisson Bishop of Exeter (AD1327–1369)* (3 vols; Exeter, 1894–99), ii, pp. 1231–4. See also Webb, *Pilgrimage in Medieval England*, pp. 154–6.

50. *Ecclesiastical History of Orderic Vitalis*, ii, pp. 346–9. See also Hayward, 'Translation-Narratives', p. 92.

51. See generally: S. Walker, 'Political Saints in Later Medieval England', in *The McFarlane Legacy: Studies in Late Medieval Politics and Society*, ed. R.H. Britnell and A.J. Pollard (Stroud, 1995), pp. 77–101.

52. R.C. Finucane, *Miracles and Pilgrims: Popular Beliefs in Medieval England* (London, 1977), pp. 131–5, 169–70; C. Valente, 'Simon de Montfort, Earl of Leicester and the Utility of Sanctity in Thirteenth-century England', *Journal of Medieval History* xxi (1995), pp. 27–49.

53. J.W. McKenna, 'Popular Canonization as Political Propaganda: the Cult of Archbishop Scrope', *Speculum* xlv (1970), pp. 608–23 (H.T. Riley (ed.), *Chronica S. Albani: Thomae Walsingham, Quondam Monachi S.Albani, Historia Anglicana* (2 vols, Rolls Series; London, 1863), ii, pp. 270–1).

54. S.B. Meech and H.E. Allen (eds), *The Book of Margery Kempe* (Early English Text Society, old series, ccxii; 1940). (For full references see *infra*, chap. 6, ix.)

55. *Book of Margery Kempe*, Bk. 2 chap. 4. The Brigittine house at Sheen had been moved in 1431 to Syon: it was this one which Margery seems to have visited (see A. Goodman, *Margery Kempe and her World* (London, 2002), pp. 118–19).

56. R.M.T. Hill (ed.), *The Rolls and Register of Bishop Oliver Sutton* (7 vols; Lincoln Record Society, xxxix–lxix; Hereford, 1948–75), v, pp. 143–4, 176, 212 (also: iii, pp. 37, 60).

57. *Ibid.*, vi, 103–4; H.C. Maxwell-Lyte and M.C.B. Dawey (eds), *The Register of Thomas Bekynton, Bishop of Bath and Wells 1443–1465* (2 vols; Somerset Record Society, xlix–l; London, 1934), i, pp. 414; Rattue, *Living Stream*, p. 86.

58. A. Hamilton-Thompson (ed.), *The Register of William Greenfield Archbishop of York 1300–1315* (Surtees Society, cli; Durham, 1940), pp. iii, 209–10, 215–17; *Calendar of the Patent Rolls* (54 vols; London, 1891–1916), *1313–17*, pp. 60, 148, 245; *1330–4*, 203; W.T. Lancaster (ed.), *Abstracts of the Charters and other Documents Contained in the Chartulary of the Priory of Bridlington* (Leeds, 1912), pp. 448–9. See W. Page (ed.), *Victoria County History, York. North Riding vol. 2* (London, 1923), p. 207; but also Webb, *Pilgrimage in Medieval England*, pp. 147–8.

59. R.C. Fowler (ed.), *Registrum Radulphi Baldock, Gilberti Segrave, Ricardi Neuport et Stephani Gravesend Episcoporum Londoniensium AD MCC-CIV–MCCCXXXVIII* (Canterbury and York Society, vii; London, 1911), pp. 25–6.

60. Adam of Eynsham, *Magna vita sancti Hugonis*, ed. D.L. Douie and D.H. Farmer (Oxford, 1985), p. 201.

61. C. Deeles (ed.), *Registrum Johannis de Pontissara Episcopi Wyntonensis* (Canterbury and York Society, xix; London, 1915), p. 238. For condemnations earlier in the thirteenth century: Powicke and Cheney, *Councils and Synods*, ii, pp. 179, 303, 722, 1044.

62. *Register of John de Grandisson*, ii, pp. 1110–11, 1157–8; and see N. Orme, 'Bishop Grandisson and Popular Religion', *Report and Transactions of the Devonshire Association* cxxiv (1992), pp. 107–18; and Haren, *Sin and Society*, p. 55.

63. Register of Bishop Ralph Ergum (Wiltshire Record Office, Trowbridge), iii, fol. 76.

64. Finucane, *Miracles*, pp. 52–3, 180.

65. M.W. Greenslade (ed.), *Victoria County History: A History of the County of Stafford*, vol. 14 (Oxford, 1990), p. 134.

66. *Register of Thomas Bekynton*, No. 648.

67. *Register of John de Grandisson*, ii, pp. 941–2.
68. See Duffy, *Stripping of the Altars*, pp. 266–98.
69. C. Louis (ed.), *The Commonplace Book of Robert Reynes of Acle* (London, 1980), No. 27 (pp. 167–9).
70. *Dives and Pauper*, 158.
71. *Ibid.*, p. 162.
72. R. Kieckhefer, *Magic in the Middle Ages* (Cambridge, 1989), pp. 182–200.
73. E.A. Bond (ed.), *Chronica Monasterii de Melsa* (3 vols; Rolls Series, London, 1866–88), iii, pp. 35–6.
74. Quoted in G.W. Owst, *Literature and Pulpit in Medieval England* (Oxford, 1961), pp. 140–1.
75. Vincent, *Holy Blood*, pp. 137–53.
76. W.H. Kelke, 'Master John Shorne, the Marston Saint', *Records of Buckinghamshire*, ii (1869), pp. 60–74; W.S. Simpson, *ibid.*, iii (1870), pp. 354–69.
77. B. Spencer, *Pilgrim Souvenirs and Secular Badges. Medieval Finds from Excavations in London* (London, 1998), p. 113.
78. W.R. Larson, 'Three Thirteenth-Century Lives of St Margaret of Antioch', in *Medieval Hagiography. An Anthology*, ed. T. Head (London, 2000), p. 677.
79. See generally S. Coleman and J. Elsner, *Pilgrimage Past and Present. Sacred Travel and Sacred Space in the World Religions* (London, 1995), esp. pp. 196–260.
80. K.L. Lewis, 'Pilgrimage and the Cult of St Katherine of Alexandria in Late Medieval England', in J. Stopford, *Pilgrimage Explored* (York, 1999), pp. 145–60.
81. *The Book of Margery Kempe*; for full references see *infra*, chap. 6 ix.
82. S.S. Morrison, *Women Pilgrims in Late Medieval England. Public Piety as Public Performance* (London, 2000), chap. 3.
83. For the following see M. Rubin, *Corpus Christi. The Eucharist in Late Medieval Culture* (Cambridge, 1991), pp. 243–72.
84. M. Aston, 'Corpus Christi and Corpus Regni: Heresy and the Peasants' Revolt', *Past and Present* cxliii (1994), pp. 3–47.
85. K.A. Winstead, *Virgin Martyrs. Legends of Sainthood in Late Medieval England* (Ithaca, 1997), chap. 3.
86. G.M. Gibson, 'Saint Anne and the Religion of Childbed. Some East Anglian Texts and Talismans', in *Interpreting Cultural Symbols*, ed. Ashley and Sheingorn (London, 1990), pp. 95–110; *Commonplace Book of Robert Reynes*, No. 49.

87. M.R. James, 'Lives of St Walstan', *Norfolk Archaeological Society Papers* xix (1917), pp. 238–67 (esp. pp. 252–3) – for lives dating to late 1400's; and Duffy, *Stripping of the Altars*, pp. 200–5, though Duffy does not comment on the social significance of Walstan's hard work.

Chapter 4: Corporate Religion: Structures and Practices

1. For references to the following, see P.H. Coulstock, *The Collegiate Church of Wimborne Minster* (Woodbridge, 1993), esp. pp. 7–24, 34–41, 94–5, 147–60, 161ff; A.D. Brown, *Popular Piety in Late Medieval England: The Diocese of Salisbury c.1250–c.1550* (Oxford, 1995), pp. 84–5, 94–5; M.K. Jones and M.G. Underwood, *The King's Mother: Lady Margaret Beaufort, Countess of Richmond and Derby* (Cambridge, 1992), pp. 233–6.
2. See especially J. Blair, 'Local Churches', pp. 265–78.
3. R.R. Darlington (ed.), *Vita Wulfstani* (Camden Society, cix; 1928), 52.
4. D.M. Smith (ed.), *English Episcopal Acta, i, Lincoln 1047–1185* (Oxford, 1980), No. 7.
5. 'The Chronicle of Crowland Abbey', in *The Church Historians of England*, ed. J.H. Stevenson (London, 1854), ii, pp. 677–8.
6. See Faith, *English Peasantry*, pp. 190–4; and the useful summary in N.J.G. Pounds, *A History of the English Parish* (Cambridge, 2000), pp. 28–9.
7. *Ibid.*, pp. 272–82.
8. Norton church (Worcestershire) had virgates of land from 'collectione rusticorum' (R.W. Lennard, 'Two Peasant Contributions to Church Endowment', *English Historical Review* lxvii (1952), pp. 230–3).
9. In 1262, for instance, a local lord granted to the 'parishioners' of St Giles's chapelry in Great Longdon two oxgangs of land to augment the maintenance of a chaplain celebrating in the chapel (H.E. Savage (ed.), *The Great Register of Lichfield Cathedral* (Staffordshire Record Society, 1924), No. 696).
10. C.N.L. Brooke, 'The Missionary at Home: The Church and the Towns 1000–1250', in *The Mission of the Church and the Propagation of the Faith*, ed. G.J. Cuming (Studies in Church History 6; Cambridge, 1970), p. 72.
11. R.A.R. Hartridge, *A History of Vicarages in the Middle Ages* (Cambridge, 1930), e.g. pp. 140–55.

12. See R.N. Swanson, 'Parochialism and Particularism: the Dispute over the Status of Ditchford Priory, Warwickshire, in the Early Fifteenth Century', in *Medieval Ecclesiastical Studies in Honour of Dorothy M. Owen*, ed. M.J. Franklin and C. Harper-Bill (Woodbridge, 1995), pp. 241–57; and Brown, *Popular Piety*, pp. 68–77.

13. The villagers of Haxby (Yorkshire), complained that they were four miles from one church and sixteen from another (J. Raine (ed.), *The Fabric Rolls of York Minster 1362–1550* (Surtees Society, xcv; London, 1859), pp. 254–5).

14. *Calendar of Entries in the Papal Registers*, vi, p. 108.

15. Quoted in Pounds, *English Parish*, p. 94.

16. *Book of Margery Kempe*, pp. 58–60.

17. C.R. Cheney and B.E.A. Jones (eds), *English Episcopal Acta, 11, Canterbury 1162–1190* (London, 1986), No. 65.

18. As at Standish (Worcs.) or Hutthorpe (Northants.) or Melksham (Wilts.) (P.M. Hoskin (ed.), *English Episcopal Acta, 13, Worcester 1218–1268* (Oxford, 1997), No. 9; F.M. Stenton, *Documents Illustrative of the Social and Economic History of Danelaw* (London, 1920), No. 465; Salisbury Cathedral, Dean and Chapter muniments, Press IV, E3, Melksham/16).

19. J.H. Stevenson (ed.), *The Edington Cartulary* (Wiltshire Record Society xlii; Devizes, 1987), p. 547.

20. Powicke and Cheney, *Councils and Synods*, i, p. 82.

21. E. Berger (ed.), *Les registres d'Innocent IV* (3 vols; Paris, 1884–97), iii, p. 131 (No. 6094).

22. C. Drew, 'Early Parochial Organisation in England. The Origins of the Office of Churchwarden', *Borthwick Institute of Historical Research. St Anthony's Publications* vii (1954).

23. See the emphasis placed on this in B.A. Kümin, *The Shaping of a Community: The Rise and Reformation of the English Parish c.1400–1560* (Aldershot, 1996), chap. 2. K.L. French prefers to emphasize 'episcopal mandate' as the catalyst in the 'formation of communal identity' (*The People of the Parish. Community Life in a Late Medieval English Diocese* (Philadelphia: University of Pennsylvania Press, 2001), p. 21).

24. Kümin, *Shaping of a Community*, p. 55.

25. Brown, *Popular Piety*, pp. 83–9; French, *People of the Parish*, chap. 4.

26. F. Somers (ed.), *Halesowen Churchwardens' Accounts (1487–1582)*, (Worcestershire Historical Society, 1952–57); Bishop Hobhouse (ed.), *Churchwardens' Accounts of Croscombe, Pilton, Yatton, Titinhill, Morebath*

and St Michael Bath 1349–1580 (Somerset Record Society, iii, 1890), pp. 208–24.

27. See generally, Morris, *Churches in the Landscape*, chap. 7.

28. William of Malmesbury, *Gesta Regum Anglorum*, p. 460.

29. C. Peters, 'The Late Medieval English Church: Parish Devotion in Buildings and the Landscape. Interior and Furnishings', in *Church Archaeology. Research Directions for the Future*, ed. J. Blair and C. Pyrah (Council for British Archaelogy Research Report 104; York, 1996), pp. 68–75. And for the importance of the liturgy generally on church building, see C.N.L. Brooke, 'Religious Sentiment and Church Design. The Later Middle Ages', in his *Medieval Church and Society: Collected Essays* (London, 1971), pp. 162–82.

30. E. Fernie, 'The Effect of the Conquest on Norman Architectural Patronage', *Anglo-Norman Studies* ix (1986), pp. 71–85.

31. J. Blair, 'Clerical Communities and Parochial Space: the Planning of Urban Mother Churches in the Twelfth and Thirteenth Centuries', in *The Church in the Medieval Town*, ed. T.R. Slater and G. Rosser (Aldershot, 1998), pp. 272–94.

32. L.J. Proudfoot, 'The Extension of Parish Churches in Medieval Warwickshire', *Journal of Historical Geography* ix (1983), pp. 231–46.

33. See Blair, 'Clerical Communities'; and Rosser, 'Cure of Souls'.

34. P. Binski, 'Murals in the Nave of St Albans Abbey', in *Church and City 1000–1500: Essays in Honour of Christopher Brooke*, ed. D. Abulafia, M. Franklin and M. Rubin (Cambridge, 1992), pp. 249–78.

35. J.J. Wilkinson (ed.), *Receipts and Expenses in the Building of Bodmin Church AD 1469–72* (Camden Miscellany vii, new series 14; 1875).

36. Brown, *Popular Piety*, pp. 105, 122–3.

37. W.P. Baildon (ed.), *Select Cases in Chancery 1364 to 1471* (Selden Society, x; London, 1896), No. 20.

38. Quoted in Owst, *Literature and Pulpit*, p. 275.

39. Because the priest at Husthwaite (Yorkshire) had to serve an outlying chapel three days a week, his parishioners in 1472 complained that mass was not celebrated often enough in the mother church.

40. R.N. Swanson, 'Problems of the Priesthood in Pre-Reformation England', *English Historical Review* cv (1990), pp. 845–69; P. Marshall, *The Catholic Priesthood and the English Reformation* (Oxford, 1994).

41. T.C.B. Timmins (ed.), *The Register of John Chandler Dean of Salisbury 1404–17* (Wiltshire Record Society, xxxix; Devizes, 1984), No. 81.

42. *Ibid.*, Nos. 81, 563.

43. P. Blickle, 'Communal Reformation and Peasant Piety: The Peasant Reformation and its Late Medieval Origins', *Central European History* xx (1987), pp. 216–28; Kümin, *Shaping of a Community*, p. 11.

44. Such seems to be the agreement reached by villagers at Horsmonden in 1338 with Blackmore priory and the bishop of Rochester (C. Johnson (ed.), *Registrum Hamonis Hethe Diocesis Roffensis AD 1319–1352* (Canterbury and York Society, xlviii; Oxford, 1948), i, pp. 354–5).

45. At Castle Combe (Wiltshire) in 1406 the parishioners appointed their own priest and paid him out of the tithes of the church because the rector had not done so (J.M. Horn (ed.), *The Register of Roger Hallum Bishop of Salisbury 1404–12* (Canterbury and York Society, lxxii; Torquay, 1976), p. 43).

46. W. Page and J. Horace Round (ed.), *Victoria County History Essex vol. 2* (London, 1907), p. 17.

47. For two short surveys see B. Hanawalt, 'Keepers of the Lights: Late Medieval English Parish Gilds', *Journal of Medieval and Renaissance Studies* xiv (1984), pp. 21–37; and especially G. Rosser, 'Communities of Parish and Guild in the Later Middle Ages', in *Parish Church and People*, ed. S.J. Wright, pp. 29–55. For a survey of guilds in one region, see: V.R. Bainbridge, *Gilds in the Medieval Countryside: Social and Religious Change in Cambridgeshire c.1350–1550* (Woodbridge, 1996).

48. M.R. James (ed.) (revised C.N.L. Brooke and R.A.B. Mynors), *De nugis curialum by Walter Map* (Oxford, 1983), p. 154.

49. An observation made for guilds in the Low Countries: P. Trio, *Volksreligie als spiegel van den stedelijke samenleving: de broedershappen te Gent in late middeleeuwen* (Leuven, 1993), pp. 300–1.

50. J. Toulmin Smith and L. Toulmin Smith, *English Gilds* (Early English Text Society, original series, xl; London, 1870), pp. 137–40.

51. H.F. Westlake, *The Parish Gilds of Medieval England* (London, 1919), pp. 16, 20.

52. K. Farnhill, *Guilds and the Parish Community in Late Medieval East Anglia c.1470–1550* (Woodbridge, 2001), pp. 30–4. Farnhill stresses the importance of guilds as sources of credit.

53. Brown, *Popular Piety*, pp. 146–57; Crouch, *Piety, Fraternity and Power*, pp. 133–40.

54. For example: G. Rosser, *Medieval Westminster 1200–1540* (Oxford, 1989), pp. 281–2; Brown, *Popular Piety*, chap. 7.

55. B.R. McRee, 'Religious Guilds and Civic Order. The Case of Norwich in the Late Middle Ages', *Speculum* lxvii (1992), pp. 69–97.

56. Rosser, 'Communities of Parish and Guild'.

57. As Rosser ('Communities of Parish and Guild') makes clear; see also Brown, *Popular Piety*, pp. 132–58.

58. G. Rosser, 'Parochial Conformity and Voluntary Religion in Late Medieval England', *Transactions of the Royal Historical Society* sixth series, i (1991), pp. 173–89.

59. For examples, see Farnhill, *Guilds*, chaps 5–7.

60. See generally: N. Orme, 'Children and the Church in Medieval England', *Journal of Ecclesiastical History* xlv (1994), pp. 563–87.

61. Examples in Blair, *Surrey*, pp. 156–7.

62. K. Mertes, 'The Household as a Religious Community', in *People, Politics and Community in the Later Middle Ages*, ed. J. Rosenthal and C. Richmond (Gloucester, 1987), pp. 123–39; K. Mertes, *The English Noble Household 1250–1600* (Oxford, 1988), pp. 139–40.

63. Brown, *Popular Piety*, p. 205.

64. C. Kerrison and L. Toulmin Smith (eds), *A Commonplace Book of the Fifteenth Century* (London, 1926), pp. 10–12.

65. C.A.J. Armstrong, 'The Piety of Cicely, Duchess of York: A Study in Late Medieval Culture', in his *England, France and Burgundy in the Fifteenth Century* (London, 1983), pp. 135–56; C.M. Barron and A.F. Sutton (eds), *Medieval London Widows 1300–1500* (London, 1994).

66. Wiltshire Record Office, Trowbridge, G23/1/213, fols. 30v–31v.

67. N.P. Tanner (ed.), *Heresy Trials in the Diocese of Norwich 1428–31* (Camden Society, 4th series, xx; London, 1977), pp. 41–50.

68. S. Rees Jones, 'The Household and English Urban Government in the Later Middle Ages', in *The Household in Late Medieval Cities, Italy and Northwestern Europe Compared*, ed. M. Carlier and T. Soens (Louvain, 2001), pp. 71–87; C. Beattie, 'Governing Bodies: Law Courts, Male Householders, and Single Women in Late Medieval England', in *Managing Power, Wealth and the Body: The Christian Household c.800–1550*, ed. C. Beattie, A. Maslakovic and S. Rees Jones (Turnhout, 2003). I am grateful to the author for allowing me cite this article in advance of publication. Also: McSheffrey, 'Men and Masculinity'.

69. See especially Duffy, *Stripping of the Altars*, chap. 3.

70. Bartlett, *England under Norman and Angevin Kings*, pp. 449–50.

71. Examples in Brown, *Popular Piety*, pp. 81–3, 214.

72. E. Duffy, 'The Parish, Piety, and Patronage in Late Medieval East Anglia: the Evidence of Rood-Screens', in *The Parish in English Life*

1400–1600, ed. K.L. French, G.C. Gibbs and B.A. Kümin (Manchester, 1997), pp. 133–62.

73. A. Hudson, *The Premature Reformation. Wyclifite Texts and Lollard History* (Oxford, 1988), p. 150; Salisbury Cathedral Dean and Chapter Muniments, Register of John Burgh, fol.1; Select Cases in Chancery, No. 132; *Testamenta Eboracensia* (Surtees Society, liii; 1869), iv, 209.

74. *Calendar of Papal Letters*, x, pp. 621–2.

75. Heath, *Church and Realm*, pp. 279–81.

76. *Register of Thomas Bekynton*, p. 149.

77. For the following, see especially: R. Hutton, *The Stations of the Sun. A History of the Ritual Year in Britain* (Oxford, 1996).

78. *Dives and Pauper*, p. 157.

79. Owst, *Literature and Pulpit*, pp. 393–4.

80. *Registrum Hamonis Hethe*, i, p. 466; Wiltshire Record Office, Register of Bishop Neville, fol. 109.

81. R. Hutton, *The Rise and Fall of Merry England* (Oxford, 1994), pp. 59–60.

82. *Ibid.*, pp. 62–6; Kümin, *Shaping of a Community*, chap. 5.

83. D. Dymond and C. Paine, *The Spoils of Melford Church* (Ipswich, 1992).

84. For this interpretation see Duffy, *Stripping of the Altars*, pp. 37–40.

85. On the so-called 'religion of the gentry', see: C. Richmond, 'Religion and the Fifteenth-Century English Gentleman', in *The Church, Politics and Patronage in the Fifteenth Century*, ed. R.B. Dobson (Gloucester, 1984), pp. 193–208; C. Richmond, 'The English Gentry and Religion c.1500', in *Religious Belief and Ecclesiastical Careers in Late Medieval England*, ed. C. Harper-Bill (Woodbridge, 1991), pp. 121–50; C. Carpenter, 'The Religion of the Gentry in Fifteenth-Century England', in *England in the Fifteenth Century: Proceedings of the 1986 Harlaxton Symposium*, ed. D. Williams (Bury St Edmunds, 1987), pp. 53–74; Brown, *Popular Piety*, pp. 252–6. Richmond's argument for a 'detachment' of gentry from parish worship is the most interesting and contentious; it seems to work best if 'detachment' is taken to mean involvement but in a socially distinctive manner.

86. Quoted in P.D.A. Harvey, 'Initiative and Authority in Settlement Change', in *The Rural Settlements of Medieval England*, ed. M. Aston, D. Austin and C. Dyer (Oxford, 1989), p. 38. The villagers probably had no option, the change being forced on them by the plans of Thomas of Woodstock, duke of Gloucester, to found there a new

collegiate church (A. Goodman, *The Loyal Conspiracy, The Lords Appellant under Richard II* (London, 1971), pp. 82–4).

87. This seems generally to be the case despite individual exceptions and arguments that churchwardens were from a 'broad social base': Kümin, *Shaping of a Community*, pp. 31–41; French, *People of the Parish*, pp. 75–9, 85–9.

88. M. Aston, 'Segregation in Church', in *Women in the Church*, ed. W.J. Sheils and D. Wood (Studies in Church History, xxvii; Oxford, 1990), pp. 237–94.

89. C. Burgess, 'Shaping the Parish: St Mary at Hill, London, in the Fifteenth Century', in *The Cloister and the World. Essays in Medieval History in Honour of Barbara Harvey*, ed. J. Blair and B. Golding (Oxford, 1996), pp. 246–86.

90. M. Rubin, 'Small Groups: Identity and Solidarity in the Late Middle Ages', in *Enterprise and Individuals in Fifteenth-Century England*, ed. J. Kermode (Gloucester, 1991), pp. 134–49.

91. C.J. Calhoun, 'Community: Toward a Variable Conceptualization for Comparative Research', *Social History* v (1980), pp. 105–29; Kümin prefers the exercise of 'common sense' (*Shaping of a Community*, p. 2); French includes elements of diversity and compulsion in a definition of 'community' (*People of the Parish*, p. 21).

92. Dyer, 'The English Medieval Village Community and its Decline'.

93. C.A. Sneyd (ed.), *A Relation of the Island of England* (Camden Society, old series, xxxvii; 1847), p. 23; Wiltshire Record Office, Register of Bishop Audley, 1st series, fol. 158v.

94. For a comprehensive overview of women in late medieval parishes see: C. Peters, 'Women and the Reformation: Social Relations and Attitudes in Rural England c.1470–1570' (Oxford D.Phil. Thesis, 1993), chaps 4, 5, 6.

95. John Mirk, *Mirk's Festial: A Collection of Homilies by Johannes Mirkes*, ed. T. Erbe (Early English Text Society, extra series, xcvi; 1905), p. 57.

96. *Register of Dean Chandler*, 21.

97. P.H. Cullum, ' "And Hir Name was Charite": Charitable Giving by and for Women in Late Medieval Yorkshire', in *Woman is a Worthy Wight*, ed. P.J.P. Goldberg (Stroud, 1992), pp. 182–211.

98. Peters, 'Women and the Reformation', chap. 4.

99. K.L. French, 'Maidens' Lights and Wives' Stores: Women's Parish Guilds in Late Medieval England', *Sixteenth-Century Journal* xxix (1998), pp. 399–425.

100. K.L. French, '"To Free them from Binding": Women in the Late Medieval Parish', *Journal of Interdisciplinary History* xxvii (1997), pp. 387–412.

101. Brown, *Popular Piety*, p. 257. And for the difficulties of interpreting what the social implications of 'hocking' might have been, see C. Humphrey, *The Politics of Carnival. Festive Misrule in Medieval England* (Manchester, 2001), pp. 52–5.

102. French, *People of the Parish*, pp. 114–36.

103. G.M. Gibson, 'Blessing from Sun and Moon. Churching as Women's Theater', in *Bodies and Disciplines*, ed. Hanawalt and Wallace, pp. 139–54.

Chapter 5: Corporate Religion: Death and the Afterlife

1. Guillaume de Deguileville, *The Pilgrimage of Human Life*, ed. E. Clasby (London, 1992); Guillaume de Deguileville, *Pilgrimage of the Life of Man Englished by John Lydgate AD 1426*, ed. F.J. Furnivall (London, 1905).

2. J. Huizinga, *The Waning of the Middle Ages*, trans. F. Hopman (1924; Harmondsworth, 1982), p. 134. But for alternative general surveys used in this section see: M. Aston, 'Death', in *Fifteenth-Century Attitudes. Perceptions of Society in Late Medieval England*. ed. R. Horrox (Cambridge, 1994), pp. 202–28; P. Binski, *Medieval Death. Ritual and Representation* (London, 1996); J. Aberth, *From the Brink of the Apocalypse. Confronting Famine, War, Plague, and Death in the Later Middle Ages* (London, 2001), pp. 109–257; C.W. Bynum, *Last Things. Death and the Apocalypse in the Middle Ages* (Penn State University Park, 2000), pp. 1–10.

3. S. Wenzel (ed.), *Fasciculus Morum. A Fourteenth-Century Preacher's Handbook* (Penn State University Park; 1989), pp. 98–105; John Mirk, *Mirk's Festial*, p. 295.

4. Quoted in N.P. Tanner, *The Church in Late Medieval Norwich 1370–1532* (Toronto, 1984), pp. 59–60 – though the source is sixteenth century. For other examples see *infra*, chap. 6 iv.

5. Tristram, *English Wall Painting*, pp. 235–6.

6. Camille, *Luttrell Psalter*, pp. 89, 103.

7. British Library, Add. MS 34193, fols. 126–130v (E.M. Thompson, 'The Vision of Edmund Leversedge', *Notes and Queries for Somerset and Dorset* ix (1904), pp. 19–25).

8. C. Burgess, 'Death and Commemoration in an English Parish', in *The Place of the Dead. Death and Remembrance in Late Medieval and Early Modern Europe*, ed. B. Gordon and P. Marshall (Cambridge, 2000), p. 52.

9. *De nugis curialum*, p. 159 (and see Bartlett, *England under Normans and Angevins*, pp. 612–4); *Saint Modwenna*, ed. A.T. Baker and A. Bell (Anglo-Norman Text Society vii; Oxford, 1947), pp. 191–2; John Mirk, *Mirk's Festial*, p. 181.

10. W.L. Bowles and J.G. Nichols, *Annals and Antiquities of Lacock Abbey* (London, 1835), p. 201 (Appendix 1 for the 'Book of Lacock' *c.*1275).

11. Cited in Bartlett, *England under Normans and Angevins*, pp. 599–601.

12. D. Crouch, 'The Culture of Death in the Anglo-Norman World', in *Anglo-Norman Political Culture and the Twelfth-Century Renaissance*, ed. C. Warren-Hollister (Woodbridge, 1997), pp. 157–80 (esp. p. 175).

13. For examples see Brown, *Popular Piety*, pp. 332–4; more importantly: D. Postles, 'Lamps, Lights and Lay Folk: "Popular" Devotion Before the Black Death', *Journal of Medieval History* xxv (1999), pp. 97–114.

14. For example, see: D. Postles, 'Defensores Astabimus: Garendon Abbey and its Early Benefactors', in *Monasteries and Society in Medieval Britain*, ed. B. Thompson (Harlaxton Medieval Studies, vi; Stamford, 1999), pp. 97–116.

15. *De nugis curialum*, pp. 72–5 (also pp. 84–113).

16. M. Lambert, *Franciscan Poverty* (London, 1961).

17. For instance: R.S. Gottfried, *Bury St Edmunds and the Urban Crisis 1290–1539* (Princeton, 1982).

18. Brown, *Popular Piety*, pp. 46–7. And more importantly, see B. Thompson, 'Monasteries and their Patrons at Foundation and Dissolution', *Transactions of the Royal Historical Society* sixth series, iv (1994), 103–25.

19. J.T. Rosenthal, *The Purchase of Paradise. The Social Function of Aristocratic Benevolence, 1307–1485* (London, 1972), chap. 4.

20. S. Raban, *Mortmain Legislation and the English Church 1279–1500* (Cambridge, 1982).

21. B. Thompson, 'Habendum et tenendum: Lay and Ecclesiastical Attitudes to the Property of the Church', in *Religious Belief and Ecclesiastical Careers in Late Medieval England*, ed. C. Harper-Bill (Woodbridge, 1991), pp. 197–238.

22. For examples, Brown, *Popular Piety*, pp. 28–31. See also C. Cross, 'Monasticism and Society in the Diocese of York 1520–40', *Transactions of the Royal Historical Society* fifth series, xxxviii (1982), p. 132.

23. L. Rollason, 'The *Liber Vitae* of Durham and Lay Association with Durham Cathedral Priory in the Later Middle Ages', in *Monasteries and Society*, ed. Thompson, pp. 277–95.

24. Brown, *Popular Piety*, pp. 28–30, 37, 47–8.

25. M. Oliva, *The Convent and the Community in Late Medieval England: Female Monasteries in the Diocese of Norwich, 1350–1540* (Woodbridge, 1998), pp. 11–27.

26. See J. Greatrex (ed.), *The Vocation of Service to God and Neighbour: Essays on the Interests, Involvements and Problems of Religious Communities and their Members in Medieval Society* (Brepols, 1998).

27. K.L. Wood-Legh, *Perpetual Chantries in Britain* (Cambridge, 1955), pp. 1–3.

28. F. Barlow (ed.), *Durham Annals and Documents of the Thirteenth Century* (Surtees Society, clv; 1948), p. 228.

29. *Chronica Monasterii de Melsa*, ii, pp. 59–63.

30. F.N. Davis, C.W. Foster, A. Hamilton Thompson (eds), *Rotuli Ricardi Gravesend Diocesis Lincolniensis* (Canterbury and York Society, xxxi; 1925), pp. 24–6.

31. Brown, *Popular Piety*, pp. 33–4, 103–4; and more generally, A. Kreider, *English Chantries: the Road to Dissolution* (London, 1979), pp. 72–5.

32. References in Brown, *Popular Piety*, pp. 92–3. And see Kümin, *Shaping of a Community*, pp. 19–22.

33. W. Sparrow-Simpson (ed.), *Visitations of Churches Belonging to St Paul's Cathedral 1249–52* (Camden Society, new series liii; Camden Miscellany, ix; 1895), 23–6. By 1297 the same church had seven lights maintained by the hiring out of over 130 sheep to seventy-four people (*Visitations of Churches belonging to St Paul's Cathedral in 1297 and 1453* (Camden Society, new series lv; 1895), pp. 29–32).

34. Westlake, *Parish Guilds*, p. 153.

35. C.M. Barron, 'The Parish Fraternities of Medieval London', in *The Church in Pre-Reformation Society: Essays in Honour of F.R.H. DuBoulay*, ed. C.M. Barron and C. Harper-Bill (London, 1985), pp. 13–37. Crouch, *Piety, Fraternity and Power*, pp. 128–33.

36. Quoted in *ibid.*, p. 61.

37. *Ibid.*, pp. 33–4.

38. 'The Stoks of Seen' Church', *Wiltshire Notes and Queries* ii (1896), pp. 528–32; Duffy, *Stripping of the Altars*, p. 335.

39. For example, at Berkeley (Glos.) parishioners in 1278 undertook to find five marks a year to maintain such a priest 'in their chantry of the Virgin' (J.W. Willis Bund (ed.), *The Register of Bishop Godfrey*

Giffard 1268–1302 (Worcestershire Historical Society; Oxford, 1902), pp. 99).

40. Wood-Legh, *Perpetual Chantries*, pp. 8–10.
41. Brown, *Popular Piety*, pp. 97–8.
42. C. Burgess, ' "For the Increase of Divine Service": Chantries in the Parish in Late Medieval Bristol', *Journal of Ecclesiastical History* xxxvi (1985), pp. 46–65.
43. M.R. James, 'Twelve Medieval Ghost Stories', *English Historical Review* xxxvii (1922), pp. 413–23.
44. C. Burgess, ' "A Fond Thing Vainly Invented" ', pp. 56–84.
45. Brown, *Popular Piety*, pp. 22–3, 154–5.
46. See for example: C. Wordsworth, 'Wiltshire Pardons or Indulgences', *Wiltshire Archaeological and Natural History Magazine* xxxviii (1913), pp. 15–33 (from bishops of Salisbury registers); N. Orme, 'Indulgences in the Diocese of Exeter 1100–1536', *Report and Transactions of the Devonshire Association* cxx (1988), pp. 25–32.
47. For references see: A.D. Brown 'The Late Medieval English Church: Parish Devotion in Buildings and the Landscape. Parish Church-Building: the Fabric', in *Church Archaeology*, ed. J. Blair and C. Pyrah, pp. 63–8.
48. C. Burgess and B. Kümin, 'Penitential Bequests and Parish Regimes in Late Medieval England', *Journal of Ecclesiastical History* xliv (1993), pp. 610–30; Brown, *Popular Piety*, p. 108.
49. S. Flood (ed.), *St Albans Wills 1471–1500* (Hertfordshire Record Society Publications, ix; Cambridge, 1993), e.g. No. 148.
50. Duffy, *Stripping of the Altars*, p. 335.
51. N. Saul, *Scenes from Provincial Life: Knightly Families in Sussex 1280–1400* (Oxford, 1986), chap. 5; and more generally: N. Saul, *Death, Art, and Memory in Medieval England. The Cobham Family and their Monuments, 1300–1500* (Oxford, 2001).
52. K.J. Allison (ed.), *Victoria County History: York; East Riding, vol i* (Oxford, 1969), pp. 81–2, 333.
53. M. Norris, 'Late Medieval Monumental Brasses: an Urban Funerary Industry and its Representations of Death', in *Death in Towns. Urban Responses to the Dying and the Dead 100–1600*, ed. S. Bassett (Leicester, 1992), p. 194.
54. Robert Mannyng of Brunne, *Handlyng Synne*, ed. I. Sullens (New York, 1983), pp. 219–20.
55. F.W. Weaver (ed.), *Somerset Medieval Wills 1383–1500* (Somerset Record Society, xvi; 1901), i, p. 68. For examples of the trend in parts

of southern and northern England, see Brown, *Popular Piety*, pp. 203–4, and Hughes, *Pastors and Visionaries*, p. 123.

56. Saul, *Art and Memory*, p. 233.

57. J. Gairdner (ed.), *The Paston Letters* (6 vols; London, 1904), v, No. 791.

58. P.M. King, 'The Cadaver Tomb in the Late Fifteenth Century: Some Indications of a Lancastrian Connection', in *Dies Illa: Death in the Middle Ages*, ed. J.H.M. Taylor (Liverpool, 1984), pp. 45–57.

59. F. Warren and B. White (ed.), *The Dance of Death* (Early English Text Society clxxxi; London, 1931); H.N. McCracken (ed.), *The Minor Poems of John Lydgate; Part ii* (Early English Text Society, original series, cxcii; London, 1934), p. 702.

60. See texts in R. Horrox (ed.), *The Black Death* (Manchester, 1994), pp. 150–4; 110–24.

61. See comments on Julian of Norwich's 'Showings' in Aberth, *From the Brink of the Apocalypse*, pp. 175–7.

62. Horrox, *Black Death*, pp. 82–4.

63. For a judicious assessment, see B. Nilson, *Cathedral Shrines of Medieval England* (Woodbridge, 1998), esp. p. 67. I would emphasize the impact of the second major visitation of plague in 1361 (see graphs and tables pp. 211–41).

64. S.K. Cohn, *The Cult of Remembrance and the Black Death. Six Renaissance Cities in Central Italy* (London, 1992); S.K. Cohn, 'The Place of the Dead in Flanders and Tuscany,' in *The Place of the Dead. Death and Remembrance in Late Medieval and Early Modern Europe*, ed. B. Gordon and P. Marshall (Cambridge, 2000), pp. 17–43.

65. Testamentary evidence from pre-Black Death England is much sparser than it is for Italy. The Salisbury figures are from admittedly small samples: 14 wills 1270–1349; 64 wills 1361–99; 48 wills 1400–49 (sources: Brown, *Popular Piety*, pp. 21, 101). Similar comments about more lavish funeral provision after Plague have been made about Bury St Edmunds and (by the early 1400s) about Hull, though absence of pre-Plague wills makes comparisons even more difficult (R. Dinn, 'Death and Rebirth in late Medieval Bury St Edmunds', in *Death in Towns. Urban Responses to the Dying and the Dead 100–1600*, ed. S. Bassett (Leicester, 1992), pp. 155, 165; P. Heath, 'Urban Piety, p. 219).

66. M. Vale, 'Piety, Charity and Literacy among the Yorkshire Gentry 1370–1480', *Borthwick Papers*, i (1976), pp. 1–32.

67. For sources used in the following section, by town or region: Bath (C.B. Pearson (ed.), 'The Churchwardens' Accounts of the Church

and Parish of St Michael without North Gate Bar 1349–1575',
Somersetshire Archaeological and Natural History Society, xxiii (1877),
1–28); Berkshire – Reading and Newbury (A.D. Brown, 'Perpetual
Chantries in Late Medieval Berkshire', in *An Historical Atlas of
Berkshire*, ed. J. Dils (Reading, 1998), pp. 30–1); Beverley (A.F. Leach
(ed.), *Beverley Town Documents* (Selden Society, xiv; London, 1900));
Bridport (Brown, *Popular Piety*, pp. 134–7, 160–2); Bridgewater
(T.B. Dilkes (ed.), *Bridgewater Borough Archives 1200–1377* (Somerset
Record Society, xlviii; 1933) vol. i; and *1377–99* liii (1938), vol ii; also
R.W. Dunning (ed.), *Victoria County History: Somerset* (Oxford, 1992),
vol vi, pp. 230–3); Bristol (C. Burgess, 'Strategies for Eternity:
Perpetual Chantry Foundation in Late Medieval Bristol', in *Religious
Belief and Ecclesiastical Careers in Late Medieval England*, ed. C. Harper-Bill
(Woodbridge, 1991), pp. 1–34); Cambridgeshire (Bainbridge, *Gilds*,
pp. 104–5); Colchester (J. Cooper (ed.), *Victoria County History: Essex*,
vol ix (Oxford, 1994), pp. 53, 64; Gloucester (N.M. Herbert (ed.),
Victoria County History: Gloucester, vol. iv (Oxford, 1988), pp. 39,
292–308); Hartlepool (W. Page (ed.), *Victoria County History: Durham,
vol. iii* (London, 1908), p. 284); Hull (K.J. Allison (ed.), *Victoria
County History: York; East Riding, vol. i*, pp. 40–1, 287–8); London
(J.A.F. Thomson, 'Piety and Charity in Late Medieval London',
Journal of Ecclesiastical History xvi (1965), pp. 178–95; Barron, 'Parish
Fraternities'); Norwich (Tanner, *Norwich*, pp. 212–9); Salisbury
(Brown, *Popular Piety*, pp. 95, 98–9, 113–4, 162–8); Wells (D.G. Shaw,
The Creation of a Community: the City of Wells in the Middle Ages (Oxford,
1993), p. 125); York and Yorkshire (Crouch, *Piety, Fraternity and Power*,
chap. 1).

68. Westlake, *Parish Gilds*, p. 50.
69. Kreider, *English Chantries*, pp. 72–5.
70. R. Hutton is less inclined to see the late medieval expansion of
the 'ritual year' as prompted by social anxieties (in *Stations of the Sun*,
pp. 412–5). But for the link made in Italian towns after the Black
Death between 'flamboyant funerals' and social competition or
fluidity, see S.T. Strocchia, *Death and Ritual in Renaissance Florence*
(London, 1992), chap. 3.
71. Crouch, *Piety, Fraternity and Power*, pp. 133–40; French, *People of the
Parish*, p. 79; Brown, *Popular Piety*, pp. 139, 179–80. For examples of
guilds operating more independently of the parish, see Farnhill,
Guilds, pp. 141–2.

72. For the following see above Introduction iv; also: S. Beckwith, 'Making the World in York and the York Cycle', in *Framing Medieval Bodies*, ed. S. Kay and M. Rubin (Manchester, 1996), pp. 254–76; S. Beckwith, 'Ritual, Theater and Social Space in the York Corpus Christi Cycle', in *Bodies and Disciplines*, ed. Hanawalt and Wallace, pp. 63–86.
73. Humphrey, *Politics of Carnival*, pp. 63–82.
74. B.R. McRee, 'Religious Guilds and Regulation of Behaviour in Late Medieval Towns', in *People, Politics and Community in the Later Middle Ages*, ed. J. Rosenthal and C. Richmond (Gloucester, 1987), pp. 108–22.
75. See *infra*, chap. 4 vi for references.
76. Morrison, *Women Pilgrims*, chap. 2.
77. M. Rubin, *Charity and Community in Medieval Cambridge* (Cambridge, 1987), esp. pp. 50–3, 289–97.
78. Brown, *Popular Piety*, chap. 8.
79. M.K. McIntosh, *Autonomy and Community: the Royal Manor of Havering, 1200–1500* (Cambridge, 1986), pp. 235–40; M.K. McIntosh, 'Local Responses to the Poor in Late Medieval and Tudor England', *Continuity and Change* iii (2) (1988), pp. 209–45; and see above, Introduction iv.

Chapter 6: Reforming the 'Inner' Life: Orthodoxy and Heresy

1. Wogan-Browne, *Saints' Lives*; Camille, *Luttrell Psalter*, p. 98; J. Catto, 'Religion and the English Nobility in the Late-Fourteenth Century', in *History and Imagination: Essays in Honour of H.R. Trevor-Roper*, ed. H. Lloyd-Jones, V. Pearl and B. Worden (London, 1981), pp. 43–55.
2. For references see chap. 2 v; and see Hughes, *Pastors and Visionaries*, pp. 64–126.
3. Henry of Lancaster, *Le livre de seyntz medicines*, ed. E.J. Arnould (Oxford, 1940); K. Fowler, *The King's Lieutenant: Henry of Grosmont, First Duke of Lancaster* (London, 1969), pp. 193–6; V.J. Scattergood (ed.), *The Works of Sir John Clanvowe* (Cambridge, 1975), esp. pp. 57, 67.
4. Walter Hilton, *The Scale of Perfection*, ed. H. Backhouse (London, 1992), Bk ii, chap. 40.
5. N. Watson, 'Fashioning the Puritan Gentry-Woman: Devotion and Dissent in Book to a Mother', in *Medieval Women: Texts and Contexts in Late Medieval Britain. Essays for Felicity Riddy*, ed. J. Wogan-Browne,

R. Voaden, A. Diamond and A. Hutchison (Turnhout, 2000), pp. 169–84.

6. Wogan-Browne, *Saints' Lives*, chap. 1.

7. D. Greenway and L. Watkiss (eds), *The Book of the Foundation of Walden Monastery* (Oxford, 1995), pp. 122–4.

8. C.W. Bynum, *Jesus as Mother: Studies in the Spirituality of the High Middle Ages* (Berkeley, 1982); C.W. Bynum, *Holy Feast and Holy Fast* (Berkeley, 1987). For challenges to the association of the women with the 'body', see K. Biddick, 'Gender, Bodies, Borders: Technologies of the Visible', *Speculum* lxviii (1993), pp. 389–418 and S. Farmer, 'The Beggar's Body: Intersections of Gender and Social Status in High Medieval Paris', in *Monks and Nuns*, ed. Farmer and Rosenwein, pp. 153–71.

9. Biddick, 'Gender, Bodies'.

10. Wogan-Browne, *Saints' Lives*, chaps 6 and 7.

11. B. Millett, 'Women in No Man's Land: English Recluses and the Development of Vernacular Literature in the Twelfth and Thirteenth Centuries', in *Women and Literature in Britain 1150–1500*, ed. C.M. Meale (Cambridge, 1993), pp. 86–103. For possible 'beguinages' in late medieval Norwich, however, see Tanner, *Norwich*, pp. 202–3.

12. K.L. Lewis, *The Cult of St Katherine of Alexandria in Late Medieval England* (Woodbridge, 2000), p. 217.

13. Wogan-Browne, *Saints' Lives*, chaps 1 and 4.

14. *Ibid.*, chap. 6.

15. *Saint Modwenna*, ed. Baker and Bell, pp. 291–2.

16. Farmer, 'Beggar's Body'.

17. R.B. Dobson (ed.), *The Peasants' Revolt* (2nd edn; London, 1983), p. 382 (from the chronicle of Henry Knighton).

18. See generally: Clanchy, *From Memory to Written Record*; J.A.H. Moran, *The Growth of English Schooling 1340–1548: Learning Literacy and Laicization in Pre-Reformation York Diocese* (Princeton, 1985); H. Spencer, *English Preaching in the Later Middle Ages* (Oxford, 1993), esp. pp. 33–45.

19. For the following see, for instance: Clanchy, *From Memory to Written Record*, esp. chaps 2, 6–8; M. Aston, 'Devotional Literacy', in M. Aston, *Lollards and Reformers. Images and Literacy in Late Medieval Religion* (London, 1984), pp. 101–33; S. Justice, *Writing and Rebellion. England in 1381* (London, 1994), pp. 30–6.

20. L.R. Poos, 'Social History and the Book of Hours', in R.S. Wieck (ed.), *Time Sanctified: The Book of Hours in Medieval Art and Life* (New York, 1988), p. 37; Lewis, *St Katherine of Alexandria*, esp. p. 184.

21. Quoted in Justice, *Writing and Rebellion*, p. 18. And see: S. Crane, 'The Writing Lesson of 1381', in *Chaucer's England. Literature in Historical Context*, ed. B. Hanawalt (Minneapolis, 1992), pp. 201–21.

22. *The Idea of the Vernacular. An Anthology of Middle English Literary Theory 1280–1520*, ed. J. Wogan-Browne, N. Watson, A. Taylor and R. Evans (Exeter, 1999), p. 119.

23. John Mirk, *Mirk's Festial*, pp. 124–9.

24. N. Watson, 'Censorship and Cultural Change in Late-Medieval England: Vernacular Theology, the Oxford Translation Debate, and Arundel's Constitutions of 1409', *Speculum* lxx (1995), esp. pp. 840–6.

25. F.J. Furnivall et al. (eds), *Hoccleve's Works: the Minor Poems* (Early English Text Society, lxi and lxxiii; 1892 and 1897; new. ed. 1970), p. 13.

26. William of Newburgh, 'Historia', i, pp. 131–4; P. Biller, 'The Earliest Heretical Englishwomen', in *Medieval Women*, ed. J. Wogan-Browne et al., pp. 363–75.

27. Bartlett, *England under Normans and Angevins*, pp. 479–80; B. Harvey, *The Short Oxford History of the British Isles: The Twelfth and Thirteenth Centuries* (Oxford, 2001), p. 260; R.I. Moore, 'Literacy and the Making of Heresy c.1000–c.1150', in P. Biller and A. Hudson (eds), *Heresy and Literacy, 1000–1530* (Cambridge, 1994), p. 34.

28. William of Newburgh, 'Historia', ii, pp. 466–73; J.I. Cate, 'The English Mission of Eustace of Flay (1200–1201)', in *Etudes d'histoire dédiées à la mémoire de Henri Pirenne*, ed. F.L. Ganshof (Brussels, 1937), pp. 67–89. And for Eustace's mission as part of a wider genre of charismatic and revivalist preaching, see Dickson, 'Encounters in Medieval Revivalism', pp. 283–4.

29. B. Stock, *The Implications of Literacy: Written Language and Models of Interpretation in the Eleventh and Twelfth Centuries* (Princeton, 1983), esp. chap. 2 (for his influential ideas on 'textual communities'). And several articles in P. Biller and A. Hudson (eds), *Heresy and Literacy, 1000–1530* (Cambridge, 1994) (esp. P. Biller, 'Heresy and Literacy: Earlier History of the Theme', pp. 1–18; R.N. Swanson, 'Literacy, Heresy, History and Orthodoxy: Perspectives and Permutations for the Later Middle Ages', pp. 279–93).

30. R.I. Moore, *The Formation of a Persecuting Society: Power and Deviance in Western Europe, 950–1250* (Oxford, 1987).

31. See generally, Langmuir, *History, Religion and Antisemitism*.

32. H. Leyser, *Hermits and the New Monasticism. A Study of Religious Communities in Western Europe 1000–1150* (London, 1984), esp. pp. 77, 80.

33. Moore, 'Literacy and the Making of Heresy', p. 34.
34. Powicke and Cheney, *Councils and Synods*, ii, p. 379.
35. Millett, ' "Women in No Man's Land" '.
36. Warren, *Anchorites*, pp. 21–2, 79–80; chaps 5–7; Hughes, *Pastors and Visionaries*, pp. 64–126.
37. For this section see generally: K.B. McFarlane, *John Wycliffe and the Beginnings of English Nonconformity* (London, 1952); Hudson, *The Premature Reformation*, chap. 2; A. Kenny (ed.), *Wyclif and his Times* (Oxford, 1986). For a useful overview see: R. Rex, *The Lollards* (Basingstoke, 2002), chaps 2 and 3.
38. Southern, *Grosseteste*, pp. 298–309.
39. J.I. Catto, 'John Wyclif and the Cult of the Eucharist', in *The Bible in the Medieval World*, ed. K. Walsh and D. Woods (Studies in Church History, Subsidia iv; Oxford, 1985), pp. 269–86.
40. A. Goodman, *John of Gaunt. The Exercise of Princely Power in Fourteenth-Century Europe* (Harlow, 1992), chap. 11.
41. K.B. McFarlane, *Lancastrian Kings and Lollard Knights* (Oxford, 1972), pp. 202–20.
42. J.A.F. Thomson, 'Orthodox Religion and the Origins of Lollards', *History* lxxiv (1989), pp. 39–55.
43. Henry Knighton, *Chronicon*, ed. J.R. Lumby (2 vols, Rolls Series; London, 1889–95), ii, pp. 179, 186–7.
44. M. Aston, 'Lollardy and Sedition, 1381–1431', in her *Lollards and Reformers*, pp. 1–47.
45. Justice, *Writing and Rebellion*, chap. 2.
46. R.G. Davies, 'Richard II and the Church', in *Richard II*, ed. Goodman and Gillespie pp. 83–106.
47. For the following see P. McNiven, *Heresy and Politics in the Reign of Henry IV: The Burning of John Badby* (Woodbridge, 1987); and especially P. Strohm, *England's Empty Throne. Usurpation and the Language of Legitimation 1399–1422* (London, 1990), esp. chap. 2.
48. *Hoccleve's Works*, pp. 47–9.
49. E. Powell, *Kingship, Law and Society: Criminal Justice in the Reign of Henry V* (Oxford, 1989), chap. 6.
50. Quoted in McFarlane, *John Wycliffe*, p. 68. And see more generally: Thomson, *Later Lollards*.
51. Hudson, *Premature Reformation, passim*. However, R. Rex (*Lollards*, pp. 75–8) is more sceptical about the implications of 'Lollard' literature for the presence of a coherent sect.

52. *Norwich Heresy Trials*, p. 45.
53. R.M. Haines, 'Reginald Pecock: a Tolerant Man in an Age of Intolerance', in *Persecution and Toleration*, ed. W.J. Sheils (Studies in Church History, xxi; Oxford, 1984), pp. 125–37.
54. Wiltshire Record Office, Salisbury Bishops' Registers: Register of Bishop Audley, 1st series, fol. 169.
55. Brown, *Popular Piety*, p. 222.
56. Hudson, *Premature Reformation*, esp. pp. 193, 279.
57. *Rotuli Parliamentorum*, v, p. 632.
58. For references to these see Hudson, *Premature Reformation*, pp. 149–50.
59. See especially, Watson, 'Censorship and Cultural Change'; and D. Aers, 'Altars of Power'.
60. Catto, 'Religious Change under Henry V'.
61. H. Spencer in particular emphasizes the 'repressive' effect of Arundel's Constitutions, but in a more qualified way (Spencer, *English Preaching*, e.g. pp. 177–86.)
62. D. Lawton, 'Englishing the Bible, 1066–1549', in Wallace (ed.), *Cambridge History*, esp. p. 455.
63. Spencer, *English Preaching*, pp. 60–6.
64. D.P. Wright (ed.), *The Register of Thomas Langton, Bishop of Salisbury, 1485–93* (Canterbury and York Society, lxxiv; 1985), p. 419.
65. D. Plumb, 'The Social and Economic Status of the Later Lollards', in *The World of Rural Dissenters, 1520–1725*, ed. M. Spufford (Cambridge, 1995), pp. 103–31; Brown, *Popular Piety*, pp. 217–8.; R. Lutton, 'Connections Between Lollards, Townsfolk and Gentry in Tenterden in the Late Fifteenth and Early Sixteenth Centuries', in *Lollardy and the Gentry in the Later Middle Ages*, ed. M. Aston and C. Richmond (Stroud, 1997), pp. 199–228.
66. Cf. Owst, *Literature and Pulpit*, pp. 482–3.
67. Warren, *Anchorites*, chaps 6 and 7; Brown, *Popular Piety*, pp. 206–7.
68. See especially: J.I. Catto, 'Fellows and Helpers: The Religious Identity of the Followers of Wyclif', in *The Medieval Church: Universities, Heresy, and the Religious Life*, ed. P. Biller and B. Dobson (Studies in Church History, Subsidia xi; Woodbridge, 1999), pp. 141–61.
69. *Register of Bishop Langton*, p. 495.
70. C. Cross, ' "Great Reasoners in Scripture": The Activities of Women Lollards 1380–1530', in *Medieval Women*, ed. D. Baker (Oxford, 1978), pp. 359–80; M. Aston 'Lollard Women Priests?', in M. Aston, *Lollards and Reformers*, pp. 49–70.

71. For the arguments in this paragraph see: S. McSheffrey, *Gender and Heresy: Women and Men in Lollard Communities, 1420–1530* (Philadelphia, 1995).

72. Armstrong, 'Piety of Cicely, Duchess of York'; A.M. Hutchison, 'Devotional Reading and the Monastery in the Late Medieval Household', in *De Cella in Seculum. Religious and Secular Life and Devotion in Late Medieval England*, ed. M.G. Sargent (Cambridge, 1989), pp. 215–27; C.M. Meale, '"... alle the bokes I have of latyn, english, and frensch": Laywomen and Their Books in Late Medieval England', in *Women and Literature in Britain 1150–1500*, ed. C.M. Meale (Cambridge, 1993), pp. 128–58.

73. Text in McCracken, *Lydgate*, pp. 173–92. See Winstead, *Virgin Martyrs*, pp. 122–4.

74. Lewis, *The Cult of St Katherine*, chap. 4.

75. M.Y. Offard (ed.), *William Caxton. The Book of the Knight of the Tower* (Early English Text Society, Special Series, ii; London, 1971), esp. p. 92.

76. F. Riddy, '"Women Talking About Things of God": A Late Medieval Sub-Culture' in *Women and Literature in Britain*, ed. Meale, pp. 104–27.

77. K. Ashley and P. Sheingorn (eds), *Interpreting Cultural Symbols. Saint Anne in Late Medieval Society* (London, 1990), introduction; Lewis, *The Cult of St Katherine*, chap. 5.

78. G. Ashton, *The Generation of Identity in Late Medieval Hagiography. Speaking the Saint* (London, 2000), esp. pp. 12, 64 (following French feminists Irigaray and Cixous).

79. F. Riddy, 'Mother Knows Best: Reading Social Change in a Courtesy Text', *Speculum* lxxi (1996), pp. 66–86.

80. See Introduction iv and chap. 4 vi for references; also, for urban legislation in Coventry in 1492, see P.J.P. Goldberg, 'Coventry's 'Lollard' Programme of 1492 and the Making of Utopia', in *Pragmatic Utopias. Ideals and Communities, 1200–1630*, ed. R. Horrox and S. Rees Jones (Cambridge, 2001), pp. 97–116.

81. Contrast Duffy, *Stripping of the Altars*, e.g. pp. 19, 109–10 with C. Richmond, 'Religion', pp. 183, 195. For the placing of Margery Kempe within East Anglian religious culture see: G.M. Gibson, *The Theater of Devotion. East Anglian Drama and Society in the Late Middle Ages* (Chicago, 1989); and for a wider context, see the splendid *Margery Kempe and her World* by A. Goodman. The literature on Margery Kempe is now so vast, that complete reference to other important contributions is impossible here.

82. A. Goodman, 'The Piety of John Brunham's Daughter, of Lynn', in *Medieval Women*, ed. D. Baker (Oxford, 1978), pp. 347–58.

83. K. Lochrie, *Margery Kempe and Translations of the Flesh* (Penn State University Park, 1991), esp. chaps 2 and 3.

84. L. Staley, *Margery Kempe's Dissenting Fictions* (Penn State University Park, 1994).

85. *The Book of Margery Kempe*, esp. Bk 1, chaps 46–8, 52.

86. *Ibid.*, Bk 1, chaps 11, 16, 23, 24, 43, 44, 60, 67, 68, 83.

87. *Ibid.*, Bk 1, chaps 46–56.

88. *Ibid.*, Bk 1, chap. 69.

89. S. Rees Jones, ' "A peler of Holy Church": Margery Kempe and the Bishops', in *Medieval Women*, ed. J. Wogan-Browne et al., pp. 377–91.

90. *The Book of Margery Kempe*, esp. Bk 1, chaps 15, 16, 45, 69.

91. *Ibid*, esp. Proem, Preface; Bk 1, chaps 58 and 62.

92. Lochrie, *Margery Kempe*, esp. chaps 1–3. See also: S. Beckwith, 'A Very Material Mysticism: the Medieval Mysticism of Margery Kempe', in *Medieval Literature: Criticism, Ideology and History*, ed. D. Aers (Brighton, 1986), pp. 34–57.

93. *The Book of Margery Kempe*, esp. Bk 1, chaps 28, 45.

94. *Ibid.*, Bk I, chap. 40.

95. Staley, *Dissenting Fictions*. Alternatively, for the 'real' Margery in the Book reflecting individualism and commercialism in the post-Black Death economy see: D. Aers, 'The Making of Margery Kempe', in his *Community, Gender and Individual Identity* (London, 1988), pp. 73–116.

Conclusion

1. For a good introduction to recent views and a work which highlights continuities in the Reformation process, see (in this series): C. Marsh, *Popular Religion in Sixteenth-Century England* (London, 1998).

Further Reading

General Background

Religion, Society and Ritual

C. Bell, *Ritual Theory, Ritual Practice* (Oxford, 1992).

C. Bell, *Ritual. Perspectives and Dimensions* (Oxford, 1997).

E. Durkheim, *The Elementary Forms of the Religious Life* (1915; London, 1964).

M.B. Hamilton, *The Sociology of Religion. Theoretical and Comparative Perspectives* (London, 1995).

D. Handleman, *Models and Mirrors: Towards an Anthropology of Public Events* (Cambridge, 1990).

G.I. Langmuir, *History, Religion and Antisemitism* (Oxford, 1990).

M.B. McGuire, *Religion. The Social Context* (4th edn; London, 1997).

B.S. Turner, *Religion and Society. A Materialist Perspective* (London, 1983), esp. pp. 78–80.

M. Weber, *The Sociology of Religion*, trans. E. Fischoff, ed. T. Parsons (London, 1965).

Gender Theory

J. Butler, *Gender Trouble: Feminism and the Subversion of Identity* (rev. ed.; London, 1999).

T. Moi, *What is a Woman? And Other Essays* (Oxford, 1999).

Medieval Society

Society and Ritual

S. Beckwith, *Christ's Body. Identity, Culture and Society in Late Medieval Writings* (London, 1993).
S. Beckwith, 'Ritual, Theater and Social Space in the York Corpus Christi Cycle', in *Bodies and Disciplines. Intersections and History in Fifteenth-Century England*, ed. B. Hanawalt and D. Wallace (Minneapolis, 1996), pp. 63–86.
C. Humphrey, *The Politics of Carnival. Festive Misrule in Medieval England* (Manchester, 2001).
M. James, 'Ritual, Drama and Social Body in the Late Medieval English Town', in his *Society, Politics and Culture* (Cambridge, 1986), pp. 16–47.
M. Rubin, 'Europe Remade: Purity and Danger in Late Medieval Europe', *Transactions of the Royal Historical Society* sixth series, xi (2001), pp. 101–24.

Social Change and Theory

J.L. Bolton, *The Medieval English Economy 1150–1500* (London, 1980).
J. Bolton, ' "The World Upside Down". Plague as an Agent of Economic and Social Change', in *The Black Death in England*, ed. W.M. Ormrod and P. Lindley (Stamford, 1996), pp. 17–78.
R.H. Britnell, *The Commercialisation of English Society 1000–1500* (2nd edn; Manchester, 1996).
G. Constable, *Three Studies in Medieval Religious and Social Thought* (Cambridge, 1995), pp. 251–341.
J. Denton (ed.), *Orders and Hierarchies in Late Medieval and Renaissance Europe* (Houndmills, 1999).
C. Dyer, *Standards of Living in the Later Middle Ages. Social Change in England c.1200–1520* (Cambridge, 1989).
C. Dyer, 'The English Medieval Village Community and its Decline', *Journal of British Studies* xxxiii (1994), pp. 407–29.
R. Faith, *The English Peasantry and the Growth of Lordship* (London, 1997).
R.H. Hilton, 'Ideology and Social Order in Late Medieval England', in his *Class Conflict and the Crisis of Feudalism* (2nd edn; London, 1996), pp. 246–52.
M. Keen, *English Society in the Later Middle Ages 1348–1500* (London, 1990).

M.K. McIntosh, *Controlling Misbehaviour in England 1370–1600* (Cambridge, 1998).

S.H. Rigby, *English Society in the Later Middle Ages. Class, Status and Gender* (London, 1995).

M. Rubin, *Charity and Community in Medieval Cambridge* (Cambridge, 1987).

R. M. Smith, ' "Modernization" and the Corporate Medieval Village Community in England: Some Sceptical Reflections', in *Explorations in Historical Geography. Interpretative Essays*, ed. A.R.H. Baker and D. Gregory (Cambridge, 1984), pp. 140–79.

Gender, Society and Religion

C. Beattie, 'Meanings of Singleness: The Single Woman in Late Medieval England' (Unpublished doctoral dissertation, University of York, 2001), part 1, pp. 27–61.

J.M. Bennett, *Medieval Women in Modern Perspective* (Washington, 2000).

K. Biddick, 'Gender, Bodies, Borders: Technologies of the Visible', *Speculum* lxviii (1993), 389–418.

C.W. Bynum, *Jesus as Mother: Studies in the Spirituality of the High Middle Ages* (Berkeley, 1982).

C.W. Bynum, *Holy Feast and Holy Fast* (Berkeley, 1987).

P.H. Cullum, ' "And Hir Name was Charite": Charitable Giving by and for Women in Late Medieval Yorkshire', in *Woman is a Worthy Wight*, ed. P.J.P. Goldberg (Stroud, 1992), pp. 182–211.

M.E. Mate, *Women in Medieval English Society* (Cambridge, 1999).

C. Peters, 'Women and the Reformation: Social Relations and Attitudes in Rural England c.1470–1570', (Oxford D.Phil. Thesis, 1993).

A. Vauchez, 'Female Prophets, Visionaries, and Mystics in Medieval Europe', in *The Laity in the Middle Ages: Religious Belief and Devotional Practices*, trans. M.J. Schneider ed. D. E. Bornstein (Notre Dame, Ind., 1993), pp. 219–29.

The Medieval Church

General

G. Constable, *The Reformation of the Twelfth Century* (Cambridge, 1996).

J. Le Goff, *La naissance du purgatoire* (Paris, 1981).

C. Morris, *The Papal Monarchy. The Western Church from 1050 to 1250* (Oxford, 1989).

A. Murray, *Reason and Society in the Middle Ages* (Oxford, 1978).

R.W. Southern, *Western Society and the Church in the Middle Ages* (Harmondsworth, 1970).

R.N. Swanson, *Religion and Devotion in Europe c.1215–c.1515* (Cambridge, 1995).

J.A.F. Thomson, *The Western Church in the Middle Ages* (London, 1998).

The Church, Clergy and Laity in England

J. Blair, *Early Medieval Surrey. Landholding, Church and Settlement before 1300* (Stroud, 1991).

R. Brentano, *Two Churches. England and Italy in the Thirteenth Century* (Princeton, 1968).

C.N.L. Brooke, 'The Medieval Town as Ecclesiastical Centre: General Survey', in *European Towns. Their Archaeology and Early History*, ed. M.W. Barley (London, 1977), pp. 459–74.

N. Brooks, *The Early History of the Church of Canterbury: Christ Church from 597 to 1066* (Leicester, 1994).

J. Campbell, 'The Church in Anglo-Saxon Towns', in *The Church in Town and Countryside*, ed. D. Baker (Studies in Church History, xvi; Oxford, 1979), pp. 119–35.

J. I. Catto, 'Religious Change under Henry V', in *Henry V: the Practice of Kingship*, ed. G.L. Harriss (Oxford, 1985), pp. 97–115.

C.R. Cheney, *From Becket to Langton: English Church Government 1170–1213* (Manchester, 1956).

C. Cubitt, *Anglo-Saxon Church Councils c.650–c.850* (Leicester, 1995).

R.G. Davies, 'The Episcopate', in *Profession, Vocation and Culture in Later Medieval England: Essays Dedicated to the Memory of A.R. Myers*, ed. C.H. Clough (Liverpool, 1982).

W.J. Dohar, *The Black Death and Pastoral Leadership. The Diocese of Hereford in the Fourteenth Century* (Penn State University Park, 1995).

M. Haren, *Sin and Society in Fourteenth-Century England. A Study of the Memoriale Presbitorum* (Oxford, 2000).

C. Harper-Bill, 'English Religion after the Black Death', in *The Black Death in England*, ed. W.M. Ormrod and P. Lindley (Stamford, 1996), pp. 79–123.

D. Hay, 'The Church of England in the Later Middle Ages', *History* liii (1968), pp. 35–50.

P. Heath, *Church and Realm 1272–1461* (London, 1988).

J. Hughes, *Pastors and Visionaries: Religion and Secular Life in Late Medieval Yorkshire* (Woodbridge, 1988).

H.R. Loyn, *The English Church 940–1154* (Harlow, 2000).

P. Marshall, *The Catholic Priesthood and the English Reformation* (Oxford, 1994).

H. Mayr-Harting, *The Coming of Christianity to Anglo-Saxon England* (London, 2nd edn, 1991).

D.M. Owen, *Church and Society in Medieval Lincolnshire* (Lincoln, 1971).

W.A. Pantin, *The English Church in the Fourteenth Century* (Cambridge, 1955), pp. 189–262.

G. Rosser, 'The Cure of Souls in English Towns before 1000', in *Pastoral Care Before the Parish*, ed. J. Blair and R. Sharpe (Leicester, 1992), pp. 267–84.

R.W. Southern, *Robert Grosseteste: the Growth of an English Mind in Medieval Europe* (Oxford, 1986).

R.W. Southern, *St Anselm. A Portrait in a Landscape* (Cambridge, 1990).

R.N. Swanson, *Church and Society in Late Medieval England* (Oxford, 1989).

R.N. Swanson, 'Problems of the Priesthood in Pre-Reformation England', *English Historical Review* cv (1990), pp. 845–69.

N.P. Tanner, *The Church in Late Medieval Norwich 1370–1532* (Toronto, 1984).

Books, Sermons and Instruction

L.E. Boyle, 'The Fourth Lateran Council and Manuals of Popular Theology', in T. Heffernan (ed.), *The Popular Literature of Medieval England* (Knoxville, 1985), pp. 30–43.

J. Frantzen, *The Literature of Penance in Anglo-Saxon England* (New Brunswick, 1983).

S. Hamilton, *The Practice of Penance 900–1050* (Woodbridge, 2001).

M.D. Legge, *Anglo-Norman Literature and its Background* (Oxford, 1963).

M. McC. Gatch, *Preaching and Theology in Anglo-Saxon England: Aelfric and Wulfstan* (Toronto, 1997).

N. Orme, 'Children and the Church in Medieval England', *Journal of Ecclesiastical History* xlv (1994), pp. 563–87.

G.W. Owst, *Literature and Pulpit in Medieval England* (Oxford, 1961).

W.A. Pantin, 'Instructions for a Devout and Literate Layman', in *Medieval Learning and Literature: Essays Presented to Richard Wilson Hunt*, ed. J.J.G. Alexander and M.T. Gibson (Oxford, 1976), pp. 398–422.

H. Spencer, *English Preaching in the Later Middle Ages* (Oxford, 1993).

R.N. Swanson, *Catholic England. Faith, Religion and Observance Before the Reformation* (Manchester, 1993).

D. Wallace (ed.), *The Cambridge History of Medieval English Literature* (Cambridge, 1999).

N. Watson, 'Censorship and Cultural Change in Late-Medieval England: Vernacular Theology, the Oxford Translation Debate, and Arundel's Constitutions of 1409', *Speculum* lxx (1995), pp. 822–64.

Religious Orders and the Laity

J. Burton, *Monastic and Religious Orders in Britain 1000–1300* (Cambridge, 1994).

C. Cubitt, 'Virginity and Misogyny in Tenth- and Eleventh-Century England', *Gender and History* xii (2000), pp. 1–32.

G. Dickson, 'Encounters in Medieval Revivalism: Monks, Friars, and Popular Enthusiasts', *Church History. Studies in Christianity and Culture* lxviii (1999), pp. 265–93.

R.B. Dobson, *Durham Priory 1400–1450* (Cambridge, 1973).

S.K. Elkins, *Holy Women of Twelfth-Century England* (London, 1988).

S. Foot, *Veiled Women I: The Disappearance of Nuns from Anglo-Saxon England; Veiled Women II: Female Religious Communities in England, 871–1066* (Aldershot, 2000).

B. Golding, *Gilbert of Sempringham and the Gilbertine Order c.1130–c.1300* (Oxford, 1995).

J. Hill, 'Monastic Reform and the Secular Church', in *England in the Eleventh Century*, ed. C. Hicks (Stamford, 1992), pp. 103–16.

D.M. Kerr, *Religious Life for Women c.1100–c.1350* (Oxford, 1999).

C.H. Lawrence, *The Friars. The Impact of the Early Mendicant Movement on Western Society* (London, 1994).

H. Leyser, *Hermits and the New Monasticism. A Study of Religious Communities in Western Europe 1000–1150* (London, 1984).

H. Mayr-Harting, 'Functions of a Twelfth-Century Recluse', *History* lx (1975), pp. 337–52.

M. Oliva, *The Convent and the Community in Late Medieval England: Female Monasteries in the Diocese of Norwich, 1350–1540* (Woodbridge, 1998).

B. Thompson, 'Monasteries and their Patrons at Foundation and Dissolution', *Transactions of the Royal Historical Society* sixth series, iv (1994), pp. 103–25.

B. Thompson (ed.), *Monasteries and Society in Medieval Britain* (Harlaxton Medieval Studies, vi; Stamford, 1999).

Religion and the Laity

'Popular' Religion: General

P. Biller, 'Popular Religion in the Central and Later Middle Ages', in *Companion to Historiography*, ed. M. Bentley (London, 1997), pp. 221–46.

P. Blickle, 'Communal Reformation and Peasant Piety: The Peasant Reformation and its Late Medieval Origins', *Central European History* xx (1987), pp. 216–28.

J. Bossy, *Christianity in the West 1400–1700* (Oxford, 1985).

N.Z. Davis, 'Some Tasks and Themes in the Study of Popular Religion', in *The Pursuit of Holiness in Late Medieval and Renaissance Religion*, ed. C. Trinkaus and H.A. Oberman (Leiden, 1974), pp. 307–36.

J. van Engen, 'The Christian Middle Ages as an Historiographical Problem', *American Historical Review* xci (1986), pp. 519–52.

A. Gurevich, *Medieval Popular Culture. Problems of Belief and Perception*, trans. J.M. Bak and P.A. Hollingsworth (Cambridge, 1988).

R. Kieckhefer, *Magic in the Middle Ages* (Cambridge, 1989).

R. Kieckhefer, 'The Specific Rationality of Medieval Magic', *American Historical Review* xcix (1994), pp. 813–37.

J-C. Schmitt, *The Holy Greyhound: Guinefort, Healer of Children since the Thirteenth Century* (1979; Cambridge, 1983).

J-C. Schmitt, 'Religion, Folklore, and Society in the Medieval West', in *Debating the Middle Ages*, ed. L.K. Little and B.H. Rosenwein (Oxford, 1998), pp. 376–87.

S.J. Tambiah, *Magic, Science, Religion, and the Scope of Rationality* (Cambridge, 1990).

K.V. Thomas, *Religion and the Decline of Magic* (1971; Harmondsworth, 1978).

'Popular' Religion in England

A.D. Brown, *Popular Piety in Late Medieval England: The Diocese of Salisbury c.1250–c.1550* (Oxford, 1995).

R.G. Davies, 'Religious Sensibility', in *An Illustrated History of Late Medieval England*, ed. C. Given-Wilson (Manchester, 1996), pp. 103–26.

E. Duffy, *The Stripping of the Altars: Traditional Religion in England 1400–1700* (New Haven, Conn., 1992).

G.M. Gibson, *The Theater of Devotion. East Anglian Drama and Society in the Late Middle Ages* (Chicago, 1989).

R. Hutton, *The Rise and Fall of Merry England* (Oxford, 1994).

R. Hutton, *The Stations of the Sun. A History of the Ritual Year in Britain* (Oxford, 1996).

K.L. Jolly, *Popular Religion in Late Saxon England. Elf Charms in Context* (University of North Carolina Press, 1996).

The Parish

M. Aston, 'Segregation in Church', in *Women in the Church*, ed. W.J. Sheils and D. Wood (Studies in Church History, xxvii; Oxford, 1990), pp. 237–94.

J. Blair, 'Secular Minsters in Domesday Book', in *Domesday Book; A Reassessment*, ed. P. Sawyer (London, 1985), pp. 104–42.

J. Blair, 'Local Churches in Domesday Book and Before', in *Domesday Studies*, ed. J.C. Holt (Bury St Edmunds, 1987), pp. 265–78.

J. Blair, 'Debate: Ecclesiastical Organization and Pastoral Care in Anglo-Saxon England', *Early Medieval Europe* iv (2) (1995), pp. 193–212.

C. Burgess and B. Kümin, 'Penitential Bequests and Parish Regimes in Late Medieval England', *Journal of Ecclesiastical History* xliv (1993), pp. 610–30.

E. Cambridge and D. Rollason, 'Debate: The Pastoral Organization of the Anglo-Saxon Church: a Review of the 'Minster Hypothesis', *Early Medieval Europe* iv (1) (1994), pp. 87–104.

C. Drew, 'Early Parochial Organisation in England. The Origins of the Office of Churchwarden', *Borthwick Institute of Historical Research. St Anthony's Publications* vii (1954).

E. Duffy, 'The Parish, Piety, and Patronage in Late Medieval East Anglia: the Evidence of Rood-Screens', in *The Parish in English Life 1400–1600*, ed. K.L. French, G.C. Gibbs and B.A. Kümin (Manchester, 1997), pp. 133–62.

S. Foot, 'Anglo-Saxon Minsters: A Review of Terminology', in *Pastoral Care Before the Parish*, ed. J. Blair and R. Sharpe (Leicester, 1992), pp. 212–25.

K.L. French, 'Maidens' Lights and Wives' Stores: Women's Parish Guilds in Late Medieval England', *Sixteenth-Century Journal* xxix (1998), pp. 399–425.

K.L. French, *The People of the Parish. Community Life in a Late Medieval English Diocese* (Philadelphia: University of Pennsylvania Press, 2001).

C.P. Graves, 'Social Space in the English Medieval Parish Church', *Economy and Society* xviii (1989), pp. 297–322.

B.A. Kümin, *The Shaping of a Community: The Rise and Reformation of the English Parish c.1400–1560* (Aldershot, 1996).

R. Morris, *Churches in the Landscape* (London, 1989).

N.J.G. Pounds, *A History of the English Parish* (Cambridge, 2000).

G. Rosser, 'Parochial Conformity and Voluntary Religion in Late Medieval England', *Transactions of the Royal Historical Society* sixth series, i (1991), pp. 173–89.

Guilds

V.R. Bainbridge, *Gilds in the Medieval Countryside: Social and Religious Change in Cambridgeshire c.1350–1550* (Woodbridge, 1996).

C.M. Barron, 'The Parish Fraternities of Medieval London', in *The Church in Pre-Reformation Society: Essays in Honour of F.R.H DuBoulay*, ed. C.M. Barron and C. Harper-Bill (London, 1985), pp. 13–37.

D.J.F. Crouch, *Piety, Fraternity and Power. Religious Gilds in Late Medieval Yorkshire 1389–1547* (York, 2000).

K. Farnhill, *Guilds and the Parish Community in Late Medieval East Anglia c.1470–1550* (Woodbridge, 2001).

B. Hanawalt, 'Keepers of the Lights: Late Medieval English Parish Gilds', *Journal of Medieval and Renaissance Studies* xiv (1984), pp. 21–37.

B.R. McRee, 'Religious Guilds and Regulation of Behaviour in Late Medieval Towns', in *People, Politics and Community in the Later Middle Ages*, ed. J. Rosenthal and C. Richmond (Gloucester, 1987), pp. 108–22.

B.R. McRee, 'Religious Guilds and Civic Order. The Case of Norwich in the Late Middle Ages', *Speculum* lxvii (1992), pp. 69–97.

G. Rosser, 'Anglo-Saxon Gilds', in *Minsters and Parish Churches: the Local Church in Transition 950–1200*, ed. J. Blair (Oxford University Committee for Archaeology, Monograph xvii; Oxford, 1988), pp. 31–5.

G. Rosser, 'Communities of Parish and Guild in the Later Middle Ages', in *Parish Church and People: Local Studies in Lay Religion 1350–1750*, ed. S.J. Wright (London, 1988), pp. 29–55.

H.F. Westlake, *The Parish Gilds of Medieval England* (London, 1919).

Saints, Cults and Pilgrimage

B. Abou-el-Haj, *The Medieval Cult of Saints. Formations and Transformations* (Cambridge, 1994).

K. Ashley and P. Sheingorn (eds), *Interpreting Cultural Symbols. Saint Anne in Late Medieval Society* (London, 1990).

K. Ashley and P. Sheingorn, *Writing Faith. Text, Sign and History in the Miracles of Saints* (Chicago, 1999).

R. Bartlett, 'The Hagiography of Angevin England', in *Thirteenth-Century England V*, ed. P.R. Coss and S.D. Lloyd (Woodbridge, 1995).

J. Bengtson, 'St George and the Formation of English Nationalism', *Journal of Medieval and Early Modern Studies* xxvii (1997), pp. 317–35.

M. Bloch, *The Royal Touch. Sacred Monarchy and Scrofula in England and France*, trans. J.E. Anderson (London, 1973).

M. Clayton, *The Cult of the Virgin Mary in Anglo-Saxon England* (Cambridge, 1990).

M. Clayton, 'Centralism and Uniformity Versus Localism and Diversity: the Virgin and the Native Saints in the Monastic Reform', *Peritia* viii (1994), pp. 95–106.

S. Coleman and J. Elsner, *Pilgrimage Past and Present. Sacred Travel and Sacred Space in the World Religions* (London, 1995).

C. Cubitt, 'Site and Sanctity: Revisiting the Cult of the Murdered and Martyred Anglo-Saxon Royal Saints', *Early Medieval Europe* ix (2000), pp. 53–83.

M.G. Dickson, 'Patterns of European Sanctity: the Cult of Saints in the Later Middle Ages' (Unpublished Ph.D thesis; Edinburgh, 1975).

D. Dyas, *Pilgrimage in Medieval English Literature 700–1500* (Cambridge, 2001).

R.C. Finucane, *Miracles and Pilgrims: Popular Beliefs in Medieval England* (London, 1977).

P.J. Geary, *Furta Sacra: Theft of Relics in the Central Middle Ages* (Princeton, 1978).

P.A. Hayward, 'Translation-Narratives in Post-Conquest Hagiography and English Resistance to the Norman Conquest', in *Anglo-Norman Studies* xxi, ed. C. Harper-Bill (Woodbridge, 1999), pp. 67–93.

T. Head (ed.), *Medieval Hagiography. An Anthology* (New York, 2000).

G. Klaniczay, *Holy Rulers and Blessed Princesses. Dynastic Cults in Medieval Central Europe* (Cambridge, 2000).

A.M. Kleinberg, *Prophets in their own Country. Living Saints and the Making of Sainthood in the Late Middle Ages* (Chicago, 1992).

K.L. Lewis, *The Cult of St Katherine of Alexandria in Late Medieval England* (Woodbridge, 2000).

S.S. Morrison, *Women Pilgrims in Late Medieval England. Public Piety as Public Performance* (London, 2000).

B. Nilson, *Cathedral Shrines of Medieval England* (Woodbridge, 1998).

N. Orme, *The Saints of Cornwall* (Oxford, 2000).

J. Rattue, *The Living Stream: Holy Wells in Historical Context* (Woodbridge, 1995).

S.J. Ridyard, *The Royal Saints of Anglo-Saxon England: A Study of West Saxon and East Anglian Cults* (Cambridge, 1988).

D. Rollason, *Saints and Relics in Anglo-Saxon England* (Oxford, 1989).

G. Rosser, 'Anglo-Saxon Gilds', in *Minsters and Parish Churches: the Local Church in Transition 950–1200*, ed. J. Blair (Oxford University Committee for Archaeology, Monograph xvii; Oxford, 1988), pp. 31–5.

M. Rubin, *Corpus Christi. The Eucharist in Late Medieval Culture* (Cambridge, 1991).

J.M.H. Smith, 'Oral and Written: Saints, Miracles, and Relics in Brittany, c.850–1250', *Speculum* lxv (1990), pp. 309–43.

B. Spencer, *Pilgrim Souvenirs and Secular Badges. Medieval Finds from Excavations in London* (London, 1998).

J. Sumption, *Pilgrimage. An Image of Medieval Religion* (London, 1975).

A. Thacker, 'Cults at Canterbury: Relics and Reform under Dunstan and his Successors', in *St Dunstan. His Life, Times and Cult*, ed. N. Ramsay, M. Sparks, T. Tatton-Brown (Woodbridge, 1992), pp. 221–45.

A. Vauchez, *Sainthood in the Later Middle Ages* (1988; Cambridge, 1997).

N. Vincent, *The Holy Blood. King Henry III and the Westminster Blood Relic* (Cambridge, 2001).

S. Walker, 'Political Saints in Later Medieval England' in *The McFarlane Legacy: Studies in Late Medieval Politics and Society*, ed. R.H. Britnell and A.J. Pollard (Stroud, 1995), pp. 77–101.

D. Webb, *Pilgrims and Pilgrimage in the Medieval West* (London, 1999).

D. Webb, *Pilgrimage in Medieval England* (London, 2000).

K. A. Winstead, *Virgin Martyrs. Legends of Sainthood in Late Medieval England* (Ithaca, 1997).

Death

J. Aberth, *From the Brink of the Apocalypse. Confronting Famine, War, Plague, and Death in the Later Middle Ages* (London, 2001).

M. Aston, 'Death', in *Fifteenth-Century Attitudes. Perceptions of Society in Late Medieval England*, ed. R. Horrox (Cambridge, 1994), pp. 202–28.

P. Binski, *Medieval Death. Ritual and Representation* (London, 1996).

C. Burgess, ' "A Fond Thing Vainly Invented": An Essay on Purgatory and Pious Motive in Late Medieval England', in *Parish Church and People: Local Studies in Lay Religion, 1350–1750*, ed. S.J. Wright (London, 1988), pp. 56–84.

C. Burgess, 'Death and Commemoration in an English Parish', in *The Place of the Dead. Death and Remembrance in Late Medieval and Early Modern Europe*, ed. B. Gordon and P. Marshall (Cambridge, 2000).

C.W. Bynum, *Last Things. Death and the Apocalypse in the Middle Ages* (Penn State University Park, 2000).

S.K. Cohn, *The Cult of Remembrance and the Black Death. Six Renaissance Cities in Central Italy* (London, 1992).

D. Crouch, 'The Culture of Death in the Anglo-Norman World', in *Anglo-Norman Political Culture and the Twelfth-Century Renaissance*, ed. C. Warren-Hollister (Woodbridge, 1997), pp. 157–80.

R. Dinn, 'Death and Rebirth in Late Medieval Bury St Edmunds', in *Death in Towns. Urban Responses to the Dying and the Dead 100–1600*, ed. S. Bassett (Leicester, 1992), pp. 151–69.

J. Huizinga, *The Waning of the Middle Ages*, trans. F. Hopman (1924; Harmondsworth, 1982).

W.M. Ormrod and P. Lindley (eds), *The Black Death in England* (Stamford, 1996).

D. Postles, 'Lamps, Lights and Lay Folk: "Popular" Devotion Before the Black Death', *Journal of Medieval History* xxv (1999), pp. 97–114.

N. Saul, *Death, Art, and Memory in Medieval England. The Cobham Family and their Monuments, 1300–1500* (Oxford, 2001).

J-C. Schmitt, *Les revenants: les vivants et les morts dans la société médiévale* (Paris, 1994).

Literacy and 'Personal' Devotion

C.A.J. Armstrong, 'The Piety of Cicely, Duchess of York: A Study in Late Medieval Culture', in his *England, France and Burgundy in the Fifteenth Century* (London, 1983), pp. 135–56.

M. Camille, *Mirror in Parchment. The Luttrell Psalter and the Making of Medieval England* (London, 1998).

C. Carpenter, 'The Religion of the Gentry in Fifteenth-Century England', in *England in the Fifteenth Century: Proceedings of the 1986 Harlaxton Symposium*, ed. D. Williams (Bury St Edmunds, 1987).

J. Catto, 'Religion and the English Nobility in the Late-Fourteenth Century', in *History and Imagination: Essays in Honour of H.R. Trevor-Roper*, ed. H. Lloyd-Jones, V. Pearl and B. Worden (London, 1981), pp. 43–55.

M.T. Clanchy, *From Memory to Written Record. England 1066–1307* (2nd edn; Oxford, 1993).

A. Goodman, *Margery Kempe and her World* (London, 2002).

A.M. Hutchison, 'Devotional Reading and the Monastery in the Late Medieval Household', in *De Cella in Seculum. Religious and Secular Life and Devotion in Late Medieval England*, ed. M.G. Sargent (Cambridge, 1989), pp. 215–27.

K. Lochrie, *Margery Kempe and Translations of the Flesh* (Penn State University Park, 1991).

C.M. Meale (ed.), *Women and Literature in Britain 1150–1500* (Cambridge, 1993).

K. Mertes, 'The Household as a Religious Community', in *People, Politics and Community in the Later Middle Ages*, ed. J. Rosenthal and C. Richmond (Gloucester, 1987), pp. 123–39.

W.M. Ormrod, 'The Personal Religion of Edward III', *Speculum* lxiv (1989), pp. 849–77.

M. Otter, 'Closed Doors: An Epithalamium for Queen Edith, Widow and Virgin', in *Constructions of Widowhood and Virginity in the Middle Ages*, ed. C.L. Carson and A.J. Weisl (Basingstoke, 1999), pp. 63–92.

C. Richmond, 'Religion and the Fifteenth-Century English Gentleman', in *The Church, Politics and Patronage in the Fifteenth Century*, ed. R.B. Dobson (Gloucester, 1984), pp. 193–208.

F. Riddy, 'Mother Knows Best: Reading Social Change in a Courtesy Text', *Speculum* lxxi (1996), pp. 66–86.

L. Staley, *Margery Kempe's Dissenting Fictions* (Penn State University Park, 1994).

B. Stock, *The Implications of Literacy: Written Language and Models of Interpretation in the Eleventh and Twelfth Centuries* (Princeton, 1983).

N. Watson, 'Fashioning the Puritan Gentry-Woman: Devotion and Dissent in Book to a Mother', in *Medieval Women: Texts and Contexts in Late Medieval Britain. Essays for Felicity Riddy*, ed. J. Wogan-Browne, R. Voaden, A. Diamond and A. Hutchison (Turnhout, 2000), pp. 169–84.

J. Wogan-Browne, N. Watson, A. Taylor and R. Evans (eds), *The Idea of the Vernacular. An Anthology of Middle English Literary Theory 1280–1520* (Exeter, 1999).

J. Wogan-Browne, *Saints' Lives and Women's Literary Culture c.1150–1300. Virginity and its Authorizations* (Oxford, 2000).

Heresy

M. Aston, *Lollards and Reformers. Images and Literacy in Late Medieval Religion* (London, 1984).

M. Aston and C. Richmond (eds), *Lollardy and the Gentry in the Later Middle Ages* (Stroud, 1997).

P. Biller and A. Hudson (eds), *Heresy and Literacy, 1000–1530* (Cambridge, 1994).

J.I. Catto, 'John Wyclif and the Cult of the Eucharist', in *The Bible in the Medieval World*, ed. K. Walsh and D. Woods (Studies in Church History, Subsidia iv; Oxford, 1985), pp. 269–86.

J.I. Catto, 'Fellows and Helpers: The Religious Identity of the Followers of Wyclif', in *The Medieval Church: Universities, Heresy, and the Religious Life*, ed. P. Biller and B. Dobson (Studies in Church History, Subsidia xi; Woodbridge, 1999), pp. 141–61.

A. Hudson, *The Premature Reformation. Wyclifite Texts and Lollard History* (Oxford, 1988).

S. Justice, *Writing and Rebellion. England in 1381* (London, 1994).

K.B. McFarlane, *John Wycliffe and the Beginnings of English Nonconformity* (London, 1952).

S. McSheffrey, *Gender and Heresy: Women and Men in Lollard Communities, 1420–1530* (Philadelphia, 1995).

R.I. Moore, *The Formation of a Persecuting Society: Power and Deviance in Western Europe, 950–1250* (Oxford, 1987).

R. Rex, *The Lollards* (Basingstoke, 2002).

P. Strohm, *England's Empty Throne. Usurpation and the Language of Legitimation 1399–1422* (London, 1990).

Index